GunDigest
SHOOTER'S GUIDE to
CONCEALED
CARRY

JORGE
AMSELLE

Published by

Gun Digest® Books, an imprint of F+W, A Content + eCommerce Company
Krause Publications • 700 East State Street • Iola, WI 54990-0001
715-445-2214 • 888-457-2873
www.krausebooks.com

To order books or other products call toll-free 1-800-258-0929
or visit us online at www.gundigeststore.com

ISBN-13: 978-1-4402-4172-7
ISBN-10: 1-4402-4172-4

Cover Design by Dane Royer
Designed by Sandi Carpenter
Edited by Gordy Krahn and Chris Berens

Printed in USA

ABOUT THE AUTHOR

Jorge Amselle is an NRA-certified firearms instructor, military veteran, bull's-eye shooter and full-time professional firearms writer for various national gun magazines, including *Combat Handguns, Guns and Weapons for Law Enforcement, Special Weapons for Military and Police, Rifle Firepower, American Rifleman and Shooting Illustrated*. He routinely tests out the latest guns, ammunition, gear and holsters from large and small manufacturers around the country and around the world. He is on the road observing, attending, participating in and reporting on law enforcement and self-defense training academies throughout the year.

Amselle has a Juris Master Degree from the George Mason University School of Law and more than 20 years of experience in communications and public policy. His articles on politics and firearms have appeared in the *New York Times, Wall Street Journal, National Review, The Daily Caller* and other national publications. He has also appeared on C-SPAN, PBS, MSNBC and FOX News and has testified before Congress and state legislatures. He practices what he preaches and has been carrying a concealed firearm on a daily basis for more than 20 years.

ACKNOWLEDGMENTS

There are a lot of holster, ammunition, concealed-carry clothing and accessory and firearms manufacturers and every one of them I contacted for assistance was incredibly helpful with products, advice and images. There are too many to list here but all of the companies featured in this book produce high-quality gear and provide excellent customer service. I am also grateful to my wife, Megan, for her help and advice and to all of those who agreed to pose for photos and let me use their property, including Skipp Galythly and Chris Lyons. Finally, a special thanks to John Frazer for writing the legal chapter.

CONTENTS

CHAPTER 1

HISTORY OF CONCEALED CARRY

A police raid confiscating illegal alcohol during the 1920s. Many firearms prohibitions and controls date to the same time period. loc.gov

PROHIBITION

Throughout most of America's history, firearms were commonplace, used by hunters, farmers, target shooters and law enforcement and military personnel. The sight of someone carrying a gun would rarely raise an eyebrow, and no one felt any need to conceal their firearms—unless they had a nefarious purpose.

Highwaymen, road agents and footpads were a constant danger to the traveler and would often conceal their weapons to gain the advantage of surprise against their unsuspecting victims. No decent person, it was thought, had any cause to conceal a weapon on his or her person. In fact, states and local jurisdictions enacted laws and ordinances outlawing the

During the 1880s, Western towns such as Tombstone, Arizona, had problems with young, drunk, single, armed cowboys. Now it's a tourist attraction. Nick Ares

concealment of weapons during the early 1800s.

In rural areas, openly carrying firearms was common, but in more populated areas, especially where problems had previously occurred, firearms regulations were enacted and enforced. One of the most well known examples took place in 1881 in Tombstone, Arizona Territory. Local ordinance outlawed the carrying of firearms in town, whether concealed or open, and an attempt to disarm some cowboys ended up as the famed gunfight at the OK Corral.

In 1911, New York passed the Sullivan Act, making it the first state to aggressively regulate firearms. It mandated that anyone seeking to own a concealable handgun had to first obtain a permit. And carrying a concealable firearm was further regulated. But as far as rifles were concerned, it was not uncommon to see someone on public transportation well into the 1950s and 1960s with a cased rifle on their way to hunt or target shoot, even in New York City.

FEDERAL LAWS

Of course the history of concealed carry is inexorably intertwined with the history of gun control in general. The Second Amendment to the Constitution, protecting the right to keep and bear arms, was not initially involved because the federal government had not taken any steps to restrict firearms; laws that did so were left up to the states. That changed in 1934 with the passage of the National Firearms Act, which implemented restrictions on machine guns, sawed-off shotguns and various other uncommon firearms.

The Gun Control Act of 1968, enacted following several high-profile political assassinations, came next and resulted in most of the modern restrictions we have today. It created a list of people prohibited from gun ownership

The National Rifle Association was established in 1871 to promote marksmanship. It's America's longest-standing civil rights organization, dedicated to protecting Second Amendment rights. Fair use logo image of NRA

(felons, drug users, etc.). It established the licensing of firearms dealers and restricted the ability of private persons to buy guns directly. It also implemented importation restrictions on "non-sporting" firearms.

It was after this point that the National Rifle Association (NRA), founded in 1871 to promote marksmanship, decided to become politically active. In 1975, the NRA established the Institute for Legislative Action (NRA-ILA) to lobby on behalf of gun rights. However, it took more than 10 years to achieve its first victory, with the 1986 Firearm Owners' Protection Act. This act established protections for federally licensed firearms dealers from abusive regulations and oversight. It protected the rights of people traveling with firearms across state lines. It prohibited the federal government from maintaining a national registry of firearms. Finally, it also prohibited the registration of any new machine guns, freezing the supply of legally transferable machine guns.

The two most significant federal firearms laws after this were the 1993 Brady Handgun Violence Prevention Act, which mandated background checks for all firearms purchases from licensed dealers, and the 1994 Assault Weapons Ban, which sunset in 2004 and is no longer applicable. It should be noted that there was a huge backlash after the 1994 Assault Weapon Ban, which directly contributed to unprecedented losses for the Democrat Party in Congress and the Republican takeover of the House of Representatives for the first time in nearly 40 years. President Bill Clinton acknowledged that the gun issue had caused irreparable harm to his party, and most politicians have been smart enough to stay away from promoting gun bans ever since. It is also why the law was allowed to die in 2004.

TURNING POINT

The mid-1980s marked the beginning of a new era for gun rights. At this time, according to NRA-ILA, only 10 states had laws that made it fairly easy for the average person to carry a concealed firearm. Then in 1987, Florida enacted a "shall issue" law, which basically stated that any law-abiding individual had the right to receive a concealed-handgun permit.

The media went nuts, ignoring the fact that 10 other states had already initiated similar laws. Newspaper headlines declared that there would be shoot-outs in the street, just like during the "Old West" days. There was even a made-for-TV movie about it called "Right of the People," which

In 1987, Florida granted any law-abiding resident the right to receive a concealed-handgun permit.
Public domain

aired during prime time on ABC (since there were only three major networks back then, prime time airing was a big deal) and starred Lando Calrissian (Billy Dee Williams).

The film was sensationalist claptrap and anti-gun propaganda. If you ever need a good laugh and have a couple of hours of your life to waste, try to find a copy. The basic storyline is that after a horrible crime, the residents of a small town decide to allow anyone who wants to carry a gun to do so. Hilarity ensues when a bunch of trigger-happy morons (which is how the media routinely portrays gun owners) get into enough shootouts that the new law is reconsidered.

SHALL ISSUE VS. MAY ISSUE

Currently all 50 states have laws that provide for residents to apply for a permit to carry a concealed handgun. In the vast majority of the states, the law stipulates that the issuing authority (the state or local police, local sheriff or judges) has no discretion. They must issue concealed-handgun permits to all applicants who meet the standards set by the state. Applicants do not have to provide a reason for carrying, or if they do, self-defense is accepted without question. This is known as "shall-issue."

In a small handful of states (currently eight of them), the issuance of concealed-carry licenses is left to

Every state has some form of a concealed-carry law, but they can vary significantly. Sue Clark

Peter Minuit had an easier time buying Manhattan in 1626 than New York City residents have obtaining a concealed-carry permit today. Public Domain-Alfred Fredericks—Popular Science Monthly Volume 75/Britannica

the arbitrary discretion of the issuing authority. These are known as "may-issue" states. In those places where the state police are in charge of permits, there's at least some uniformity and guidelines that residents can clearly learn and follow. In Maryland, for example, the state police issue permits. And while it is extremely difficult to get one and applicants must show a compelling reason, at least the system is transparent and uniformly applied.

In states where local authorities issue permits, you get a complete hodgepodge. In California, for example, issuing a concealed-handgun permit is left to the arbitrary discretion of the county sheriffs. If you live in a small rural county and are best buds with the sheriff, then there's no problem. If you live in one of the state's more populous and urban counties (where you might feel more inclined to need a gun to protect yourself), tough luck. Each county establishes its own criteria for issuing permits, or the sheriff might decide that he or she doesn't want to issue any permits, period.

An analysis of gun permits in New York City conducted a few years ago yielded no surprises. Gun permits were concentrated in the wealthiest neighborhoods where the rich, famous, and socially and politically well connected live. The poor had the most difficult time getting gun permits, because they couldn't afford an expensive attorney to navigate the maze of restrictions the city imposes.

WHY WE NEED "SHALL-ISSUE"

Florida passed its new concealed-carry law despite the media uproar and nothing happened. And over the next decade, 29 other states passed similar laws. I had already moved to Virginia from Maryland when Virginia enacted a shall-issue concealed-carry weapon (CCW) law in 1995, and it made me appreciate my new home that much more. The average person still cannot get a concealed-handgun permit in Maryland without convincing the state police you absolutely need one (and self defense is not a valid reason).

When I was in college, I worked as a security guard in Maryland, and one of the other guards was a former police officer who took early retirement as the result of an on-the-job injury. He had several documented death threats against him from convicted felons he'd arrested and was provided a concealed-handgun permit by the Maryland state police, which was good for 3 years. When he went to renew it, they refused because there had been no new death threats against him.

In the eight remaining states without shall-issue laws, getting a concealed-handgun permit is left up to the arbitrary discretion of state or local law enforcement agencies. This means, with rare exception, the average person cannot get a concealed-

handgun permit unless they're politically connected, wealthy or famous. Even if they qualify for one, it might contain a lot of restrictions. In Maryland, for example, you might be able to get a permit if you have a cash-based business and routinely make large deposits at the bank. But then the permit only applies when you are actually making those deposits. Essentially, you can get a permit in Maryland to protect your money but not your life.

Fortunately, most of the states that have liberalized concealed-carry laws also recognize each other's permits and issue nonresident permits. So if you live in a restrictive state, at least you can protect yourself when you travel.

COURT CASES

Historically, court cases on Second Amendment grounds rarely gained any traction and the last time the Supreme Court had looked at the matter was in United States vs. Miller in 1939. This was a case with mixed results

Cases involving Second Amendment rights often find their way into the court systems. Chris Potter/StockMonkeys.com

and upheld the National Firearms Act (NFA) as constitutional. The question was over a sawed-off shotgun, and the Court found there was no constitutional right to own one because it was not a suitable militia weapon. It should be noted that the NFA did not outlaw possession of sawed-off shotguns or machine guns; rather it simply stated you had to register them and pay a tax.

Then, in 2008, everything changed. The Supreme Court agreed to hear a challenge to the gun laws in Washington D.C. The District of Columbia falls directly under federal jurisdiction but was granted "home rule" (the ability of residents to govern their local affairs) in 1973. The new D.C.

government immediately set out to impose gun restrictions and an onerous licensing and registration scheme for gun owners living in the city. In 1976, they simply stopped accepting applications for new handguns. They also mandated that all firearms stored in the home had to be kept unloaded and locked away or disassembled. It's probably unrelated, but during the 1980s Washington, D.C., became known as the murder capital of the United States.

A D.C. resident named Dick Heller sued the city on Second Amendment grounds and in District of Columbia vs. Heller (2008) the Supreme Court ruled in his favor. For the first time,

The U.S. Supreme Court got one right in the case of District of Columbia vs. Heller in 2008, declaring that the Second Amendment guarantees an individual the right to own a gun and that self defense is a legitimate use and reason for gun ownership. Mark Fischer

Illinois was the last state to enact concealed-carry legislation. Deepak

the Court declared that the Second Amendment guarantees an individual the right to own a gun and that self defense is a legitimate use and reason for gun ownership. The Court required that the city allow residents to register and possess handguns once again and specifically threw out the city's laws against keeping a loaded and accessible gun in the home. This decision applied only to federal areas however, not to the states.

In 2010, the Supreme Court revisited this issue in McDonald vs. Chicago. The city of Chicago, Illinois, had banned handgun possession in the early 1980s. After the Heller decision, Chicago resident Otis McDonald sued the city. The Court agreed and extended the holding in Heller to the states. Now states had to honor the same Second Amendment right as the federal government.

As a direct result of these decisions, more lawsuits were brought and continue to be litigated that challenge all sorts of firearms restrictions at the local and state levels. The most notable example is Moore vs. Madigan (2013), decided by the U.S. Court of Appeals, 7th Circuit, against the State of Illinois. Illinois was the last holdout, with no provision to allow for concealed carry for any reason. The court ordered the state to come up with a law that would allow concealed carry, and now Illinois is a shall-issue state, where any law abiding person who meets the requirements cannot be denied a concealed-carry permit.

California provides another example: In 2014, a panel of the 9th U.S. Circuit Court of Appeals in Peruta vs. County of San Diego held that refusing to reasonably issue concealed-carry permits to residents violated the Constitution. That decision is being appealed by the state, although it's unclear if it has grounds to do so. I will be surprised if this decision stands, but the sheriff of San Diego County has already said he will not appeal and has started issuing permits for self-defense reasons.

GETTING A PERMIT AND RECIPROCITY

If you live in a shall-issue state and decide to apply for a concealed-carry permit, the experience will vary from state to state. The fees and requirements in these states vary significantly but are generally not onerous. They

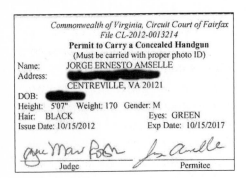

Some concealed-carry permits look very official, like a driver's license. Others look like they came inside a cereal box. Jorge Amselle

always include a criminal background check and a training requirement. In some states, military service is accepted as proof of training. There was a case in Virginia where a World War II veteran applied for a concealed-carry permit and the judge refused because he deemed that the man's training was not current enough. The legislature fixed that very quickly in the veteran's favor.

Training in some states can be as simple as watching an online safety video and taking a short quiz. In other states, it can be 16 hours of safety and legal training, as well as a qualification on the range. The cost of the permits can vary, but range between $50 and $100 in most cases. Some permits can include fingerprints and photographs and look like a driver's license, or they can be a plain paper card with your name and address and signed by a judge.

If you travel a lot, you might want to get more than one permit. Since some states recognize the permits of other states (known as reciprocity), in order to carry in the highest number of areas, you can apply for multiple nonresident permits. Utah and Florida are usually the most popular and provide the highest level of reciprocity. If you combine these two with your own state, you could conceivably carry in nearly 40 states. Obviously, state laws change constantly, and it's always best to check before traveling. UsConcealedCarry.com/travel/ is a good source for up-to-date conceal-carry reciprocity information.

CONCEALED CARRY VS. OPEN CARRY

This book is about concealed carry, but the subject of open carry is an important one even if you never carry a firearm openly. What if the wind blows your coat open and your gun becomes exposed for only a second but someone notices? What if someone can see the outline of your gun through

In most states, carrying a gun in open sight is allowed. Teknorat

your clothing? What if you are simply moving your gun from your holster to your glove box and it becomes visible to a passerby? These are all real-world examples that can get you in trouble.

When I was working as a security guard at a shopping mall (hey, a job is a job), we received a call about someone who might have been carrying a gun. It turned out the guy was carrying a wallet in some type of odd shoulder holster. The fact is that today we live in a far different America, where the sight of someone (who is obviously not a hunter or a police officer) carrying a gun in open sight scares some people.

Still, in most states carrying a gun openly is allowed. But just because something is legal doesn't mean it's always a good idea or appropriate. If I'm heading to the range on a hot day and don't have any other stops planned, I might open carry. If I'm going shopping, I prefer to keep my gun concealed. Many experts on this matter discourage open carry because it can actually make you a target for

Many open-carry holsters are extremely comfortable to wear all day. Blackhawk

criminals. Others feel it dissuades criminals. I guess it depends on the bad guy's intent and state of mind.

There's also the issue of public perception. Many people believe that anyone with a gun other than a police officer is a bad guy, and whenever they see someone with a gun (or what they think is a gun), all hell breaks loose. In Boston, a shopping mall was evacuated and the SWAT team and a police helicopter were called in—all for a man carrying an umbrella.

Funny, right? It wasn't so funny for a shopper who was shot and killed by Las Vegas police officers as he was exiting a Costco because store security called 911 and reported that he was carrying a gun. He had a permit and was legally armed, but a tragic case of miscommunication cost him his life.

When scared people call the police and report they see a man with a gun, the police respond. Police officers do a tough job in a professional manner, but they are also human and can make mistakes or have bad days. This can result in a lot of unpleasantness, as police must respond to these calls without knowing the circumstances or the armed suspect's intent. I can't blame the police for being on edge, but over-reacting can and does occur and sometimes lawful citizens are detained, harassed, arrested or killed as a result.

There are those who advocate open carry in order to get the public used to the sight of guns. Although I think that would be great, I doubt that efforts to return urbanites to a 19th century mindset regarding guns are going to succeed anytime soon—and I don't care to make myself a guinea pig in the process.

This can also backfire politically. In California, open carry of loaded guns used to be legal, until the Black Panthers started marching around with loaded guns back during the 1960s. Then only the carrying of unloaded guns was allowed, which gun-rights activists immediately took advantage of and began doing so as a confrontational form of protest and filming their encounters with police. The result was not an expansion of gun rights but rather legislation banning open, unloaded carry as well.

CHAPTER 2

CHOOSING THE RIGHT GUN

Too many people think a gun is a gun is a gun. This is incorrect. A gun is a tool and you need the right one for the job. But you also need to consider that unlike most other tools, guns are made to fit the individual, not just the task at hand. The gun you would use to hunt pheasants could be used for self defense but probably not for concealed carry. Likewise, a gun that might be great for home defense might not be well-suited for concealed carry. The gun that a full-grown man can shoot and carry comfortably might not be the right gun for a smaller-statured person.

That said, high-quality firearms can be expensive, and it's imperative you train regularly with each gun you carry. While it would be nice to have the resources to own a different gun for various clothing options and for all four seasons, and to have the time to train and become proficient in their use, this is not realistic for most people. Most people who carry a concealed firearm stick with one or two guns. What follows are a few basic ideas and suggestions for finding the gun that will best suit your needs the majority of the time.

REVOLVERS

One of the earliest single-barrel repeating handguns was the revolver,

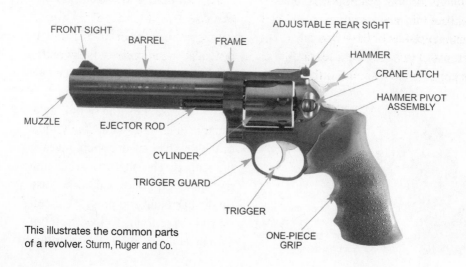

FRONT SIGHT
BARREL
FRAME
ADJUSTABLE REAR SIGHT
HAMMER
CRANE LATCH
HAMMER PIVOT ASSEMBLY
MUZZLE
EJECTOR ROD
CYLINDER
TRIGGER GUARD
TRIGGER
ONE-PIECE GRIP

This illustrates the common parts of a revolver. Sturm, Ruger and Co.

This Taurus eight-shot .357 Mag. with custom paint and decal might be a bit much for everyday concealed carry. Custom Digital Designs

so named because the cartridges are stored in a cylinder that revolves to line each cartridge up with the barrel in turn. The oldest self-contained, cartridge-firing revolvers operated in single-action mode, meaning the user had to manually cock the hammer for each shot in order to fire the gun. These types of single-action revolvers are still being made, but are relegated to use by collectors and history buffs, as well as cowboy action shooters. While they can certainly be used for self defense and concealed

The Taurus Judge, chambered in .410/.45 Colt, is a popular revolver but a bit on the large side for concealed carry. Taurus

carry—and many were used that way in the past—they are not ideal for the modern handgun user.

The modern, double-action revolver was developed more than 100 years ago. Pulling the trigger both cocks and releases the hammer to fire the gun. The result is that double-action revolvers are very easy to operate. They don't have a safety latch you need to disengage before you can fire or a lot of other extraneous controls.

ADVANTAGES

Simplicity is the hallmark and main advantage of using a revolver for self defense. Pushing or pulling a simple latch can swing the cylinder of the revolver swung open, revealing the separate chambers that each hold one cartridge. To unload it, you just tip the barrel up and press the extractor rod in the front. To load, you tip the barrel down, insert the cartridges

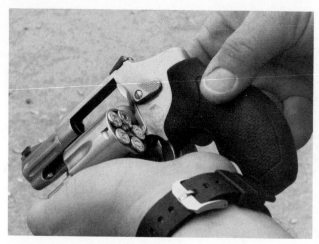

Revolvers are easy to load and operate. Jorge Amselle

and then close the cylinder. The revolver is now ready to fire.

Even those with weak hands or other ailments can easily accomplish this simple operation. Since there are no other buttons or mechanisms, the revolver, now loaded, is always ready to be fired and the user doesn't have to worry about doing anything other than aiming the gun and squeezing the trigger. If a cartridge malfunctions in an emergency, the user can squeeze the trigger again and the cylinder will rotate to the next cartridge and fire that one. Note: If a cartridge fails to fire on the range, keep the gun pointed downrange and wait 30 seconds before proceeding.

Many revolvers are also more versatile in the ammunition they can use. Since the chambers are individual, bullet shape can be more varied. Also, each chamber is sized primarily for width, so it's easy to use smaller-caliber cartridges that are the same diameter. The most common revolvers used for personal defense are chambered in .357 Mag. and .38 Special, which have the same diameter. The Magnum is longer and more powerful.

If you buy a revolver chambered in .357 Mag., you have the option of shooting .38 Special ammunition, which is cheaper and has a lot less recoil. A revolver chambered in the more powerful cartridge will have a slightly longer cylinder and is generally larger and heavier than one built for .38 Special ammunition. However, the ammunition versatility enables you to switch among cartridges if ammunition of one type is harder to find. The other advantage is that different people with different sensitivities to recoil can use the same gun by simply changing the ammunition.

Be aware that while you can load the shorter .38 Special cartridges in a revolver chambered for .357 Mag., the inverse is not true and should never be attempted.

You also have much more versatility on grip selection with a revolver. Underneath the grips of most revolvers there's a small metal frame. The grips simply fit around this, and you can choose between a small grip, which is easier to conceal, or a larger grip, which makes the gun more comfort-

Replacement grips, such as these from VZ Grips, make it easy to adjust the revolver for a custom fit. Fred Simons

able and easier to shoot. A grip can be selected to fit the shooter's individual hand size and shooting preferences.

Revolvers are much less prone to jamming or malfunctioning, and they can be fired through clothing (such as from inside a pocket) if needed with much less risk of the clothing interfering with the operation of the gun. They are easier to clean because there is no disassembly—you just open the cylinder, unload and clean it. Finally, in a worst case scenario, where there's a struggle and you have to fire at contact distance (the barrel of the gun is pressed against an assailant), this pressure will not stop the revolver from functioning.

DISADVANTAGES

One of the main disadvantages of a revolver for per-

sonal protection is its limited cartridge capacity. Revolvers typically accommodate six rounds in the cylinder, but smaller pocket-sized revolvers might have only a capacity of five rounds. There are larger revolvers that will fit as many as eight rounds, but these are generally ill-suited for concealed carry because of their size. The other disadvantage is that revolvers are slower

Most concealed-carry revolvers accommodate only five rounds, so it's important to make them count. Jorge Amselle

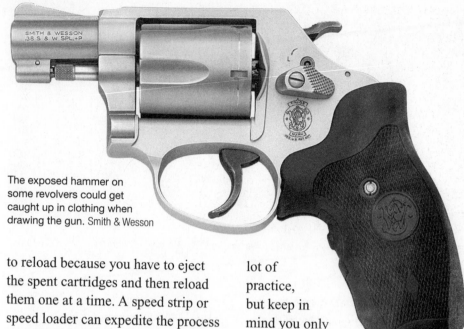

The exposed hammer on some revolvers could get caught up in clothing when drawing the gun. Smith & Wesson

to reload because you have to eject the spent cartridges and then reload them one at a time. A speed strip or speed loader can expedite the process somewhat.

Because of the cylinder, revolvers are also a bit wider, which can make them somewhat harder to conceal. In a double-action revolver the only "safety" is the pull-weight of the trigger and the length of the trigger squeeze. For most double-action revolvers, the amount of pressure the shooter needs to apply to the trigger in order to fire the gun can vary from 9 to 17 pounds and require an inch of travel. For some people, this might be too much to comfortably handle, but even for the most experienced shooters it can sometimes pose a problem.

The more pressure you have to apply to the trigger and the more time you spend squeezing the trigger, the harder it is to keep the sights on target. Shooting a double-action revolver both rapidly and accurately takes a lot of practice, but keep in mind you only need to achieve combat accuracy for self defense, meaning center mass hits at very close distances.

One consideration that applies to concealed carry in particular is with revolvers that have an exposed hammer. An exposed hammer gives the shooter the option of firing the gun in the standard double-action mode or in single-action mode by manually cocking the hammer. In single-action mode, the trigger becomes much lighter to fire and has much less distance to travel. This makes it easier to fire with greater accuracy, but it's very seldom needed in a self-defense situation. The disadvantage is that the exposed hammer can get caught up in clothing when you draw it from a holster quickly.

The S&W 340PD is an excellent and very lightweight choice for revolver carry. Smith & Wesson

While revolvers are generally very reliable, they are not jam proof (contrary to popular perception). Jams or malfunctions can occur as a result of an ammunition issue that can lock up the cylinder and prevent it from turning. Likewise, if dirt or debris gets stuck underneath the cylinder extractor, the cylinder won't turn and the gun will not fire. Clearing these malfunctions requires opening the cylinder (if you can), dumping the entire contents, clearing the debris and reloading. If you have no spare ammunition, you will need to salvage the dumped rounds that are still good. This will be time consuming.

BEST CHOICE

Small, pocket-sized revolvers are popular for concealed carry by both beginners and experts alike for their simplicity, ease of use and conve-

nience. My recommendation in this category is to look for a lightweight, small frame, five-shot revolver with a hidden (best), shrouded (next best) or bobbed hammer. Get one chambered in .357 Mag. if possible but at least in .38 Special.

Select a model that fits your hand comfortably and has a smooth and consistent trigger squeeze that's not too heavy for you to handle. Keep in mind that lightweight revolvers produce significantly more felt recoil than heavier models and might be uncomfortable to shoot, even with .38 Special loads.

SEMI-AUTOMATIC

A modern semi-automatic handgun is an entirely different animal, and there are several features of note. First, there's a magazine contained inside the grip that holds the cartridges, the

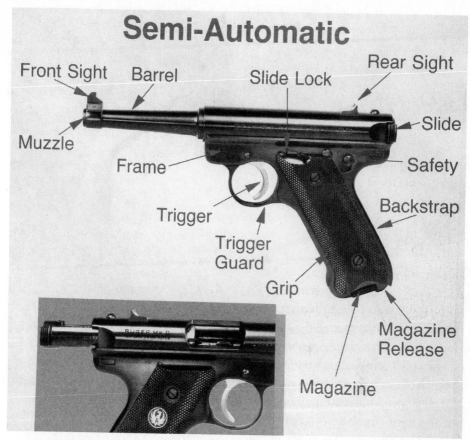

Semi-Automatic

This illustrates the common parts of a semi-automatic pistol. NRA

number of which depends on the size of the magazine, the size of the gun and the size of the ammunition. Above the grip and frame is the slide, which operates the gun. Inside the slide is the barrel with a chamber that holds one cartridge at a time located at the rear.

Operation of a semi-automatic is as follows. First, load the desired number of rounds one at a time into the magazine, up to the maximum it will accommodate. The magazine is spring loaded, so the more rounds you load the harder they are to push down.

Many people prefer to use a loading tool that makes the job much easier on the thumbs. Also, note that it's very easy to load the rounds in backward and that the gun won't work if you do, so pay attention that the rounds face the front of the magazine.

Next, insert the magazine fully into the bottom of the grip until it clicks in place. Chamber the first round by fully retracting the slide and then releasing it. This strips the top cartridge from the magazine and feeds it into the chamber at the rear of the barrel. At

The classic Walther PPK has been a solid concealed-carry pistol since well before World War II. Walther Arms

this point the gun is ready to fire, and when you squeeze the trigger, the slide will retract on its own, expelling the empty cartridge case, and then go forward to load a fresh cartridge into the chamber. The gun will fire with each squeeze of the trigger until it is empty.

There is significant variety in design for semi-automatics (far greater than for revolvers) and the choices can seem daunting. It's important to understand the basic design differences and their advantages and disadvantages in order to select the handgun that will best fit your individual needs and preferences.

ADVANTAGES

There's a good reason why police departments across America made a determined switch from revolvers to semi-automatics: firepower. A full-sized pistol can accommodate as many as 17 rounds or more plus one in the chamber. An officer usually carries two spare magazines as well, so he can easily and quickly reload by simply pressing the magazine release button (which drops the empty magazine) and inserting a full magazine.

Of course, most people are not going to select a full-sized pistol for concealed carry. But even with a very compact pocket pistol with only a six-round magazine, when you count the round in the chamber, the carrying capacity is seven rounds—two more than in a pocket revolver. And you can also carry a very flat and compact spare magazine should you need to reload quickly.

Due to their design, semi-auto pistols are flatter and smaller than any defensive revolver, which makes them easier to conceal. The way the slide operates also helps to reduce recoil relative to the cartridge and the size and weight of the pistol. Many

Semi-automatic pistols can accommodate more ammunition than revolvers, thanks to their use of a magazine. Custom Digital Designs

pistols will also go to slide lock—the slide locks to the rear and the action is open—on the last shot. This provides immediate visual confirmation that the gun is empty.

Like revolvers, semi-automatic pistols can be had in single-action, double-action or both. The key difference is that a single-action pistol needs only to be cocked for the first shot. The slide operation automatically cocks the hammer for each subsequent shot. A double-action-only pistol might have a hammer (visible or internal) or might be striker-fired. The advantage to both single-action-only and double-action-only pistols is that the trigger pull is the same for every shot.

Singe-action and striker-fired semi-autos also have the benefit of a relatively light trigger squeeze, with a short trigger pull in the case of the single-action and a long trigger pull in the case of the striker-fired pistol. They both also generally have short resets so the trigger doesn't have to go all of the way forward before it can be squeezed again to fire it. This makes it easier to shoot faster, which is an advantage in a close-range defensive scenario.

The use of a magazine means the shooter can reload a pistol quickly and easily. Jorge Amselle

Some guns, such as the Glock and Springfield XD shown here, use a striker mechanism instead of a hammer. Custom Digital Design

Many semi-automatic pistols use both double-action and single-action operation. Typically, the hammer will be in the down position for the first shot, making it a longer and heavier double-action trigger squeeze. The gun will operate in the single-action mode for all of the following shots. The advantage with this system is that you have the safety of a long, heavy trigger pull for the first shot and the accuracy and speed of a single-action trigger squeeze for all of the following shots. You do need to get used to two different trigger pulls, however.

DISADVANTAGES

The main disadvantage of the semi-automatic pistol is that there's a steeper learning curve for beginners. Each pistol might have controls that are different from others. The magazine release, which allows the user to remove the magazine, might be in different locations and might be located on different sides of the gun. Many semi-automatics (less so on small pocket pistols) will also have a slide lock/release lever that locks the slide to the rear. Each will have its own method of disassembly for cleaning and maintenance, and some of these can be a bit complicated.

Different semi-automatic pistols have different safety mechanisms, ranging from grip safeties that require a firm grip to operate to thumb safeties that must be manually deactivated. Some pistols have trigger safeties that prevent the trigger from moving backward unless squeezed from the middle. Others have various internal safeties that are always in effect until the trigger is squeezed.

The grip size on a pistol is also largely fixed, although there are replacement grips and other accessories that can help adjust the grip to suit the individual better. Many pistols also include replaceable panels, but this is found mostly on the midsize and larger pistols. Operating the slide

The Remington 1911 (above) and Glock have very different controls and disassembly procedures. The 1911 is more complex. Jorge Amselle

might also be difficult for someone with smaller hands, hand injuries or poor hand strength, although some manufacturers make pistols with slides that are easier to manipulate. With practice most people can handle slide manipulation.

Reliability can also be a concern. If anything obstructs the movement of the slide, such as clothing, it likely will not cycle properly. Pistols are also much more sensitive to ammunition selection, and some types of ammunition might not function reliably in some pistols. With certain types of pistols, it's possible to inadvertently hit the magazine release and then be left with the one shot in the chamber

and a magazine on the ground.

Clearing jams is typically faster with a pistol, depending on the nature of the malfunction. The types of malfunctions that can occur with a pistol are more varied, although there is a generally accepted standard method for dealing with these quickly. First, slap the base of the magazine to make sure it is fully and firmly inserted. Next, rack and release the slide to clear the malfunction. These steps should be done while maintaining your focus on the threat (and not looking at the gun). If this fails to correct the malfunction, look at the gun to diagnose the nature of the problem and correct it. Note: If possible, taking

There is a standard procedure for clearing malfunctions with a semi-automatic pistol. Jorge Amselle

Many popular pocket pistols, such as this Kel-Tec P-3AT, have no hammer drop safety and should be carried with caution. Jorge Amselle

cover at this point might be a good idea.

Most modern pistols are designed with what is called a hammer drop safety. This is an internal mechanical device that prevents the gun from firing if it's accidentally dropped. It is unusual, but if you drop a loaded gun at just the right angle on a hard surface with just the right amount of force, there's a chance it will fire. The hammer drop safety is designed to prevent this.

However, there is no such safety on some pocket pistols and some older pistols. In these cases, the manufacturer recommends carrying the gun with an empty chamber. This means that for concealed carry, you would have a full magazine in your gun but no round in the chamber. If you needed to use it, you would first have to chamber a round, which will slow you down and is not ideal. Most people (myself included) ignore this warning and prefer speed over the very slight risk. The choice is yours, however, and if you opt for one of these pocket pistols, you have been warned.

Finally (speaking of dropping a handgun), *never* try to catch a falling gun in midair. The danger of pulling the trigger without intending to is far greater than the chance of the gun discharging when it hits the ground.

SEMI-AUTOMATIC BEST CHOICE

Speaking strictly for concealed-carry use, I prefer a pistol no larger than mid-sized, preferably compact or sub-compact in double-action-only or striker-fired with a single-stack magazine. This means you have fewer rounds in the magazine, but it also means the gun is lighter and thinner, making it easier to carry a spare magazine. For the smallest pocket pistols, I use nothing chambered smaller than .380 ACP; for larger pistols, 9mm is my ideal choice, although some might prefer a larger caliber. Note that the larger the caliber, the greater the recoil and in very small guns this can be unpleasant.

BIG GUN VS. SMALL GUN

Big guns are easier to shoot (especially with larger calibers) and accommodate more ammunition, but they are also heavier and more difficult to conceal. If you are going to select a full-sized gun to carry concealed, you will need to adjust your methods of carry and/or clothing choices to keep it hidden and easily accessible. Finding a way to carry a full-sized gun comfortably might also involve some trial and error.

As you move down the scale to smaller handguns, trade-offs begin to surface. Smaller guns are more difficult to shoot and have more limited caliber selection, but are also easier to conceal and more comfortable to

The Diamondback DB9 might be the smallest and lightest 9mm pistol on the market. It's ideal for pocket carry and packs plenty of power. Diamondback Firearms

carry. A mid-sized or even a compact gun can split the difference between a good home defense handgun and one that's appropriate to use for concealed carry. It might be the best choice for those who want only one handgun for both uses.

HANDLING RECOIL

Recoil is the real-world application of Newton's Laws of Physics, specifically the second and third laws. These state that force is equal to the mass of an object multiplied by its acceleration, and that for every force there is an equal and opposite force. A 9mm cartridge, for example, will produce the exact same amount of force regardless of the gun it is fired from (assuming the bullet weight and velocity are the same). The exception being that a gun with a longer barrel will produce higher velocities from the same cartridge and, thus, more force as well.

The force coming back against your hand is also equal to the force of the bullet going forward. But remember that force is a factor of mass and acceleration, and what you actually feel is the acceleration. The smaller the gun, the less weight or mass it has and the higher the acceleration you will feel against your hand. This is why a small gun seems to kick so much harder than a larger gun in the same caliber.

You can reduce the recoil you feel in several ways. First, you can select a different ammunition type. Not a different caliber, but ammunition specifically designed to kick less either as a result of the bullet weight or its velocity. You can also change how you perceive the recoil by altering the grip size. Very small, narrow grips well-suited for concealed carry drive all of the recoil into a small portion of the web of your hand, causing you to feel it more. A larger grip spreads the recoil across a larger surface area of your hand, softening the blow. Think

Recoil from a small 9mm, such as this Ruger LC9, can be stiff, but it doesn't feel as bad as this photo makes it look. Jorge Amselle

of catching a baseball bare handed versus with a glove.

Some grips are also made of softer material with more elasticity. These not only spread the acceleration across a wider area of your hand, they also reduce the acceleration and thus the perceived recoil. Reducing recoil not only makes shooting much more comfortable, it also helps shooters avoid flinching or anticipating the shot. Anticipation causes shooters to push the gun forward and down against the expected recoil before the gun goes off, sending shots low and causing misses.

My wife sometimes carries a Smith & Wesson 340 PD revolver with a scandium alloy frame. It weighs less than 12 ounces and is very compact and easy to carry. Even when loaded, the weight is negligible. This revolver will handle .357 Mag. ammunition, which is a very powerful round. However, because of its small size and light weight, firing full-power magnum loads from this revolver is brutally painful. I fired four rounds of .357 Mag. ammunition through it and could not bring myself to fire the fifth. She loads it with self defense .38 Special ammunition specifically designed to produce lower recoil (and it is still unpleasant to shoot).

A large gun, such as this full-sized 1911 chambered in .45 ACP, kicks less than a petite gun in a smaller defensive caliber. Jorge Amselle

Just because it's pink or small doesn't make it an ideal handgun for a woman. This SIG P238 is a good choice. SIG Sauer Academy

GUNS FOR WOMEN

As a firearms instructor, I routinely had women in my classes who had a gun for self defense that had been given to them by a husband, boyfriend or father. In many cases, the gun was a very small pistol chambered in a cartridge smaller than .380 ACP (what most consider the minimum for self defense). Sometimes these guns were overly complex, difficult to maintain and provided a poor fit in the hand. Small guns are good for concealed-carry use, but they are also more difficult to shoot and not ideal for beginners.

There are several areas of particular concern for women regarding handgun selection. First, there's the grip size and shape. Be sure to find a gun that

feels good in the hand, allows you to have a firm grip and that you're able to reach the controls. The weight of the trigger, meaning how hard you have to squeeze it for the gun to fire, is another concern. When selecting a handgun, make sure to dry fire it a few times (aiming in a safe direction and ensuring the gun is unloaded) to get the feel of the trigger and determine if it's comfortable for you. It's considered polite to ask before dry firing a handgun, however.

For semi-automatics, you will want to check the weight of the slide, or how much force is needed to pull it all the way back to chamber a round, clear a malfunction, check the chamber to make sure the gun is empty, and/or lock the slide to the rear. Some

This Ruger LC380 was specifically designed for less recoil and an easy-to-operate slide.
Jorge Amselle

manufacturers, specifically Remington and Ruger, make pistols with slides that are easier to retract.

Women tend to have smaller hands, so it's also important to take note of the position of any controls on the pistol. How easy are they to reach and operate? You will have to occasionally clean your gun, so it's also important to understand how the pistol disassembles. Some are much more complicated and more difficult to disassemble than others.

Finally, consider the magazine. A double-stack magazine holds more ammunition, but it also makes the gun wider and loading the last few rounds can be difficult, requiring a lot of force. There are loading tools that can help, but you should also consider a single-stack magazine that will be easier to load fully. In small, concealable handguns, recoil will be more severe, so make sure to factor caliber and handgun weight into your selection as well.

TROUBLESHOOTING

There are a lot of companies making handguns, and most of them offer compact and concealed-carry models. The choices can frankly seem overwhelming. As with most things, the general rule is that the higher-quality guns are also the most expensive, but that's not always the case. There are several manufacturers making high-quality concealed-carry guns at very reasonable prices.

My advice is to do your research before you buy and stick with well-regarded, well-known brands. As a gun writer, I review dozens of guns every year. I take them to the range and put hundreds of rounds through them. I test them using at least three different

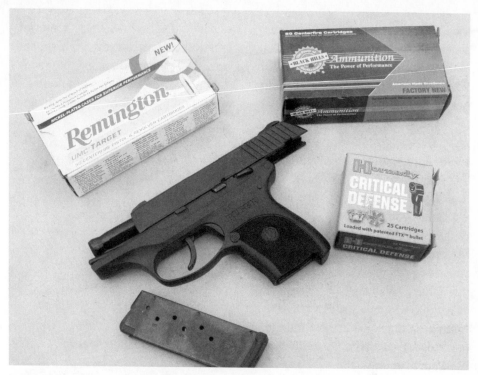

Try different brands and types of ammunition to see what works best. Jorge Amselle

types of ammunition. I check their accuracy at different distances. I take them apart to see how they work.

When I receive a gun for testing, I expect it to work flawlessly right out of the box with no cleaning or maintenance needed, regardless of the brand of ammunition I use. From a concealed-carry handgun, I expect good combat accuracy at 7 yards (3- to 4-inch five-shot groups at worst) for the smallest of them and farther out for the larger models.

At least 10 percent of the handguns I test fail to meet my initial expectations. The problems are often simple things, such as the failure of an empty cartridge to eject, the fail-

ure of a round to feed into the chamber from the magazine, double feeds, stovepipes, a failure of the trigger to reset properly, etc. Sometimes these issues are caused by poor-quality ammunition or ammunition that the handgun just doesn't like for whatever reason. Sometimes the magazine might have a manufacturing defect or dent that prevents proper and reliable functioning. This is why it's so important to give any gun you intend to use for self defense a thorough run though at the range.

Solutions vary, but the first thing I always try is using a different magazine. I also test different types of defensive ammunition to make sure they cycle properly, and if I find one specific type or brand that does not work well, I avoid using it. Handguns will have been test fired at the factory, but this is usually only a few rounds. New guns benefit from a breaking-in period. I would never carry a gun for self defense without first having fired a minimum of 200-300 rounds though it to make sure it's functioning properly and reliably.

Firing this many rounds helps to smooth out the contact points inside the gun and improves the cycling of the action as well as the trigger pull. Many of the guns I test that initially exhibit malfunctions do so within this break-in period, and it generally sorts itself out afterward.

User error is another factor that shouldn't be overlooked. Make sure you understand how to properly operate your handgun. I've seen magazines and rounds inserted backward, barrels installed upside down, parts removed and not replaced during cleaning, and possibly worst of all, using the wrong ammunition. (And I'm not talking about unreliable ammunition, but am-

A bad magazine can be the source of feeding problems. Use a different magazine to check if this is causing the malfunctions. Jorge Amselle

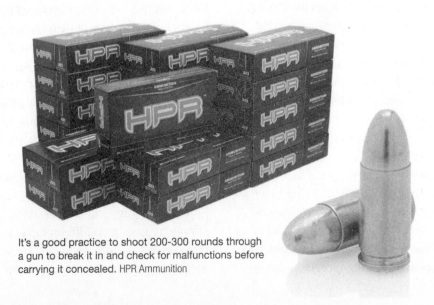

It's a good practice to shoot 200-300 rounds through a gun to break it in and check for malfunctions before carrying it concealed. HPR Ammunition

Debris between the ejector spur and the cylinder can lock up a revolver so that it will not fire.
Jorge Amselle

munition designed for a completely different gun.)

For the most part, the minor issues that occasionally come up either resolve themselves during a break-in period or might require a replacement magazine or just a thorough cleaning. Very rarely, the problems are more severe and require that the gun be returned to the manufacturer. The vast majority of manufacturers will make things right and either repair or replace guns that don't function properly at their expense.

During several years of professionally reviewing firearms, I've had only three occasions when a gun did not function properly, reliably or safely and the manufacturer was either unable to fix the problem or refused to do so.

The astute reader will notice that I have not mentioned any revolver malfunctions. That's because problems with revolvers fall into two basic categories. The first involves extremely minor issues that either do not affect the function of the revolver or are easily resolved with a quick cleaning. The second category is major malfunctions that are almost impossible to miss during the final manufacturer's inspection, so it's extremely unlikely you will encounter these with a new revolver. Malfunctions can occur with older revolvers that might require the services of a competent gunsmith, but in general this will be the result of a lot of use.

However, a minor malfunction that prevents your revolver from working in the middle of an emergency situation will certainly not feel minor at the time. The worst of these is if the cylinder fails to rotate and locks up.

No amount of squeezing the trigger will get the gun to fire. This can be caused by a small amount of debris between the back of the cylinder and the extractor. On a clean gun that is kept in a holster, this should never happen. Even a gun that's kept in a pocket and exposed to a lot of lint shouldn't have a problem.

I have only ever seen this problem with a revolver once, and that was during a training class after firing hundreds of rounds with no cleaning. The solution is to open the cylinder and dump out all of the empty cases and live ammunition. Flick the ejector rod a few times to clear any debris and then rapidly reload. If you don't carry spare ammunition, you'll need to conduct the ammo dump into you hand and pocket the live rounds for your reload. This is a slow process even when experts do it, and it would be advisable to run and seek cover before attempting it in a self-defense situation.

I mentioned earlier that it's best to stick with well-known brand names when buying a handgun. However,

If the cylinder fails to rotate and locks up, dump the ammo and hit the ejector rod a few times to clear any debris that might be causing the problem. Jorge Amselle

I've encountered malfunctions in all types of firearms from all sorts of manufacturers. No one is immune, but you do get what you pay for, and major manufacturers tend to have fewer issues with their products and are more likely to stand behind their guns. On the other hand, small manufacturers often take extreme pride in their work and offer faster and better customer service than some of the larger, busier and more bureaucratic gun companies.

CHAPTER 3

BUYING A GUN AND TRAVELING WITH A FIREARM

TRY BEFORE YOU BUY

Most of us would not buy a car without considering its options and taking it for a test drive. A firearm purchase is really no different. You want to consider how the gun will be used, the reputation of the manufacturer, the features that are important to you, reviews of the various guns you are considering, and, of course, the cost.

Many first-time gun buyers rely on recommendations from friends or family members. They might attend a basic firearms class (which I highly recommend) and follow the advice

A retail gun shop will have a large selection of new guns to choose from. Dannielle Blumenthal

A large, well-stocked gun store will have knowledgeable staff, an on-site gunsmith, plenty of accessories, and can help with any issues or questions. Marcin Wichary

of an instructor. Many people simply walk into a gun store and ask the clerk for advice (which could be good or bad).

If you are truly new to firearms, my best advice is to try before you buy. If you have friends who shoot, ask to go with them to the range and try some of their handguns. If you take a firearms class, ask the instructor about trying out different guns on the range. Most instructors have a variety of loaner guns available. There are also private shooting ranges that rent firearms.

Keep in mind that renting a firearm or asking an instructor to provide one for you can be an expensive proposition. You will have to pay range fees and for ammunition. Instructors will charge for their time as well, or a rental fee for their guns. Ranges also charge rental fees. It would be like taking a car for a test drive and having to pay for a car wash and a full tank of gas. I suspect fewer people would opt for the test drive if this were the case. However, a high-quality handgun will cost hundreds of dollars, so making the right choice is important.

NEW OR USED

I gave up buying new cars a while back. I like new cars, but my practical and cheap side won out and now I buy only used vehicles. Of course with a used car, your options are more limited and the car's features might not include everything you want. Also, you don't really know how well the previous owner maintained the car or what mechanical issues might arise.

When you opt to buy a new gun, you have the liberty to select exactly what you want. You can choose the size, caliber, color, sights, grips, accessories, manufacturer, etc. Most guns stores will special order anything you want if they don't have it on hand, and you get the benefit of a manufacturer's warranty should anything go wrong. With a new gun purchase, many gun stores will also stand behind the product and assist you in dealing with the manufacturer if you have any issues.

When you buy a new gun, you also get all of the extras the manufacturer wants you to have. This includes the original box or case. Most modern gun boxes are made from polymer and offer secure protection for your gun. Many can be locked shut with a simple padlock, making them good for transportation or even basic home security.

A trigger or cable lock will also be included for added safety, and all of the accessories will be included as well: cleaning rods, disassembly tools, spare magazines, warranty cards and, perhaps most important, the owner's manual. Of course, buying a new gun means paying full price and for some guns that are in high demand and hard to find, you might even pay more than full price.

When you buy a used gun, you can save 20 or 30 percent or more from the

This gun might be a bit too used, but it was a great concealed-carry gun in its day. D.C.Atty

When buying a used gun, check the barrel for excessive wear or damage to the rifling.
Custom Digital Designs

cial care to note how the trigger feels. It should not be overly heavy or gritty. Make sure the gun fires in both the single-action and double-action modes if so designed. If there's a de-cocking mechanism, try it out as well.

Check the takedown lever for proper functioning and disassemble the gun. If the gun is very dirty, it's a good indicator that it was not properly maintained. Sometimes guns that are having issues just need a thorough cleaning, or there might be a more severe problem. If the gun is already dirty, it will be more difficult to determine the situation you're dealing with.

You also want to check the barrel. There should be no bulges anywhere along the outside. Inspect the rifling and look for rust, pitting or uneven wear. If you see a ring inside the barrel, that's a bad sign. Check the muzzle end of the barrel, especially where the rifling ends. It should be sharp and crisp. Look for excessive wear in this area. The gun should fit together well without excessive play in any of the parts. Check the slide to frame fit.

Most manufacturers offer a transferable lifetime warranty on their guns no matter who owns them and will repair any problems. However, if the previous owner has tampered with the gun or made gunsmithing changes, the warranty might be void.

For revolvers, the cylinder lock-up and timing is the most important consideration. Make sure the chambers are aligning properly with the barrel

cost of the same gun new. This is for a used gun in good working condition. However, it's up to you to determine whether the used gun you are considering is indeed is good condition. Make sure all of the controls on the gun function as they are intended to.

For semi-automatic pistols, make sure all the safety devices are fully functional. If there's a grip safety, squeeze the trigger without pressing it to make sure it works. If there's a thumb safety, activate it and try to squeeze the trigger, then deactivate it and try to dry fire the gun. Take spe-

When buying a used revolver, check the cylinder for proper timing and alignment as well as excessive wear.
Custom Digital Designs

have concerns, questions or problems you can easily return and ask for assistance.

A gun store will generally be welcoming, well-lit and well-appointed, with organized and labeled merchandise. Prices are clearly displayed, and the staff will generally be knowledgeable and helpful. If you go to a gun store where this is not the case, you might want to go elsewhere.

The biggest advantage of shopping at a gun store is that the staff will have plenty of time to talk with you and answer your questions. They will have a good selection of handguns for you to hold and try out to see what you like and what works for you. They will have a full selection of ammunition, holsters and accessories to match your gun. There is simply no substitute for being able to handle a variety of guns and products before deciding which to purchase.

and there's no play in the cylinder, especially when the revolver is cocked. Make sure the trigger is functioning properly and that you cannot push it forward once it's cocked. Check the trigger squeeze in single- and double-action, making sure it is neither too heavy nor too light. The gun's cosmetics can also be an indicator of proper care and maintenance.

WHERE TO BUY

A gun store is the most obvious place to purchase a gun and where most people start. This makes sense, because a gun store will have fixed hours of operation and requires little advance planning to visit. It is a formal business that occupies a fixed physical location, so if you

There are a lot of very large gun shows where good deals can be had. Just don't expect any hand-holding. Michael Coté

Many gun stores will also have an on-site gunsmith or access to one who can make repairs or adjustments or customize your gun any way you prefer. Because of the Internet, gun stores have had to adjust and become more competitive in their pricing. However, you will still generally pay a premium for the convenience and the service, but for many folks it's money well spent.

Many gun shops have ranges and gun rentals where prospective buyers can try different guns before making a purchase. Gander Mountain Academy

Some gun stores will not handle transfers of guns you bought online or will charge an exorbitant fee, especially if it's a gun they have in stock themselves. But many others will handle transfers of firearms from other sources to you for a reasonable fee.

Gun shows are another great place to shop. There are usually dozens of dealers and vendors selling guns and everything gun-related, including holsters, clothing, ammunition, safes, cleaning kits and accessories. At some of the larger shows, there are hundreds of tables full of guns and gear, and some vendors offer on-site training and gunsmithing services, as well as making custom holsters while you wait.

The selection and opportunity to see and touch all of this equipment is unmatched by any gun store, and because there are so many dealers competing for your business, the prices are very competitive. Gun shows can be extremely entertaining to walk around and see new and interesting products. For the beginner, they can also be overwhelming.

Vendors at guns shows are usually very busy and have little time to answer questions or demonstrate their products. Some are even downright impatient, to be honest. If you want to go the gun show route for your purchase, it's best to have done all of your homework in advance and know exactly what you want. The vendors are only there for the weekend, so if you have a problem, you are on your own.

If you want something custom or out of the ordinary, you are also unlikely to find it, since the vendors will focus on the most popular guns and won't be around to special order anything for you. Many of these dealers also have physical locations where you

Gun shows, such as the Houston Gun Show at the George R. Brown Convention Center, are a good place to shop for new or used firearms. M&R Photography

can go to make a purchase or special order after the show, but they might be located far away from you.

There will be a lot of buying and selling of used guns at these shows. There's plenty of room to haggle, and good deals can be found. But again, as with any used gun purchase, there's no sure way to know if the gun is in good working order. If you buy a used gun from a dealer or anyone else at a gun show, they're typically sold "as is." The best prices will be for used guns from private sellers. Usually, there will be some folks walking around with a sign stating that they have a gun to sell, and they are open to haggling.

You can also expect to save money on new guns at gun shows. In my experience, the gun show price for new guns is generally about 10 percent less than the gun store price. This difference might not be worth it if you have a lot of questions or prefer a calmer buying experience.

The Internet is

Dealers at gun shows have a variety of new and used guns for sale and typically allow browsers to handle them. Jorge Amselle

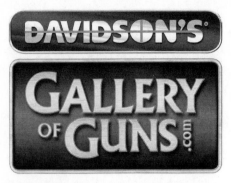

Wholesaler Davidsons' Gallery of Guns lets you shop online and ships new guns directly to a dealer in your area. (GalleryOfGuns.com) Davidsons

GunBroker.com is very similar to other online auctions, where you bid on the new and used guns and gear you want. Gunbroker.com

another excellent resource of information and reviews for different guns. There's no shortage of bloggers who will tell you exactly what they think of a gun. Some are better than others and it's best to read a variety of reviews. You can also purchase a firearm online and have it shipped to a local dealer who can then transfer it to you.

The Internet is especially helpful for locating rare or hard-to-find guns, and you can find the absolute best prices. Keep in mind that you will have to cover shipping (which on handguns has to be overnight) as well as the transfer fee your dealer charges, so you might not save as much as you think.

The Internet is also a great place to purchase holsters and accessories but again, when you buy stuff without first handling it, sometimes it doesn't work out for you. In most places you can also order and receive ammunition directly to your door from Internet vendors.

There are several websites that host firearms auctions and sales such as GunsAmerica.com and GunBroker. com. There are also major firearms distributors who sell customer direct from their websites and ship the gun to a dealer close to you who has already agreed to handle the transfer for them. GalleryOfGuns.com is one good source with a vast selection of guns. Some manufacturers make special editions of their guns that are exclusive to certain distributors.

KNOW THE LAW

Caveat: You want to do the right thing and follow the law. Ask your local licensed gun dealer and also check with the state and local police either online or by calling if you have specific questions about the laws regarding purchasing and owning a gun. Remember that having the law in writing from the police website or the actual text of the law from your state legislature is better. Simply saying that you called the police and the officer

The police won't care what a gun dealer said is legal if they think a law has been violated.
Scott Davidson

The Bureau of Alcohol, Tobacco, Firearms and Explosives is in charge of Federal Firearms Licenses for dealers, manufacturers and collectors.
Public Domain

told you X or Y is not good enough. Neither is saying that your gun dealer told you X or Y is legal.

Neither your local gun dealer nor the state or local police know all of the gun laws with certainty. For that, you need a lawyer familiar with gun laws and licensed in your state. Also keep in mind that politicians get elected to do stuff, and changing gun laws is one thing they really like to do. Every year the guns laws change—some for the better and some for the worse.

There are many laws and regulations at the federal, state and local levels that govern firearms sales and transactions. It is very important to stay on the right side of the law at all times, or you risk losing your gun rights altogether. The easiest resource is to simply visit a local gun store and ask about the legal requirements for making a purchase where you live.

All handgun purchases must be made from a federally licensed dealer in your state. You will complete a federal form asking for your personal information and answer a series of questions to determine if you are disqualified from owning a gun. There might be a state or local form to complete as well. In some cases, if you are purchasing multiple firearms, there could be additional forms.

You will need to show a government-issued ID with your photo and address and in some cases you might need two forms of ID. The dealer will call either the state police or the National Instant Criminal Background Check System to make sure you are not a prohibited person. This check takes a few minutes in most cases. In some states, there could be a waiting period, additional licensing requirements, safety training or other conditions that must first be met before you can take possession of a firearm.

If you buy a handgun from an out-of-state seller, it will have to be shipped to an in-state dealer to handle the transfer. If you buy a handgun at a gun show or gun store, the process is the same. The only exception is when you buy a firearm from a private individual, which can be done with no paperwork as long as you are both

When traveling with a firearm, especially when flying and crossing state lines, be sure to know and follow all the laws.
Grant Wicks

residents of the same state. In some states, however, this is not allowed and a licensed gun dealer or law enforcement must handle such private transfers.

TRANSPORTING AND TRAVELING WITH FIREARMS

OK, you have your gun, and you need to get it home. Depending on where you live, this might be easier said than done. Generally speaking, even the most anti-gun states will allow you to transport a gun you legally own from the place of purchase or repair or a shooting range back to your home. Of course, this only applies if you are a resident of that state and have all of the required paperwork, licenses, permits, etc., and the gun is in a locked container, unloaded and inaccessible to you. I would also check with the state and local police and the dealer where you bought the gun to make sure you are in compliance with the law.

In some states, you are allowed only to transport your legal firearms to and from a shooting range, gun/repair shop and your home with no stops in between. Don't stop to get a snack or gas or to pick up your friend. Keep the gun unloaded in a locked case in the trunk with the ammunition stored separately. This might include keeping any magazines unloaded as well. In fact, I highly recommend keeping your magazines empty, because some jurisdictions might interpret a full magazine carried in the same vehicle as a firearm that's equal to a loaded gun, even if they are separate and locked up.

Most of the northeastern states have strict regulations regarding the ownership and transportation of firearms. Beware of local laws when traveling with a gun. Christopher Connell

Most states have significantly looser requirements than these for transporting firearms within the state. Make sure to familiarize yourself with the laws in your state. Also be aware that in some states, localities can enact their own gun control ordinances. By simply driving from one jurisdiction in your state to another, you might go from law abiding citizen to criminal without knowing it. It is for this reason that several states have enacted pre-emption, which outlaws any local restrictions on firearms and provides their residents with only one statewide set of laws governing guns.

If you are from out of state, God help you if you transport your guns into or through the most hostile states in regard to firearms regulations. Places to avoid include most of the northeastern United States. The 1986 Firearm Owners Protection Act includes a safe passage provision so that if you legally possess your gun at your place of origin and can legally possess it at your destination you are protected from prosecution for transporting it in between. The gun has to be unloaded and locked up, but as long as you don't stop (other than for gas or food, but not to rest or sleep), you can't be prosecuted.

You *can* be arrested, harassed, threatened, searched, your gun confiscated and otherwise made to feel bad, but not prosecuted. If you are traveling with a firearm between states, always transport in the strictest way: unloaded, locked up, ammunition separate, in the trunk or as far away from the driver as possible.

FLYING WITH A GUN

You are allowed to fly with firearms in your checked luggage. An airline may potentially refuse, but I haven't seen any that do not allow you to check a firearm. Make sure you're allowed to legally possess the firearm in the city/state where the airport is located. The gun must be unloaded and inside a locked, hard-sided case (a plastic case is OK). Any ammunition must be in an approved container (check the airline's website). You must declare the firearm at the ticket counter to an agent. They will have a TSA agent or an approved person ask you

Airlines allow travelers to check unloaded guns in their checked baggage. Be sure to declare them at the ticket counter. That Hartford Guy

to open the case and check the gun to make sure it's unloaded.

When you get to your destination, you can claim your gun at the regular baggage check (sometimes it will be located with other oversized baggage) with the rest of your checked bags. Make sure you can legally own the gun at your final destination. Do not take possession of your luggage with a gun in it if you are at an airport in a state or city where you cannot possess the gun. There have been numerous instances of people trying to check guns in at airports located in areas where they are not allowed to possess a firearm and getting arrested for their trouble.

Specifically, travelers from other states who do not have the

A lockable, hard-sided case is required for air travel with guns. Seahorse Protective Equipment

This single gun steel combination safe from Gun Vault is inexpensive and perfect for securing a gun while traveling. Gun Vault

required permits to own a gun in New York have been arrested trying to declare and check unloaded and locked guns at New York airports. What if your connecting flight is cancelled and the airline offers to put you up at a hotel until the next day and returns your luggage to you, saying you can recheck the next day? If your luggage has a gun in it and you are stuck someplace where you can't legally have your gun, do NOT accept your luggage back. Demand that the airline retain it and check it through to your final destination.

SHIPPING A GUN

If you sell a gun to a person in another state, you must ship it to a licensed dealer in that state who will handle the FFL transfer. The U.S. Postal Service does not accept handguns for shipping, but they will accept rifles and shotguns. Visit their website to double check all of the rules. To ship a handgun, you must use a private carrier such as FedEx or UPS. You must declare that you are shipping a firearm and that it's being legally shipped. Long guns can go by ground, which is cheaper and takes longer. Handguns must be shipped by overnight delivery, which is more expensive.

Some hunters and travelers I have met don't like to fly with their firearms because of the hassle. Instead, they ship their guns to themselves at their destination. According to the Federal Bureau of Alcohol, Tobacco, Firearms and Explosives website, "A person may ship a firearm to himself or herself in care of another person in the state where he or she intends to hunt or engage in any other lawful activity. The package should be addressed to the owner. Persons other than the owner should not open the package and take possession of the firearm."

CONCEALED-CARRY PERMIT HOLDERS

If you have a concealed-carry permit, you can carry a loaded gun on your person or in your car within the state where it was issued. It is not advisable, however, to leave an unsecured firearm in your vehicle. I know many people who like to keep a handgun or rifle stored in their vehicle with ammunition at all times. If you do this, make sure it's legal to do so where you live. Also make sure the

Map of states recognizing Texas permits:

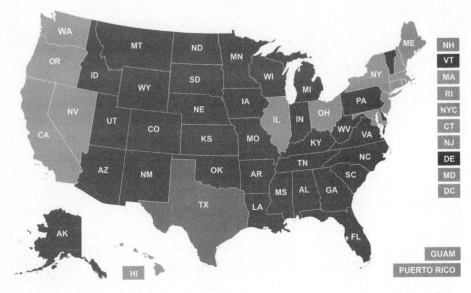

This is a map of states that recognize concealed handgun permits issued to Texas residents. This might already be out of date, so always double check. NRA-ILA

firearm is secured in some manner so that only authorized persons have access. If you're going to drive some place where you're not allowed to possess the firearm, remove it from your vehicle. Make sure if someone borrows your vehicle, they are allowed to be in possession of the firearm.

Even if you have a concealed-weapons permit, the laws in your state might have particular conditions regarding transportation in a vehicle. Make sure you have read and understand the laws in your state. Consult with an attorney if you have any questions.

Many states have what are called reciprocity agreements with other states and will recognize each other's concealed-carry permits. There are several online resources that list which states recognize each other's permits. A few states have "constitutional carry" where no permit is required to carry a concealed firearm. The rest, however, maintain a list of which state permits they will honor. These lists change often, usually expanding but sometimes shrinking.

If you have a concealed-carry permit issued in your home state, you will be able to carry concealed in other states that recognize your permit. However, you must still follow the laws of the state you are in. If you are traveling, it's always best to check the state police website for the state you're visiting as well as any states you are driving through to make sure that the reciprocity agreements are still valid

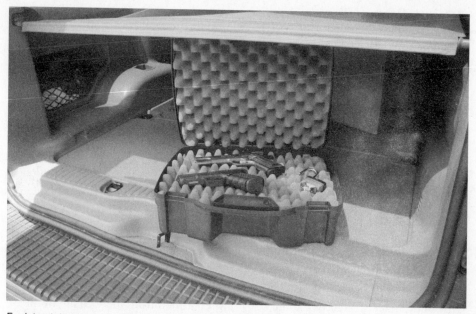

For interstate travel, guns have to be cased, unloaded and inaccessible. Jorge Amselle

and to familiarize yourself with their specific carry laws, which might be different from the ones in your state.

Each state has its own rules regarding driving with a gun or where and when you can and can't carry. Also be aware that just because it says something on the state police website doesn't mean the information is accurate or current.

If you are driving across state lines and have a CCW permit that's recognized in both states, you do not need to unload and lock up you gun for transport. However, do not assume that every police officer in your neighboring state will be aware that there's a reciprocity agreement. Print out the state police website information on reciprocity and concealed carry and bring it with you.

If you travel a lot or if the state you like to visit doesn't recognize your state's permit, you have several options. You could apply for a non-resident permit in that state (but keep in mind that in some states, it is easier to get a permit for a backyard rocket launcher business than a concealed-carry permit). Or you could apply for a permit in another state that does have reciprocity with the state you want to visit.

Florida has had state-issued concealed-carry permits longer than almost any other state, so they have had a lot of time to form these reciprocity agreements. Utah has also been very aggressive in securing reciprocity agreements. If you get nonresident permits from these two states—which is easily done—plus your own state permit, you may be able to carry concealed in up to 40 states.

DUTY TO INFORM

The job of a police officer is difficult, demanding and dangerous. When it comes to firearms, many officers are especially sensitive regarding their safety. In many states, the information on your license plate and driver's license is connected with the concealed-carry permit database. If you get pulled over, a police officer might already know that you have a CCW before he approaches your vehicle.

In some states, you have the duty to inform a police officer that you are carrying a legally concealed firearm during any official interaction (such as a traffic stop). In other states, you do not have this duty. Make sure you are aware of the laws in each state where you are carrying. In my home state of Virginia, there is no duty to inform, but your CCW information is pulled up when they run your license plate or driver's license. In Ohio it's your duty to promptly inform an officer if you're legally carrying.

Here's some good advice on proper and safe law enforcement interactions when armed from the website of the

In some states the law requires informing a police officer of a concealed firearm, others do not.
Jorge Amselle

Many states require motorists to inform an officer if they're legally carrying a gun. Be sure to know the laws of each state you travel in.
Dave Conner

Stark County Sherriff's Office in the state of Ohio:

"Person/driver/occupant has the duty to inform law enforcement officers or motor carrier officers that they are armed when approached in a vehicle. Licensee must keep hands in plain sight at all times while in motor vehicle and armed and do as directed by law enforcement officer.

DO NOT attempt to remove weapon from holster, box or compartment unless directed to do so by law enforcement officer.

DO NOT knowingly grasp, attempt to grasp or touch loaded weapon while in vehicle unless directed to do so by law enforcement officer.

DO NOT exit vehicle unless ordered to do so by law enforcement officer.

DO NOT fail to comply with all directions of law enforcement officer."

My advice is that if you're going to tell a police officer you are legally armed, start by informing the officer that you have a current concealed-handgun permit issued by your state

and *then* that you are lawfully carrying a loaded firearm concealed on your person in accordance with the conditions on your permit.

PLACES WHERE YOU CAN AND CAN'T CARRY

A permit to carry a concealed firearm is not a carte blanche to do as you please. Each state has a set of criteria governing where you can and cannot carry your firearm. Not surprisingly, these vary from state to state. Be sure to check the laws in your state and any state where you want to carry.

As far as federal laws are concerned, a state-issued concealed-carry permit is not valid inside any federal building, including post offices. You can't carry onto many federal lands either, such as military bases. You can carry in some national parks, but not into any of the buildings in the parks and not in all parks. Each park follows the concealed-carry laws of the state in which they are located, so I can carry at the Manassas National Battlefield in Virginia (but not into the museum located there). I cannot carry onto the Antietam National Battlefield in Maryland at all.

While the restricted carry places vary from state to state, there are some commonalities. Generally speaking, you cannot carry in a school or daycare facility. You cannot carry in a courthouse or jail. You may not be able to carry in the state capitol or state-owned buildings, and some state-

Even in states where it's legal to carry concealed in a bar, it is illegal to consume alcohol while carrying a firearm. Roger Blackwell

It is unlawful to carry concealed onto private property or businesses that have posted signs restricting it. Cory Doctorow

owned lands and parks might be off-limits as well. Public universities and colleges are often off-limits for concealed carry. Sometimes public festivals or sporting events, public performances and fairs are off-limits.

Airports and places of worship as well as hospitals might be restricted. It is not unusual for establishments that serve alcohol to be off-limits either. You will likely be forbidden from drinking alcohol while carrying as well, which is logical. In Virginia, the law was changed so that you can carry concealed in a bar or restaurant as long as you do not consume any alcohol. Finally, you cannot carry onto any private property that does not allow it, usually with a sign posted at the entrance. Many businesses are un-

In most places, it's OK carry in a church (with some exceptions), but schools are off-limits everywhere. Mike Procario

der pressure to post signs forbidding concealed carry, especially national chains.

Again, make sure to familiarize yourself with the list of places where you cannot lawfully carry in any state where you intend to carry and be aware that this can change from state to state and year to year.

CHAPTER 4

HOLSTER MATERIALS AND RETENTION

The whole point of concealed carry is concealment. One of the greatest things about America is its entrepreneurial spirit of free enterprise, which has delivered a veritable cornucopia of choices in all sorts of consumer products. And when it comes to the firearms industry this energy is exponentially more abundant, and there's a huge selection of holster choices available with more being developed almost daily.

If anyone thinks the number of choices we have in firearms is overwhelming, try to imagine what it's like for holsters. For each gun that's produced, there are dozens of manufacturers making holsters for it. Hol-

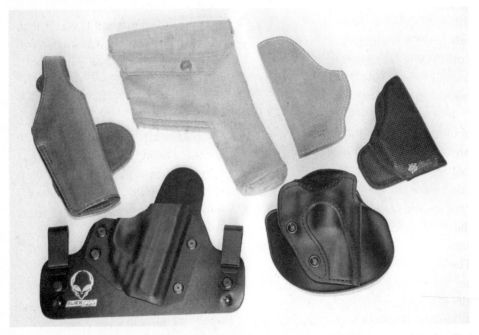

There are more holster choices than there are gun choices—something to suit everyone. Jorge Amselle

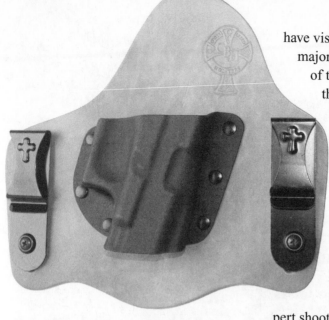

Mark Craighead started CrossBreed holsters at home and developed his own innovative inside-the-waistband holster. Jorge Amselle

have visited vast factories where major companies produce tens of thousands of holsters for the military, for police departments and for civilians around the globe. These companies use very high tech computer modeling, hire experienced graphic designers and engineers, and spend millions on the latest molding machinery and equipment. They hire expert shooters to test their gear and to act as spokespersons. Their processes are closely guarded corporate secrets, and tours for gun writers are closely monitored with photography tightly regulated.

At the other extreme, I've met with holster manufacturers that started out as one guy with a unique idea making holsters at home as a hobby—a hobby that eventually led to a hugely successful business. You can also find DIY holster kits online and dozens of individual holster makers: some who are true artists working with exotic leathers and others who keep things simpler using molded Kydex. If you visit local gun shows, you'll see holster makers custom-molding Kydex holsters on the spot while you wait.

Holsters have been around for a long time, but not all are created equal and not all serve the same purpose. Holsters designed for military or law

sters made from different materials, in different styles, to accommodate different types of carry, for right- and left-handed shooters, and built to accommodate each of these guns with a wide variety of different lights and laser attachments as well.

Gun and accessory manufacturers know this and don't want to sell products for which there are no holsters available. As soon as a new gun or accessory gets close to its final production, samples are sent to all the major holster makers so they can start setting up molds and machinery. The key is to release a new gun or accessory with a full line of holsters already available for it.

Holster making doesn't have to be complicated either. At one extreme, I

enforcement use might not be suitable for concealed carry. Look for a holster specifically made for concealed carry. And just because something is branded "concealed carry" doesn't mean it is. Like selecting a handgun, you need to find the right holster that best suits your individual needs.

HOLSTER MATERIALS

Nylon holsters can be found almost anywhere. They are inexpensive and plentiful. Many are designed for casual use and the simplest ones fit on the belt, secured by a belt loop or steel clip. These simple holsters will typically have a Velcro or snap strap that goes over the grip of the gun to secure it in the holster. Many have an extra pouch in the front for a spare magazine.

Besides being inexpensive, they have the advantage of a fairly universal fit. Like a sweat shirt, one size fits most. Most of these types of holsters are also padded to hold their shape or contain a plastic insert. Another advantage of nylon is that it's largely weather-proof, won't stretch or rip easily, won't break and is very lightweight. As far as cheap belt holsters are concerned, these types of holsters are fine for casual range use but are not ideally suited for concealed carry.

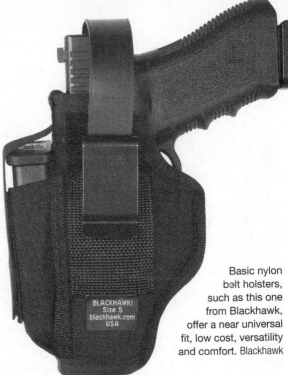

Basic nylon belt holsters, such as this one from Blackhawk, offer a near universal fit, low cost, versatility and comfort. Blackhawk

However, there are some very good nylon concealed-carry holsters available. Specifically, most pocket holsters are made from nylon and many are extremely effective and well-suited for this task. Also, there are high-quality concealed-carry holsters that are nylon-covered for added protection and durability. Nylon is used extensively in covert-style holsters, designed to look like a fanny pack or cell phone case, for example.

Leather holsters are very attractive and have a traditional feel. Since leather is a natural material—literally animal skin—it acts like skin and the quality is very dependent on the skill of the manufacturer. Leather is very pliable and most leather holsters come

police trade-in gun, you probably noticed the distinct wear on the finish from holster use.

A Leather holster can be a lot quieter during the draw, but some tight-fitting leather holsters can also squeak as you move, which announces, "Hey, I'm wearing a holster." Leather also costs more, especially for good quality, and requires some care. Keep your leather holster clean and dry as much as possible, but avoid using any sort of leather care product—just wipe it clean.

with a very snug fit. Since leather changes its shape, it will take a certain break-in period before your gun slips easily in and out of the holster. Many manufacturers suggest leaving your gun in the holster for a full day or two to get the proper fit.

Leather holsters will also contour to your body, which makes them comfortable to carry, especially concealed. The downside is that eventually any leather holster will get stretched to the point it no longer offers a secure fit for concealed carry and will need to be replaced. Leather can also attract moisture (although treated and coated leathers less so). And leather will rub against your gun and eventually wear the finish. If you've ever seen an old

Try to keep sweat off the holster. If you carry inside the waistband, wear an undershirt as a layer between your body and the holster. If the holster gets wet, it's best to just let it air dry, but don't let it dry like this if it has lost its shape. Use one of those plastic dummy Blue Guns when drying to help the holster maintain its original shape if necessary. Keep in mind that a holster that has been exposed to water or submerged in water for a long period of time might well be ruined permanently and need replacing. Extreme heat can also damage leather, so avoid leaving leather holsters in hot vehicles for long periods of time.

Soft suede holsters with more of

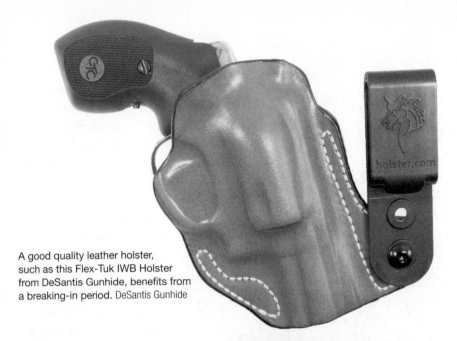

A good quality leather holster, such as this Flex-Tuk IWB Holster from DeSantis Gunhide, benefits from a breaking-in period. DeSantis Gunhide

a universal fit are also common and inexpensive. These are suitable if you have a gun for which you can't find a specifically designed holster, but they do not offer the same level of retention as a properly fitted holster. The only time I opt for a suede leather holster is for pocket carry, and there are some very good models available. Also note that leather can come from a lot of different animals and some are very exotic. For standard concealed carry, cow leather works best, although horse leather is more durable and has moisture resistant properties.

Kydex and other plastics/polymers have largely become the standard for holsters and are very popular for concealed carry. From a manufactur-

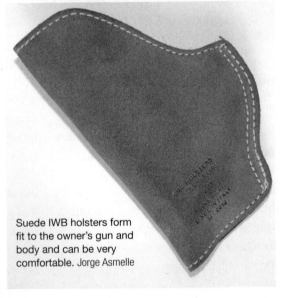

Suede IWB holsters form fit to the owner's gun and body and can be very comfortable. Jorge Asmelle

er's perspective, this is great because once you have a mold of a gun, you can churn these out very quickly and easily. However, their popularity is due to customer satisfaction, not manufacturer convenience.

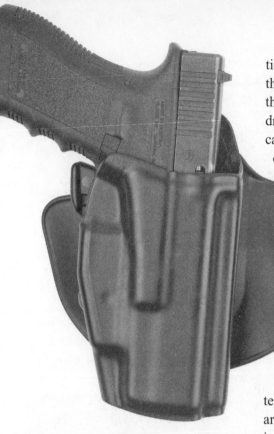

Kydex holsters are popular because they're relatively inexpensive, durable and offer good retention. Safariland

Kydex is impervious to heat, cold, moisture and rough usage. This material never loses its shape and can be molded to the exact specifications of the gun. It is strong and can be made lighter and thinner that other materials. Because it can't collect moisture, there's no chance it will cause your gun to rust. And it won't collect dust and debris, so it won't mar the finish on your gun.

These holsters are also very easy to clean—just like you would any other piece of plastic—and since the mold can be made to exact dimensions, it can have its own internal snap reten-

tion without the need for any external thumb brakes or releases. This gives the user both security and a faster draw. Since Kydex holds its shape, it can also be easier to re-holster, especially with IWB carry. And because they're mass-produced, Kydex holsters are less expensive than many other options.

While polymer and Kydex holsters do have some give, they can also be stiffer than some of the alternatives, so a proper fit to your body is important for comfort. Because of the nature of Kydex holsters, there's generally less variety in terms of styles or types of carry. They are most popular for waistband and inside-the-waistband carry. With certain types of Kydex holsters, you can also get expanded adjustability. By removing and replacing some screws, the same holster can be converted from one type of carry to another and the retention can be adjusted as well.

Cloth holsters, including those made from canvas and other materi-

Belly band holsters, such as the Galco Under Wrap, are made from cloth and Velcro and are very versatile and comfortable. Galco

als, have been around for a long time. However, when it comes to concealed carry, they tend to be seen in a specialized niche. They are designed to carry a gun very close to the body and underneath your normal garments. Most common cloth holsters are found in what are known as "belly bands." These cotton and elastic bands have two or more simple pockets to hold one or more handguns and spare ammunition. The band secures around your waist with a Velcro strap.

Another option is a cloth shoulder holster that fits close to the body and is attached with straps. They often have a thumb strap to secure the gun into the holster with Velcro. Some bra holsters are also made from cotton and secure a gun at the centerline of the chest attached to the bra just under the breasts.

The advantage of cloth is that it's inexpensive and can be very comfortable, almost like wearing a snug T-shirt. These holsters are usually a sewn cloth pocket, so they fit a wide variety of handguns. The downside is that cloth attracts moisture, especially if it's against the body. The loose fit can also mean the gun might not be as secure as one might like, and there's an issue with durability.

For a while, I carried a small .38 Special snub-nosed revolver in a jacket pocket with no holster. This was very easy and convenient and provided me quick access. Over the space of about 6 months, however, the barrel of the revolver wore a hole in the cloth lining of the pocket and was starting to wear a hole through to the outside of the pocket. If you use a cloth holster, be sure to inspect it regularly and replace it as necessary.

Clip holsters are designed with an eye toward minimalism. These are

Clip holsters that attach directly to the gun are an exercise in minimalism. I Love My Glock

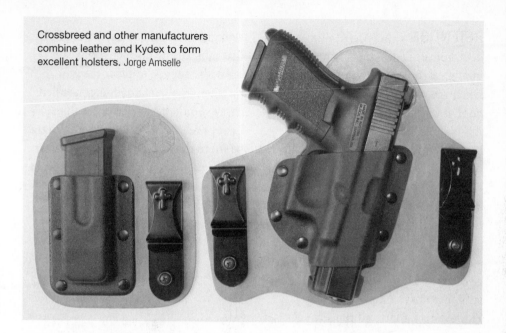

Crossbreed and other manufacturers combine leather and Kydex to form excellent holsters. Jorge Amselle

simple spring-steel clips that attach directly to the frame of the gun, usually by replacing one of the assembly pins, and allow the user to tuck the gun directly into the waistband. The clip prevents the gun from coming loose and sliding down your pants leg or slipping out. The advantage here is that there's no holster, so you can carry a concealed handgun with the absolute minimum amount of extra bulk. For inside-the-waistband carry, this can be more comfortable.

One disadvantage of using a clip holster is that the gun is placed directly against your body and exposed to moisture. Wearing a T-shirt or other undergarment is advisable. The other concern is that the trigger is left completely exposed (albeit inside your pants). Some handguns have light triggers and lack sufficient external

safeties. If any material gets caught in the exposed trigger of such a handgun, catastrophic results could ensue.

Hybrid holsters provide the best combination of materials, and there are many excellent, high-quality examples. Most common are those that mix leather and Kydex. Some IWB holsters have more comfortable soft leather backing against your body with a Kydex-molded holster on the outside, providing the advantages of both.

For improved looks, some waistband holsters feature a Kydex interior with a leather covering. Sometimes these hybrid holsters mix Kydex and Neoprene with polymers. Still others combine polymer and nylon with sheepskin. There are many combinations designed to fit a variety of needs.

RETENTION

A holster is designed to hold your gun in place so you have access to it when you need it. It won't do much good it if allows your gun to simply fall out every time you run, jump or bend over. From the earliest holsters, there was always some form of retention device, which could be as simple as a length of leather string hooked over the grip of the gun.

Old military and police holsters featured a strap or a flap closure, and this was deemed sufficient for a long time. However, as improved reporting made it clear that weapon retention was a concern, especially for police officers, some manufacturers developed much more secure retention systems to prevent unauthorized access to an officer's handgun.

A standard for the different levels of retention was developed as well. Level I retention means that there's one mechanical lock that keeps the gun inside the holster. Typically, this is a thumb break strap over the back of the handgun. Level II holsters add a secondary lock that must also be deactivated before the gun can be drawn. This typically takes the form of a button that's pushed or pressed located somewhere on the holster. Level III retention is the most secure, with three separate locking devices on the holster that must all be disengaged in the proper sequence to draw the gun.

No civilian engaged in concealed carry should ever need more than Level I retention, and even that might be more than most of us need, unless you're concerned that someone might try to snatch your gun out of its holster and use it against you. This would only be a concern if you carry a gun

This Law Enforcement holster from Blackhawk has multiple levels of retention to keep the gun securely in place. Blackhawk

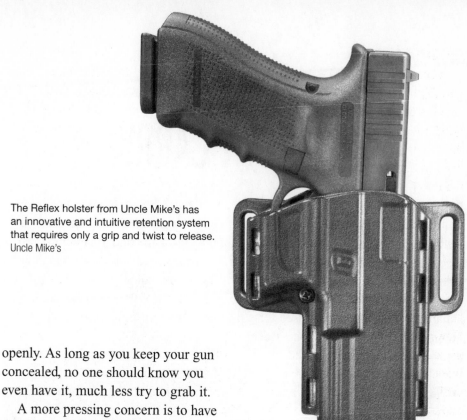

The Reflex holster from Uncle Mike's has an innovative and intuitive retention system that requires only a grip and twist to release. Uncle Mike's

openly. As long as you keep your gun concealed, no one should know you even have it, much less try to grab it.

A more pressing concern is to have quick access to your handgun, and trying to remember a Rubik's Cube-like sequence of mechanisms in order to release your gun from its holster is not conducive to this need. Still, you want to be certain your gun stays in the holster during your normal activities and even during more strenuous activities such as running and jumping. Make sure that whatever holster you select has enough retention to keep the gun in place. Most Kydex holsters have built-in ledges that offer a secure "click" when you holster your gun, and then snap out of place when you firmly grasp and draw your gun.

Many leather holsters utilize thumb or finger snap strap retention. There are also some new Level I Kydex retention holsters that feature intuitive unlocking mechanisms that are activated with your trigger finger or are deactivated with a proper grip, or which only require a simple grip and twist.

Regardless of which method you select, it's important to train with it using an empty or plastic gun. Practice drawing at home in a safe direction until the draw and retention system becomes second nature. In a situation where you need your gun and your adrenaline is pumping, fine motor skills become more difficult. The more you train and the simpler your gear is, the better.

CHAPTER 5

ON-BODY CARRY

There has been a long-standing debate about why people own guns. Historically (when America was a much more rural society), people had guns primarily for hunting. These were predominantly rifles and shotguns that could also be used for home defense if the need arose. But as we became a largely urban and suburban nation, this changed.

According to a 2012 Congressional Research Service report on gun control legislation, "By the same year, 2009, the estimated total number of firearms available to civilians in the United States had increased to approximately 310 million: 114 million handguns, 110 million rifles and 86 million shotguns."

Clearly, the number of rifles and shotgun combined is still larger than that of handguns. But individually,

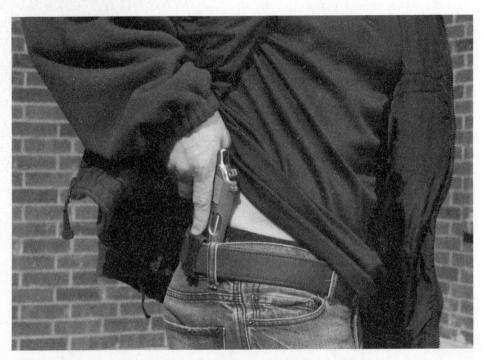

The best place to have a gun is concealed on the body at all times. Versacarry

handguns now make up the largest category of firearm. While handguns can certainly be used for hunting, target practice, competition and recreational shooting, their primary purpose is personal protection. Most gun owners today do not hunt or shoot competitively; they are driven instead by an intense interest in self defense.

If you have gone through the expense, time and trouble of getting trained, applying for a concealed-carry permit and paying for all the associated costs—not to mention the cost of the firearm, holster and ammunition—it stands to reason that you take personal protection very seriously. The whole notion behind concealed carry is to have your gun with you should you need it. As a responsible gun owner, you also need to maintain control of your firearm at all times. The best way to do this is to either keep it locked up or keep it on your person.

On-body carry offers the user full control of his or her firearm. You know where your gun is at all times, and you know it is in a safe condition, holstered. You have the fastest and most direct access to your firearm if you need it, which is why you are carrying it in the first place. There is also much less risk of someone taking the gun from you if it's concealed and on your person.

The downside is that on-body carry can be uncomfortable, and can limit your clothing options. It might also limit your choice of gun because of the limitations in terms of comfort and size, as well as concealability.

HOLSTERLESS CARRY

For some, the most convenient way to carry a handgun is to simply slip it into a pants pocket or coat pocket or just tuck it into your waistband. Depending on the type of gun you want to carry, this could either be OK or a very bad idea. A gun that's simply tucked into your waistband is not very secure, and as you move there's a good chance it could get loose and either fall out the top or slide down your pants with bad consequences.

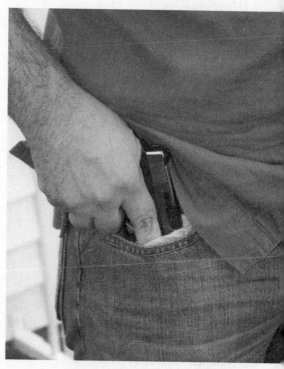

A small gun can be easily carried in a pocket without a holster, but this can be dangerous and should be avoided in most cases. Jorge Amselle

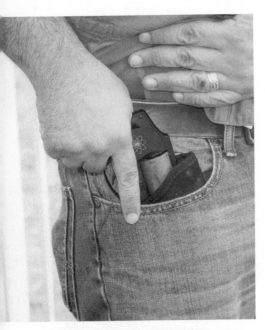

A double-action revolver is one of the safest options for pocket carry. Adding a good pocket holster makes it an even better choice. Jorge Amselle

Dirt, lint, sweat and debris are also much more likely to get into the workings of a pocketed handgun and cause a malfunction. Heaven help you if you decide to multi-task and use the same pocket for your gun, chap stick, pocket knife, keys, assorted hard candies, etc. These items will entangle themselves in your gun and very likely put pressure on the trigger with predictable results.

Some guns are far more dangerous to carry unsecured in a pocket than others, especially those with a light trigger pull. Any gun with a light trigger, especially one that lacks additional safety mechanisms, should never be carried in this manner. The only gun I'd feel comfortable carrying without a holster would be a double-action revolver with a long, heavy trigger squeeze and less susceptibility to malfunctions. Even in this case, there are plenty of holster options that should be considered.

WAISTBAND CARRY

Simply put, waistband carry means you have a holster on the outside of your belt regardless of where along your belt you choose to position it. I find this to be the most comfortable way to carry a holstered handgun and the method that gives me the quickest access to my firearm. It also provides for a wide range of handgun options—from full-sized revolvers and pistols to subcompacts and even pocket-sized guns.

The downside is that you need a cover garment to keep the gun con-

In 2008, NFL football player Plaxico Burress shot himself in the groin when the gun he had tucked into his waistband slid down the inside of his pants. He managed to squeeze the trigger as he tried to stop the gun's movement. He survived, but since he was carrying the gun illegally in New York City at the time, he went to jail.

Simply sticking a gun in your pants pocket is not much better. Again, there are plenty of news stories of people doing this and shooting themselves, sometimes fatally, when reaching into their pocket or just fidgeting about. A gun in your pocket without a holster can also change its orientation so the barrel could be pointed in any direction.

Belt or waistband carry might be the most comfortable method, but concealment is more difficult. DeSantis Gunhide

PADDLE HOLSTERS

Paddle holsters are very convenient because you don't have to remove or undo your belt to put them on or remove them. As the name implies, paddle holsters have a large flat curved paddle on the side of the holster that goes against your body. The holster portion stays on the outside of your belt, while the paddle slips over your belt between your pants and your body.

The paddle itself is usually made from some type of polymer material, often covered in leather or rubber for improved comfort and retention. Manufacturers of these types of holsters typically mold the paddle to include tabs that catch underneath the belt from either the inside of the pants or tabs on the holster that catch the belt from the outside. This keeps the holster securely at the waist when you draw your gun. There are few things more embarrassing or inconvenient than drawing your handgun only to see that the holster is still attached to it.

The securing tabs are typically under tight spring pressure, and you might need to pull the holster away from the paddle in order to put it on. I've run into tabs with a hooked design that were too firm and caught on the inside of the pants. These are more difficult to put on and remove and require a particular technique. Start by putting the paddle holster on at an angle rather than straight down. It also helps to remove it this way, essentially releasing one tab at a time.

cealed. This might entail a sport coat or jacket or simply an un-tucked shirt. But cover garments are needed with most types of carry. Waistband carry positions the firearm slightly farther away from the body, which can make concealment more difficult. Printing, which means the outline of your gun is visible against your clothing, can become more prevalent with waistband carry. This necessitates a loose enough or heavy enough cover garment to conceal the gun's shape.

Another consideration is that if you need to go someplace where your firearm is not allowed, you have to remove the holster as well as the gun, because even an empty visible holster might draw unwanted attention.

A basic paddle holster, such as this one from Fobus, is easy to put on or take off and is comfortable to wear. Fobus

The curved and malleable shape of the paddle makes it comfortable, and these types of holsters are designed in most cases to place the gun at the hip. The wide curve of the paddle is not conducive to placing the gun at the front of the waist or small of the back, although a holster with a smaller or flattened paddle might be usable in this fashion.

The holster and the paddle are only connected to each other at the very top and it's important to select a sturdy, well-constructed holster where extra care has been taken to ensure a strong build. Also, while paddle holsters are easier to put on and remove, you want to maintain a tight fit to hold the paddle in place. This might necessitate loosening your pants to put the holster on or take it off. In fact, doing so will make the process much easier.

BELT HOLSTERS

A more secure and more traditional type of holster attaches to your belt. Some simple holsters clip right onto your belt using spring steel clips. These are very easy to put on and take off and don't require that you remove your belt. They are relatively inexpensive, but the retention of the holster to the belt is not ideal. This is not to say clip-on belt holsters are unsuitable or don't work, but

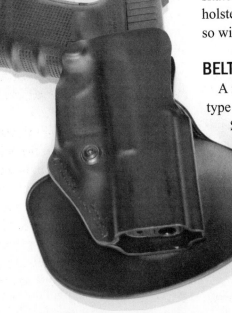

Here is a good view of the curvature of the paddle on this Safariland holster. Jorge Amselle

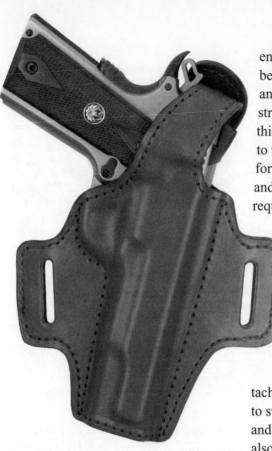

A basic leather holster from Bianchi with belt clips and thumb break retention. Bianchi

ends of the holster will be larger, because the loops are farther apart and actually outside the main holster structure. The advantage here is that this actually brings the gun in closer to the body, and the extended loops force the holster to wrap around and hug the body much more. They require more real estate on your belt, however. The other advantage, especially with leather or nylon holsters, is that both sides of the holster are attached to and part of the belt loops, which makes them more sturdy.

There are also hybrid holster systems that use Kydex and screws with interchangeable attachment systems that allow the user to switch between a paddle holster and a belt holster. Many of these will also include adjustments for the cant and height of the holster. The cant is the angle at which the holster sits on the belt and you can select between a straight up and down or slightly grip-forward orientation.

they are not my preference in terms of retention.

The most common type of holster in this category will have belt loops built into the back or sides of the holster. Belt loops on the back of the holster are common and very sturdy, but since they are attached to only one side of the holster, they might exhibit a greater amount of give and not have as tight a fit to the body. This can be particularly true with leather or nylon holsters, but much less so with a rigid Kydex holster.

Belt holsters with the loops at the

The removable screws can also be adjusted to raise or lower the holster on your waist for a custom fit, depending on the length of your arms, torso and your general comfort. Some basic leather holsters with extended belt loops also include additional loops to allow you to adjust height and cant, depending on which loops you chose to use with your belt.

Some belt holsters are designed so you don't need any cover garments.

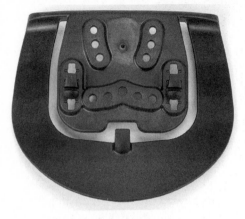

Some Kydex holsters are switchable between belt loops and a paddle, and can be adjusted for height and cant. Blackhawk

For compact and sub-compact handguns, there are holsters that fit on your belt and look like a large cell phone case or PDA holder. (Does anyone still have a PDA?) Some gun companies actually include this type of belt holster with the gun—simple nylon rigs with a zippered enclosure. They are convenient and cheap, but not especially fast if you need your gun in a hurry. The Sneaky Pete Holster is made from leather and has magnetic closures that provide quick access and complete concealability.

INSIDE-THE-WAISTBAND CARRY

If you want to carry a larger gun, there's no better option for superior concealability than inside-the-waistband carry (IWB). As the name implies, this method of carry places the gun and holster inside your pants so that only the grip of the gun is exposed. The majority of the gun and holster remain covered by your pants.

Obviously, this means that concealing the firearm is much easier. It also means you can carry a larger firearm because the length is completely covered. The only concern with a larger gun is keeping the larger grip area concealed, which is still easier than with almost any waistband carry method.

The main advantage of IWB carry, besides being able to conceal a larger gun, is that this method places the gun as close to your body as possible. In fact, it's directly against your body. Because all of us sweat and none of us likes hard, rough objects constantly rubbing against our bare skin, it's best to wear some sort of undergarment with IWB carry. This makes it more comfortable and protects the gun from moisture.

With the gun so close to your body, you also have better retention and more control. Concealment can be as simple as wearing an untucked T-shirt.

Inside-the-waistband carry makes it easier to conceal a larger gun.
Galco

Just make sure it's long enough to keep the gun concealed if you have to reach up for something or bend down. It should also be loose enough so you don't print and show the gun through your clothing. If your cover garment is too small or tight, it might also interfere with drawing the gun.

For proper and comfortable IWB carry, you'll need to make some wardrobe adjustments. First of all, your tight disco pants are out. You will need to wear pants at least one or two sizes larger in order to carry IWB comfortably. You might also need to adjust where you place the waist of your pants. If you wear your belt below your spare tire, IWB will not be very comfortable. You will want to place the holster along your belt line where it is both easy and convenient to reach, but not where it rubs your skin raw throughout the day as you move about. I experience the most discomfort when I'm sitting with IWB carry. Depending on your choice of cover garments, IWB carry can also mean a slightly slower presentation of your firearm.

For comfortable inside-the-waistband carry, pants should be a size or two larger than normal. Uncle Mike's

IWB HOLSTERS

Inside-the-waistband holster models vary significantly. The simplest consist of a plain pocket or pouch for your gun with a spring steel clip on the outside that goes over your belt while the holster goes inside your pants. Besides the grip of the gun, all that's exposed is a metal clip on your belt. Retention here is purely from friction. These types of holsters are small and usually inexpensive and convenient. They also take up very little room on your belt, so there are more options in regard to placement. If you get a holster with a metal belt clip on the outside, make sure it's high-quality and has good retention to you pants. Otherwise, you'll find it's still attached to your gun when you draw.

Some leather IWB holsters have leather loops that go around your belt and snap on. This is both very secure (keeping the holster on your belt) and convenient if you have to remove the holster. The downside is that these loops are visible on the outside.

It generally does not feel good to have the butt of your gun rubbing against your belly fat or ribs all day, so some IWB holster makers have developed a large backing to protect you from your gun and your gun from you. This shield is often leather, but new products are always being developed with neoprene or with various soft and durable materials that wick away moisture and offer a soft, padded surface for improved comfort.

Most of these IWB holsters with a backing are a lot wider, which again takes up a lot more real estate on your waistline and limits placement options. They also have two belt loops or clips

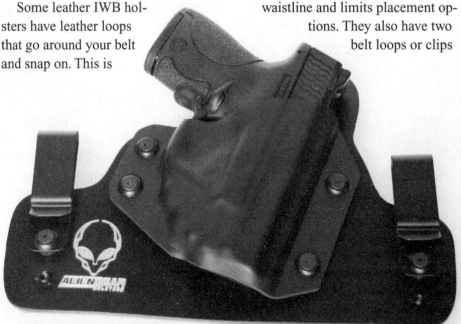

The high leather backing on an IWB holster protects both the gun and the owner. Jorge Amselle

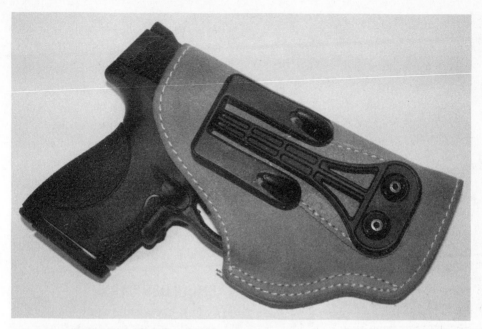

A narrow inside-the-waistband holster takes up less room on the belt, and this one from Blackhawk also allows for tucking a shirt in around it. Jorge Amselle

that come over the side of the holster to attach to your belt. Some of these are your standard spring steel clips, and some are polymer clips that hook over the outside of the belt. Others are designed for more concealability and will actually loop over the pants and underneath the belt, so all that's visible are two small catches at the bottom of your belt.

Further improvements come from what are known as tuckable IWB holsters. There are designed so the belt loops connect to the holster much lower down and leave a gap at the top between the holster and your pants. This allows you to tuck your shirt into your pants and over the gun. From the outside it just looks like you have on regular pants and a tucked-in shirt. The

gun is completely hidden from view. The main disadvantage here is that this can really slow down your draw, because you have to grasp your shirt and untuck it before you can reach the gun.

CROSS-DRAW CARRY

As the name implies, cross-draw carry means the gun is placed grip forward opposite your strong side. If you're right-handed, this means that the gun is in a holster on your left side with the grip angled toward your front or right hand. Several of the same holsters designed for IWB and waistband carry can also be used to cross-draw carry and there are also cross-draw-specific holsters.

Concealment for cross-draw carry is the same as for IWB and waistband

Cross-draw carry can be positioned on the belt or inside the waistband. This is a good way to carry when sitting or driving. Galco

arm. This draw is also generally slower than a straight up and out draw from the strong side, because you have to swing the gun to the target, and there's a chance of over swinging and missing the target.

If you are carrying in a standard friction retention holster with this method and confront someone at contact distance, it is also easier for them to attempt to grab the gun out of your holster, since it's already presented to them grip forward.

SHOULDER CARRY

Just like a cross draw, shoulder carry keeps the gun on the support side. Except in this case, instead of having the gun on the belt line, it's carried in a suspension shoulder holster system, Miami Vice style. Most of the shoulder holsters designed for this method of carry are made from high-quality leather and include a thumb snap retention system to keep the gun in place. To draw the gun, grasp the grip and flick off the thumb snap. To keep the gun from slapping around loosely, many of these holsters also include a belt loop or tab to secure it.

Since the gun is carried underneath the armpit—either vertically with the grip up or horizontally with the grip forward—you have your entire torso to hide the gun. This makes it possible to carry a much larger gun than usual and still keep it concealed. Think of Dirty Harry and his 8-inch Smith & Wesson .44 Mag. Model 29 revolver.

carry. Many find this type of carry to be very comfortable, especially when sitting. The main advantage to cross-draw comes when you need to draw your gun from a sitting position, especially in tight quarters. Those who spend a lot of time driving will find this is among the easiest methods of carry for a fast draw from a vehicle.

The main and significant disadvantage to this method of carry is that the barrel of the gun is pointed behind you and to your side as you draw the firearm to bring it in line with the target. This increases the chance that if you prematurely squeeze the trigger, a shot could go in an unsafe direction. If you are not careful in the draw, you also end up sweeping, or muzzling, your support

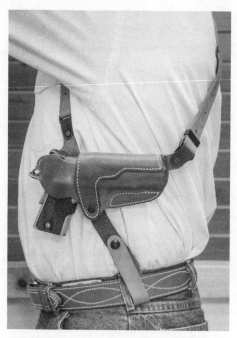

This is a high-quality leather shoulder holster from Diamond Custom with spare magazines on the opposite side. Diamond Custom

You will, of course, need a proper cover garment that conceals the gun and provides quick access.

The shoulder holster places the weight of the gun on the shoulders (where else?) like a backpack. To offset the weight of the gun on one side, many of these types of holsters also include spare magazine holders on the opposite side. This is a very easy and comfortable method of carry and requires no adaptation to your wardrobe other than the aforementioned cover garment. It has the same advantages and disadvantages as cross-draw carry, but it's a bit harder to keep the gun concealed in this manner. You also need to keep your support arm well clear of the muzzle when you draw.

One drawback with cross draw and shoulder holsters is that the shooter ends up muzzling those behind him. Galco

APPENDIX CARRY

As the name implies, this method of carry places your gun somewhere between your belly button and your hip, usually on your strong side and almost always using an IWB holster. The greatest advantage here is that your gun is in the front and under your most immediate control. You can also make sure it stays concealed and does not print against your clothing, because it's easier for you to see and feel it yourself. Your draw will also be much faster, since it's common to keep your hands along your centerline and this places the gun naturally closer to your hands.

Placing the gun directly in front of you in this manner also gives you more control and helps prevent anyone from trying to snatch it away from you. There is one very important caveat that applies to all holster use, but to this one in particular: Take very close care in re-holstering, because your gun is pointed at your groin (an area with a lot of blood vessels). If anything gets caught in the trigger and the gun goes off, there's a good chance you will bleed out before help can arrive.

For the sake of comfort, if you select this method of carry, you will need a holster that is dimensionally smaller and takes up less space on your belt. Appendix carry might not be comfortable with larger handguns, because when you sit or bend, the barrel will hit your sensitive areas while the grip pokes your ribs. This method of carry might not be comfortable for those with more of a spare tire, and it might take some getting used to.

BACK CARRY

This is basically the opposite of appendix carry and refers to carrying your gun somewhere between your strong side hip and small of the back.

Appendix carry positions the gun closer to the belly button and makes for a faster draw. TUFF Products

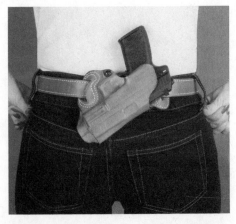

Small-of-the-back carry might feel comfortable, but it's difficult to tell if the gun is printing through a cover garment. DeSantis Gunhide

If you carry a gun on your waistline—either belt carry or IWB—you will likely find this method to be the most comfortable, and many people naturally gravitate to it. My own preference is to keep the gun right at my hip, but invariably the holster and gun migrate slightly back to where it's more comfortable. Frankly, there's just more room and less fat back there.

Carrying a gun just behind your hip or at the small of your back still provides quick access and keeps the gun completely concealed from the front. Even from a sitting position, you can reach your gun by simply leaning forward. However, you have less control of your gun, and you cannot see what people behind you can see. It is more difficult and requires a much greater conscious effort to keep your gun concealed in this manner, since your cover garments can ride up without your knowledge. In fact, every time you bend over, you will likely be printing through your clothes. Depending on the type of cover garment you have, it will also be more difficult to reach behind you to get it out of the way in order to draw your gun.

It will also be more difficult to re-holster, because you can't see the holster or make sure there are no obstructions to get in the way of the trigger. At least if you shoot yourself from behind, it will only be in the gluteus maximus (which is largely a survivable injury).

POCKET CARRY

The names of these methods of carry are not meant to confuse, but simply to be as descriptive as possible, and in this case, pocket carry means carrying a gun in your pants pocket. Pocket carry is incredibly popular, and even people who carry in other ways often have a backup pistol in their pocket. But unless you wear clown pants, you will be limited in terms of the size gun you can carry. Pocket pistols and revolvers are available in a wide variety of calibers, but they will all be fairly small guns.

Ideally, you should carry your pocket pistol on your strong side, but either side is fine, and if you are using it as a backup pistol, it might actually be better to carry it on the support side. If you are injured on your strong side or in a struggle against an assailant, you can still reach your backup gun with your support hand. Also, you will not be able to wear your skinny jeans when you pocket carry. You need pants that are loose enough so you can easily reach into your pocket.

Having looser pants with larger pockets also provides more versatility in terms of the type and size of gun you can use for pocket carry. It provides for a much faster draw, and it prevents the gun from printing through the material of your pants. This leads to one of the big advantages of pocket carry. It is possible, if you sense trouble, to have your gun in your hand ready for a very fast draw

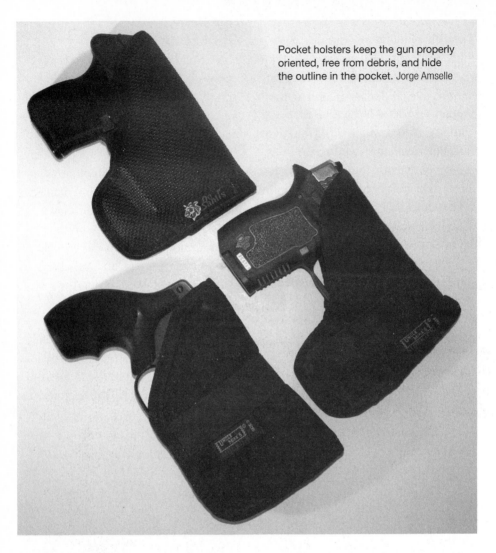

Pocket holsters keep the gun properly oriented, free from debris, and hide the outline in the pocket. Jorge Amselle

because from the outside, it just looks as though you have your hand in your pocket. This is actually a faster draw even than from a belt holster.

It is essential with pocket carry to use a proper pocket holster. These are available in nylon, Kydex and leather, but be sure to get a suitable holster and practice your draw. Otherwise, when you draw your gun, the holster will still be attached. The good hol-

sters will have a small tab that catches on the pocket when you draw, separating the holster from the gun. Others will have a tacky material sewn onto the sides to "grip" the pocket and keep the holster inside when you draw. My preference is to use my second finger to help flick the holster away from the gun as I draw.

A good pocket holster does several things. First, it protects the gun from

With pocket carry, pants should be loose enough and pockets large enough to provide easy access to the gun. Jorge Amselle

This Recluse pocket holster completely shields the gun on the outside to prevent printing while still allowing fast access. Recluse

pocket lint and debris, which can affect the functioning and reliability of the firearm. Second, it keeps the gun properly oriented (grip up) so you can quickly grasp and draw it. Third, the holster masks the outline of the gun, so it prevents printing and gives the impression you have a wallet in your front pocket.

The main drawback with pocket carry, besides that it limits the size of gun you can carry, is that it makes drawing a gun from a sitting position very difficult and almost impossible if you're driving. To draw your gun, you have to straighten your leg so you can reach into your pocket deeply enough.

This pocket holster is entirely self contained and completely hides the gun, even when moving it from place to place or handing it to another person. EZ Holsters

Of course, if you are driving, you're in control of a 4,000-pound weapon, and if you are sitting in a normal chair at home, at a restaurant, or at work, straightening your leg is not difficult. Also note that when you are sitting, the fabric of your pants stretches against your leg more and the gun is therefore more likely to print.

They also make pocket holsters specifically designed to fit in your rear pants pocket. Some of these have a hard flat leather outer cover to prevent printing and still provide very fast access to your gun. EZ Holsters offers a unit that completely hides the gun inside a hard-sided case with a snap closure. It is spring loaded, and when you open the snap, the gun pops up enough to where you can easily grip it. One advantage of the EZ Holster is that you can remove it and pass it to someone or store it right in the open, and it just looks like a case or a book, because the gun is hidden inside and completely covered.

Back-pocket carry might be more convenient for some and the gun easier to reach from a sitting position, but you lose some of the advantages of being able to stand with your hand in your pocket (on your gun) and getting the super-fast draw of front-pocket carry.

One final note of caution that applies to all types of concealed carry, but especially pocket carry: Be aware that on some guns, the magazine release can be activated without you realizing it. This depends on the design of the gun and the placement and length of the magazine release, as well as on the thickness and design of the holster. As you move, stand and especially sit, the holster and gun move around a bit in your pocket, and the material of your pants or your leg can press against the magazine release hard enough to free the magazine.

If this happens (and it has happened to me), when you draw your pocket pistol, the magazine will fall out and you will be left with the one round in the chamber (assuming you have a loaded chamber and assuming the gun does not have a magazine safety). In an emergency situation, you might not even realize your magazine is gone, and even if you do, you might not be able to find it on the ground. As a force of habit, I periodically reach into my pocket and make sure the magazine is fully inserted. This also makes carrying a spare magazine that much more important.

ANKLE CARRY

Ankle carry means that you have a gun strapped to your leg below the knee. Obviously, you will have to wear long pants to keep the gun concealed. This method of carry has some advantages. There is no burden or change to the way you dress at your waist or pockets. With the right holster, it can be very comfortable and totally unobtrusive, because most people will not be looking at your feet.

Out of the way and unobtrusive, ankle holsters offer versatility, especially for a backup gun. Uncle Mike's

The downsides to ankle carry are that you need to stick with a smaller-sized handgun and that you need to select pants that are both long enough to keep the gun concealed when you sit down and wide enough to provide access to the gun when you need it. Quick access is another sacrifice you make with this type of carry. The gun is located as far away from your hand as possible. If you are sitting down, especially in a vehicle, you can get fast access, but if you are standing, you'll have to bend over or kneel down completely to access your gun. For this reason, this type of carry is sometimes considered secondary and best suited for a backup handgun. If you carry in this manner, it's best to carry the gun on the inside of the leg on your support side.

Holster selection is also very important, because having a hard object

With ankle carry, method of draw will need to be adjusted. Galco

rubbing against your anklebone all day is far from comfortable. Most ankle holsters use an elastic material and Velcro to make the right fit and adjust to your leg. Some holsters have thick padding or sheep skin to cushion the area against your leg. Others use a garter system to help keep the holster and gun in place. Some people prefer the holster lower down on the ankle and others prefer it above the ankle. My preference is to wear an ankle holster with a black gun, black holster and a black boot, helping to keep everything comfortable and concealed.

It is also very important to select a holster with good retention, because as you walk, run or jump, the gun is more likely to come out of the holster. There was a story I heard from a police officer about a fellow patrolman who liked to carry a backup revolver in an ankle holster. During a highway traffic stop, he was involved in a bit of a scuffle. He did his job and went on

about his business. A few days later, a concerned citizen stopped by the police station with a gun he'd found on the side of the highway. It was rather beat up, undoubtedly from being run over multiple times. As it turned out, this was the backup ankle revolver of the aforementioned officer. It fell from his holster during the traffic stop, and he didn't notice that it was missing until much later. He could not find the gun and never reported it. He got in trouble.

While this is a testament to how comfortable his ankle holster was—to the point that he did not notice when the gun fell out—don't let this be you. I once had an ankle holster that, in my estimation, lacked sufficient retention. My quick fix was to fold the top of my sock down over the grip of the gun to keep it in place. Needless to say, sock retention is not ideal. Buy a good holster from the start, and if you do something that might result in the gun getting loose, check to make sure it's still there.

BELLY BANDS

Belly bands have been around for a long time and offer deep concealment with a lot of comfort. These wide elastic bands—available in a variety of colors so they don't show through your outer shirt—include pockets on both sides for ambidextrous use of a gun and spare ammunition or extra magazines. The bands fit anywhere around your torso that you find comfortable and are adjustable with a Velcro strip. You will want a snug fit. I find them most comfortable with an undershirt but in the summertime they can be used against bare skin.

The biggest advantage to belly bands is that they keep the gun tight against the body, so there's minimal chance of printing and you always know where your gun is. Many people find them to be especially well suited for strenuous activities such as jogging. You certainly don't want to be unarmed when you go for a run, and belly bands make it easy and comfort-able to keep your keys, ID, cell phone and gun on your person. They are also easily washed. They are not, however, built to last forever and if you use one a lot, replace it at least yearly, before the elastic wears out.

One drawback for many belly bands is that they lack any retention beyond the elastic. This is fine if you are not very active, but when running and jumping, it's best to find a belly band that at least includes a Velcro strap for handgun retention.

As with most types of carry, you will also need to adjust the way you

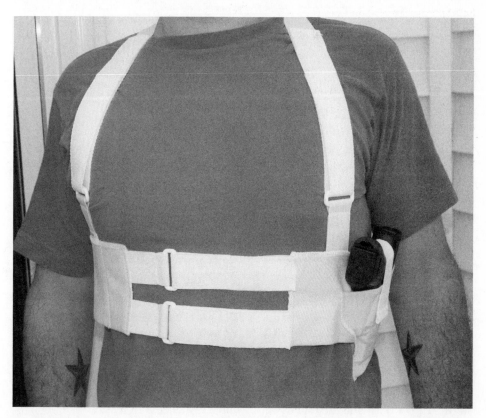

The Deep Conceal belly band holster combines elements of a shoulder holster and has retention as well. Jorge Amselle

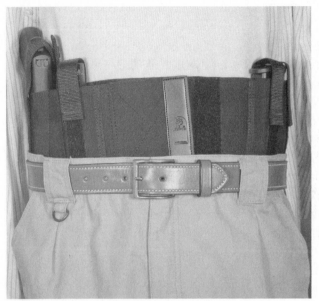

Belly bands keep the gun very close to the body and can be adjusted in a number of different ways. DeSantis Gunhide

support arm. You can, of course, orient the belly band to any position: strong-side carry, appendix carry, small of the back, etc. I personally find that a belly band offers the highest concealment when I wear it high on my torso and keep the gun located close to my armpit. However, I also find it a bit more comfortable to wear it around the waist. In a pinch, the belly band can also be used as an expedient IWB holster by simply moving it down below the belt line. Some belly bands are specifically designed for IWB use.

FANNY PACKS

Fanny packs are the ultimate accessory for the unfashionable. If you ever feel the need to relive the 1980s or just announce to the world that you have a gun, then a fanny pack holster is ideal. It's basically a purse you wear around your hip, and you'll want the pouch near your front to be able to access the gun. These types of holsters are very obvious to anyone who knows what to look for, but to the average person, you will just look like a tourist. This is just fine if your goal is to stay comfortable, keep your gun concealed and have fast access to it.

Fanny pack holsters are very

dress and practice drawing your firearm. If you wear a belly band under a loose shirt, it's a simple matter of lifting the shirt and reaching underneath for a fast draw. If you wear it underneath a tucked-in shirt, this will be much slower unless the shirt has buttons (in which case you can unbutton to reach the gun or in an emergency just rip the buttons). Deep Conceal makes shirts with fake buttons and Velcro underneath, allowing you to quickly access your gun without ruining your shirt.

Also be aware that with most types of belly bands, you will be cross drawing, so take extra care where your muzzle is pointed and keep your finger off the trigger until you are on target. Otherwise you risk perforating your

Fanny packs and belt bags allow for comfortable carry and will keep even a large gun completely hidden. But they do stick out in some environments.
DeSantis Gunhide

comfortable and require no adjustments in your normal clothing. Many of them are also roomy enough to carry spare ammunition, keys, a cell phone, pepper spray, a knife, etc. The main caveat here is to buy a fanny pack specifically designed for use as a holster, and not just to try and repurpose a standard fanny pack.

Holster fanny packs have a specific holder to keep your gun oriented for a proper draw, and they have a dedicated pocket for your gun so it doesn't get caught up with other items. Many specifically designed fanny pack holsters also have a quick opening system, either zippered or Velcro, to provide you with quick access to your gun.

Weapon retention is also not an issue, because the gun is completely enclosed inside the fanny pack. Most of the holster fanny packs on the market have an ambidextrous design for right-

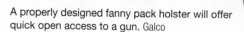

A properly designed fanny pack holster will offer quick open access to a gun. Galco

The Sneaky Pete holster is a great compromise— a belt holster that looks like a cell phone case. SneakyPete Holsters

and left-handed shooters. This method of carry is not only comfortable, but also extremely convenient if you have to remove your handgun when you are entering a restricted area. You can also hand the fanny pack off to another person and remain completely inconspicuous.

Drawing from a fanny pack holster is very simple and fast, because the pack rides on the outside of your clothing. Most people will opt to keep the fanny pack directly in front of them just below the belly button. Others prefer to keep it more toward the hip. It is important to make sure that whichever position you select, you can easily reach the fanny pack and open it quickly to access your gun. Also be aware that most fanny packs are designed for cross draw so again, try to not muzzle your arm, hand or other people when you draw, and keep your finger off the trigger until you are on target.

CHAPTER 6

OFF-BODY CARRY

Carrying a gun on your person is always best. However, it's not always convenient, and off-body carry has always been a popular option for many people. The single biggest reason for its popularity is comfort. Women often carry purses rather than trying to stuff all of their personal items into various pockets. This is because women's clothing is generally not designed with a lot of pockets. In terms of style, men and women's clothing are worlds apart.

Likewise, seeing a man with a briefcase, backpack, day planner or shoulder bag doesn't raise any eyebrows. It's very easy and convenient to carry a large handgun and spare ammunition in this manner. You have the benefit of convenience, because you can have a gun with you regardless of your clothing and you have relatively easy access to it. It's also easy to simply leave your carry device locked

Carrying a gun in a bag or case means not having to make any wardrobe adjustments. Remember, airports require that guns are checked in before going through security checkpoints.
Mobile Edge Laptop Cases

up in a vehicle, desk or locker.

Accessing your gun from a purse, briefcase or backpack can be done very quickly and easily. If you sense there might be trouble brewing, you can even prep your draw by reaching into your bag and from the outside, it just appears as though you're looking for something or perhaps grasping your keys. Depending on your gun and the type of carry you use, you also have the option of being able to fire your gun right through the material of your bag.

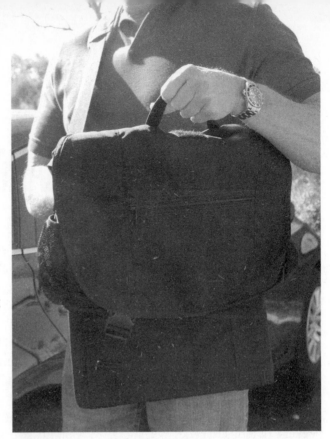

Well-designed cases make it easy to inconspicuously reach in and grab a gun. Santan Gear

My wife sometimes walks to the mailbox in the evening to check the mail (since I'm too lazy to do it during the day), and she always brings her purse with her gun in it. If she sees anyone who appears suspicious, she reaches inside and places her hand on the grip of her gun, ready to draw. If she were suddenly attacked from a different direction than the one she expects (criminals often will use misdirection to their advantage), she could fire quickly through her purse in an unexpected direction.

There are several caveats, however, which should illustrate exactly why this method of concealed carry is not ideal. First of all, you have to maintain 100 percent awareness of where your gun is located at all times. This method of carry is so convenient that it's easy to forget you even have a gun with you. How many times have you forgotten a briefcase or backpack? If you are a woman, have you ever left your purse someplace and forgotten it?

This actually happened to my wife one time while I was with her. She carries a gun in her purse routinely, and once after we were done eating at a restaurant, she left her purse under the table and forgot it. Partly this was because she doesn't always bring her

Don't leave a gun bag where someone could get to it who shouldn't. David McSpadden

ing officer or security guard is not going to react well when they find your abandoned bag with a gun in it. At the very least, you will suffer embarrassment and possibly a lot worse.

How do you prevent unauthorized access if you put down your bag—say you leave it in your office while you go to the rest room? I used to work in an office building where thieves sometimes snuck into the building pretending to be repairmen or delivery people and went into unattended offices to dig though women's purses and steal wallets. Imagine how happy some ne'er-do-well would be to find a gun he could sell on the streets for hundreds of dollars.

Let's say you keep your gun in a bag all of the time, but it's not always on your person—maybe you put it in the closet when you get home. If you have small children or a guest with small children, there's a chance they might find your gun and injure themselves or others. **If your gun is not in your immediate control, you need to take measures to secure it.**

If you take your gun to work in a bag, lock it up in your desk or a locker when it's not in within your reach. If

purse when I am with her (since I usually pay) and part is just normal forgetfulness we all have. We only realized our mistake about halfway home and immediately returned. Luckily, the waitress had noticed the abandoned bag and held onto it until we returned. If you leave your bag behind, immediately call and ask that it be located and retained someplace safe until you arrive.

Nowadays, we are being constantly warned to be on the lookout for terrorism and abandoned bags. There are news stories of travelers who forgot they had a gun or ammunition in their carry-on bags as they tried to go through security. It has happened to friends of mine who are experienced and knowledgeable, fortunately without serious repercussions. A respond-

Locking a gun in a desk drawer is a good means of securing it if it's necessary to leave it unattended. Gabriel Saldana

you leave it in your car, make sure your car is locked. When you are home, it should also be on your person or secured. Many concealed-carry off-body holsters have locking zippers or other ways to secure the gun inside the bag, box, case or purse. This certainly helps prevent unauthorized access, but it doesn't prevent someone from stealing your bag.

This also significantly slows down your draw, because the case or zipper must first be unlocked before you can access your gun. If you have warning enough to retrieve your gun in this situation, you should really have used the time to call for help or leave the area. A gun at work locked up in your desk, locker or car is not easily accessible when you need it, which defeats the purpose of concealed carry.

The final problem is that thieves are often attracted to whatever they think holds your valuables, such as

your briefcase or purse. The whole notion of concealed carry is to be able to respond to an assailant without anyone knowing you are armed. But what happens when an assailant is interested only in snatching your

福岡県警察・福岡県防犯協会連合会・福岡県バス協会
県警察ホームページ：http://www.police.pref.fukuoka.jp/
県防犯協会ホームページ：http://www.fukuboren.com/

Be aware that a thief will be attracted to an off-body-carry bag. Stealing it and discovering a gun inside will be a welcome bonus. Photocapy

purse or backpack, which they can do without warning and when you are least aware? I can only imagine the feeling if the bag where I keep my gun is stolen from me—leaving me poorer, defenseless and with the knowledge that I just armed some miscreant.

If you're going to carry using this method, the level of situational awareness required is very high. That's not a bad thing—anyone who wants to avoid being victimized should have a higher than average level of awareness, but this method of carry is less forgiving if you slip up.

I don't want to leave a negative impression of this method of concealed carry. If done properly and with due attention, it's very effective, comfortable and convenient. Depending on your clothing selection, especially for specific events or types of weather, off-body carry might be your best option. For many people it's the only convenient or comfortable way to go about their day armed. It's far better to have a gun in a bag or purse than to not have one at all.

BACKPACKS

A backpack is an easy and comfortable way to carry a concealed handgun, especially in casual settings such as college (at universities that allow concealed carry), hiking, sightseeing, etc. The key is to be unobtrusive and inconspicuous. Unfortunately, many backpacks designed for concealed carry give the impression you are about to help Chuck Norris invade Vietnam and rescue some POWs. But with tactical chic being what it is today, you will tend to stand out less than days gone by but still, these types of bags scream, "I have a gun!"

Specially designed conceal-carry backpacks, such as this one from Blackhawk, have a quick access pistol compartment and blend in well. Blackhawk

Recognizing that a tactical backpack defeats the whole "concealed" part of CCW, some enterprising souls have taken it upon themselves to repurpose more sporting or civilian-looking bags. In response, manufacturers such as Blackhawk have produced an entire line of what they call "Diversion" bags—those specifically designed to hold a gun, while appearing very casual and "civilian."

The advantage of a specifically designed CCW backpack is that you have a quick access, a dedicated pocket for a gun and likely have a built-in holster to keep it properly oriented and secured. Of course, most of these backpacks can also be used as regular backpacks to hold all of your stuff. Some are designed to carry compact carbine rifles, which is probably not what most people view as a concealed-carry firearm.

Frankly, I use these sorts of bags a lot when I go to the range, just because I don't want to raise any eyebrows or worry my neighbors. As far as anyone is concerned, I'm going for a hike, to play tennis or to the gym, and that's just fine with me.

BRIEFCASES

In a more formal setting, such an office or business meeting, a briefcase might be a more inconspicuous container for your concealed handgun. If quick access is a concern, there are soft-sided briefcases with specifically designed access panels that have a Velcro closure or a special zippered

Many conceal-carry briefcases allow for quick access but still fit in with business attire. Santan Gear

pocket that provides fast access to your handgun. The main advantage to these types of briefcases is that you still have access to the materials you need for your normal business, without having to reach into the gun pocket.

It is also possible to repurpose a standard briefcase by placing a zippered gun case inside with your other items. Of course, this will drastically slow down your draw. My father used to own a briefcase with the sole purpose of concealing a Heckler and Koch MP5 submachine gun with a trigger tab that was engaged when you squeezed a special trigger on the briefcase handle. In this manner, he could fire the gun through a special open-ing on the side of the case without ever having to open the case (except to reload). This is likely more than is needed by most of us for CCW use.

DAY PLANNERS

You used to see day planners and schedulers in the hands of nearly every business person or office worker. Now, with smartphones and apps, you rarely see them anymore, but they still won't raise any eyebrows, except from people who might laugh at you for being so old school. The nice thing about day planners is that they're the perfect size and shape to hide a handgun, even a large handgun with spare ammunition.

The basic day planner holsters serve only to hold your gun in place. Look for one with an interior holster, so your gun isn't bouncing around in there and making a lot of noise. The best day planners are fully functional as intended and will allow you to take notes, schedule meetings, etc. The gun is kept in a hidden compartment underneath. As with other off-body carry methods, many of these will also have inter-

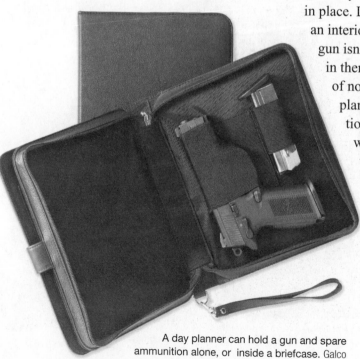

A day planner can hold a gun and spare ammunition alone, or inside a briefcase. Galco

nal locks to secure them when they're not in your immediate control.

I recall using day planners a lot (back in the day), and they were always on the heavy side. Should someone pick up your day planner holster, the weight of the gun will most likely not be noticeable. You can walk around all day holding your day planner, and it will not alarm anyone, and will provide quick access to your gun. This type of carry is also convenient if you go out to a restaurant and have to leave your gun in the car, or if you carpool and have to leave it in another person's car. Just make sure it's locked up.

Day planners are available in various sizes, and so are day planner holsters.

This means you can comfortably carry a full-sized handgun that provides a better grip, more firepower (in terms of ammunition capacity) and is easier to shoot accurately. You don't have to adjust your clothing choices, and they're equally convenient for men and women.

HIDDEN TRANSPORT

As they say: Out of sight, out of mind, and there are a variety of everyday items that can be used to hide a gun. Book holsters are a good example, and there are several styles available. Most of the ones I've seen are a bit on the large size and designed more for hiding valuables. Consequently, they don't hold the gun in place if the book is moved around a lot.

There's a huge selection of hidden and disguised gun storage solutions available.
Go Outdoors Products

If you were going to use one of these secret books to carry your gun, I would cut a piece of foam and fit it inside to secure your gun properly. Also, be aware that most of these books do not close very securely and don't have locks on them, so if you drop it or aren't careful, your gun could become exposed or worse still, fall out.

You could also make your own book holster out of an old hardcover book. Anything written by a politician is a great candidate for this, and you can usually find them at a thrift store or discount bin, or even under a table leg to keep it from wobbling. All you need to do is cut out a hole in the pages to fit your gun. Glue the rest of the pages shut for a more secure holster.

There are also holsters designed to look like a box of tissues, a first aid kit, a container for road flares and a roadside emergency kit. You might look a bit odd carrying these things around with you, but they are perfectly suitable for carrying a hidden gun in your car. Many of these have a zippered area to secure your firearm and extra ammunition.

SHOULDER BAGS

If a backpack is too much, the fanny pack too unstylish, and you don't want to carry something in your hands all day, then the man purse is ideal. Of course, no one is going to buy a man purse, so manufacturers make these shoulder bags look as tough and tactical as possible. Some of them even have tactical names such as "active shooter" bags with AR magazine pouches and MOLLE webbing all over them. Not exactly the height of discretion.

Shoulder bags offer versatility and extra room for other gear. It's not a man purse! Maxpedition

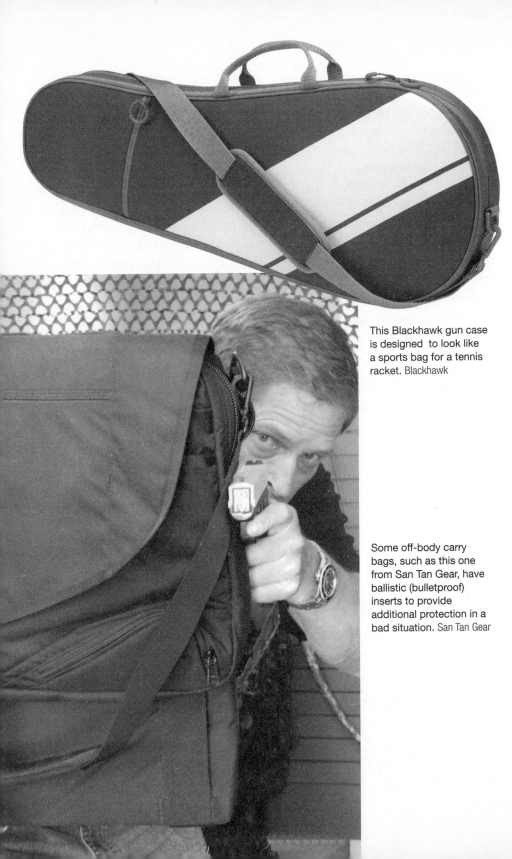

This Blackhawk gun case is designed to look like a sports bag for a tennis racket. Blackhawk

Some off-body carry bags, such as this one from San Tan Gear, have ballistic (bulletproof) inserts to provide additional protection in a bad situation. San Tan Gear

These shoulder bags are extremely practical, however, and usually fall in size between a messenger bag and a camera case. They are so convenient that it makes you wonder why men don't carry purses. They not only allow you to carry your concealed handgun in a dedicated holster pocket, but they also provide ample room for spare ammunition and other self defense items. Some manufacturers are developing more discreet shoulder bags with various colors and casual designs.

Shoulder bags are excellent for activities such as hiking or bike riding, as well as for travel and sightseeing when you would normally be carrying a map, camera, water bottle, etc. Some of these shoulder bags are also scalable and can be attached to larger backpacks. Many also feature a quick access holster compartment secured with Velcro or a fast zipper. Most of the ones I've seen don't have an internal locking mechanism, so take extra care not to leave your bag unattended.

For the extra cautious, it should be noted that some manufacturers have developed backpacks, briefcases, computer bags and shoulder bags with built-in ballistic panels that can stop most handgun ammunition. These shields will add to the cost of your off-body carry bag, but they offer a level of protection equal to that of most police vests in a compact system. Body armor is legal almost everywhere but again, check local laws before using it.

One option in this hybrid body armor/shoulder bag/holster category is the Exec Pro bag from San Tan Gear. On the outside, it looks like a computer bag, and will indeed hold your computer and other peripherals. It also contains a hidden pocket with an internal ambidextrous holster for a full-sized handgun and spare ammunition.

Internally, it has an NIJ (National Institute of Justice) certified Level IIIA ballistic insert panel, which will stop all standard shotgun and handgun ammunition. A simple pull of a tab at the bottom releases a second ballistic panel for 270 square inches of protective shield. Two handles at the rear let you hold it as a shield and maneuver out of harm's way or take a defensive position. The bag also includes a flashing strobe light for signaling others or identifying yourself to first responders.

VEHICLE CARRY

Most people don't think of their car or truck as part of their concealed-carry system. But keeping a gun in your car, especially a shotgun or rifle, can absolutely be part of your personal defense plans. I would caution anyone doing this to be mindful of local and state laws, especially if you cross state lines.

Living close to the Maryland/Washington, D.C. border—two of the least gun-friendly places in the United States—and conducting business and having family in both places, I do not keep a gun in my car. I don't want to take the chance that I might forget

Vehicle carry is ideal for long guns. CaseCruzer

that my gun is in my car and end up arrested. In D.C. it's a felony to even have ammunition.

A close friend put it better than I could regarding why vehicle carry is a good idea. The fact is, he explained, a handgun is completely unsuitable for self defense. The only reason anyone carries or uses handguns is that they are smaller and more convenient than rifles or shotguns. A handgun, for him, was primarily a tool to use in an emergency and could help him get to a "real" gun. Rifles and shotguns are far more powerful than handguns, and accurate from longer distances.

Vehicle carry of long guns is especially appealing when traveling. If you're planning a weeklong getaway

to the mountains or the beach—even if you have no plans to go shooting—it's a great comfort knowing you have the means with you for serious personal protection. Likewise, if you are on a drive far from home where there's a possibility of being stuck or stranded, you might feel under-armed with just your pocket pistol.

Keeping a loaded (or unloaded, depending on local laws) rifle and/ or shotgun in a case in your vehicle is a good backup for times when your handgun might not be enough gun. With this type of carry, make sure to keep your long gun cased and preferably locked or secured in some manner, in case your car gets stolen or broken into. You will also want to keep the case out of sight, because thieves will often smash and grab what they can see of value.

There are rifle cases for carbines designed to look like a tennis racket case. Blackhawk makes a whole line of these "Diversion" bags. Renegade Ridge Tactical makes a great diversion bag for a carbine rifle that fits on the back of the driver's or passenger's seat in a vehicle and allows for very fast access of a loaded rifle.

Of course, many people also choose to carry handguns in their vehicles. Depending on your state and local laws, you may be able to carry a loaded or unloaded gun with you at all times in your car. You may be able to keep it unlocked and within reach, say in a center console or glove box. Of course, if you have a concealed-carry permit, you will have more options in this regard.

Several companies make cases specifically for carrying a handgun in a vehicle. One innovative design comes from Titan Gun Vault, which has a locking steel case that pops the gun up grip first when you open it. It also has a separate area for a loaded magazine so you can carry an unloaded gun and load it very quickly if needed. Be aware that in some areas, a full magazine within reach of a semi-automatic pistol could be considered a loaded gun.

There are other car holster systems available. Some actually secure the gun, such as The RAC, which looks like a bike lock. Some only hold a gun in place with a simple holster or magnet, such as the one from Magna-Arm. This type of carry might also be suitable for people who are not allowed to carry at work. At least you can be armed while going to and from work.

This discreet rifle case from Renegade Ridge Tactical makes it easy to transport a long gun.
Jorge Amselle

One of my concerns with keeping a gun in my car—besides the fact that if it's the only gun I carry, I'm defenseless when I'm away from my car—is that it could get stolen. For this reason, you probably shouldn't keep your most expensive guns or family heirlooms in your vehicle on a full-time basis. A friend keeps a cheap but reliable shotgun and rifle in his vehicle, what some folks refer to as "trunk" guns.

Unless you are always parked in a climate-controlled garage, your vehicle will be subject to temperature extremes, humidity and the usual bumps and shakes as you drive. All of this is harmful to guns and ammunition over the long term—the more exposure, the worse the problem becomes.

My recommendation is to check on your gun at least every couple of weeks to make sure it's still there and that it has not developed any rust or maintenance issues. Any ammunition you keep in your car should be replaced at least annually, if not every 6 months. Take it to the range and

The Titan gun case allows for a locked gun within easy reach in a vehicle. Titan Gun Case

There are plenty of gun storage solutions for cars or trucks. Du-Ha

shoot it up. This will help improve your shooting while ensuring that your ammunition is as functional as possible at all times.

Finally, there's a very important caveat. If you lend your car to anyone, make sure they are aware that you keep firearms inside, that they are not a prohibited person or will not be violating any laws by transporting the firearms, and that they will not be traveling to any place where the firearms are not legal to transport or possess. Better yet, remove the firearms from your vehicle before lending it to anyone if there are any doubts at all.

CHAPTER 7

WOMEN'S HOLSTERS

By Megan and Jorge Amselle

Firearms being the great equalizer they are, it should come as no surprise that the fastest-growing segment of concealed-carry applications are coming from women. There are also a plethora of firearms training courses and programs offered specifically for women that provide a more comfortable and supportive learning environment.

Of course, having a concealed-carry permit isn't going to do you much good if you don't actually carry a gun, and the most important factor that determines whether you carry a gun or leave it at home is comfort. It's not only important to choose the right gun but also the right holster, and thankfully manufacturers are catering to the specific needs of women.

Women who carry concealed were once limited to using the same holsters as men, which were often a bit oversized and generally not very feminine. However, as the ranks of conceal-carry ladies swelled, manufacturers began creating holsters designed specifically to fit women's bodies. Most women shooters today have multiple holster systems available that correspond to a variety of conceal-

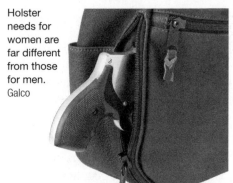

Holster needs for women are far different from those for men. Galco

Women are the fastest-growing segment of the concealed-carry market. Viridian Green Laser-Oleg Volk

ment scenarios: everyday casual, business, evening and even exercising.

Buying a holster is not that different from buying clothes. You need one that's comfortable, fits your body and is concealable under what you're wearing. And just like shopping for clothes, you should try out several holster types to find one or more that feel comfortable and natural to you. Remember, if your holster is uncomfortable, chances are you won't wear it.

As a cautionary tale, consider what the late Nobel Prize winning economist Milton Friedman wrote about the four ways to spend money. You can spend your money on yourself, in which case you get exactly what you want at the lowest price. You can spend your money on someone else, in which case you get a good price and they probably don't get what they want. You can spend someone else's money on yourself, in which case you get exactly what you want with no regard to cost. And you can spend someone else's money on another person, in which case cost and need go right out the window. My point is: If you are buying something as personal as a holster for another person, be sure to keep the receipt.

Don't be fooled by the shenanigans of some manufacturers trying to capture a share of the women's market. Unfortunately, there are those who simply make things in pink and expect women to buy them, or expect men to buy them for their wives, daughters, mothers, sisters, girlfriends, etc. It makes no sense to spend hundreds of dollars on a high-quality handgun and then try to save a few bucks on a holster, which can be just as important to effective self defense.

For each of the categories listed here, there are manufacturers who have specifically designed concealed-carry holsters for women. All of these manufacturers have women shooters who work with them. Some of them sponsor competitive female shooters who help design their gear and really put it to the test. If something doesn't work or is not comfortable, you can bet they will hear about it.

Many of these manufacturers also cater to law enforcement, including female police officers who carry everyday on- and off-duty. When your life is on the line, you take a very dim view of equipment that doesn't deliver.

BELT HOLSTERS

The classic model is the outside-the-waistband holster, attached by a clip, paddle or belt loop. It offers the best access to the gun and is the easiest to draw from. OWB holsters are versatile and can be used in a variety of positions on the waist: strong side, cross draw, small of the back, appendix, etc. Its downside is that it's not very easy to conceal, particularly because few women appreciate a bulky mass right on their waistline. This type of holster is used mostly in cooler weather, when jackets and sweatshirts

Holsters specifically designed for women, such as this one from Safariland, compensate for curves and improve comfort. Safariland

women's belt holster doesn't just place the gun higher on the hip, it also angles it slightly outward to prevent discomfort.

Safariland's Model 329 is designed to ride close to the body for concealment but allow the holster to angle outward when drawing. It also features a low-cut opening in the front so the gun can clear the holster much more easily without having to raise it up too far. This is important because the holster is already placed higher on the hip, so a high draw would be difficult.

Safariland's Model 6378 ALS Paddle Holster features Level 1 retention, with the holster automatically locking the gun in place and releasing it via a thumb button, which can be

easily cover it. In hotter weather, a very loose shirt is required to conceal its shape.

Hip carry for many women can be a challenge, but Safariland and Bianchi both produce a line of holsters that are designed for women who tend to wear their gun higher on the hip. For men, the hip is mostly a straight up and down affair—not so for women. Because of the angle of the hip, a standard belt holster designed for men will tend to dig into the ribs on a woman. A well-designed

Women's holsters compensate with a lower ride and enlarged opening in the front. Safariland

operated very quickly with little practice. Several Bianchi paddle holsters designed for women feature a slight offset to increase comfort for female users and are available in standard and retention styles.

I personally prefer paddle holsters for their ease of use and the ability to remove or replace them with minimal effort, especially when I have to go someplace that doesn't allow firearms, such as the Post Office. However, women might prefer a standard belt holster that avoids having to place anything inside the pants or against the skin, which can be less comfortable. Many paddle holsters have a tendency to pinch the skin on the inside, especially if the pants have a tight fit.

INSIDE THE WAISTBAND

As with men's inside-the-waistband holsters, IWB holsters for women require pants or skirts that are slightly larger in order to fit comfortably and accommodate the extra space needed for a gun and holster. Also, like belt holsters, women will find that IWB carry will be most comfortable with the gun high on the hip, although depending on body shape and clothing choices, some women prefer a low rise

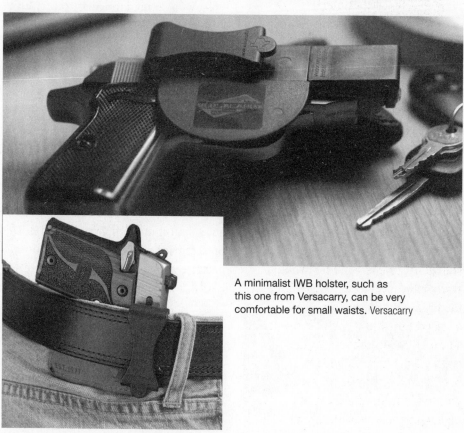

A minimalist IWB holster, such as this one from Versacarry, can be very comfortable for small waists. Versacarry

waistline and lower IWB carry.

With high IWB carry, a full draw can be difficult if the gun is riding high on the hip. However, Crossbreed Holsters are a very popular and comfortable choice because they feature a thick leather pad between the gun and the body and provide excellent concealment and a fast draw.

Holsters that fit inside the waistband offer many of the same advantages as OWB holsters. They're fairly easy to access and can be placed at several positions on the waist. But they are more concealable than an OWB holster because the fabric of the

A belly band is a comfortable and effective IWB holster. Galco

wearer's pants shields the outline. It's very important to ensure that an IWB holster is well-padded and comfortable, because it will be pressed against your skin with minimal cushioning.

The one major drawback of IWB holsters is fitting them inside your pants. If you have the room to spare, then there's no problem. If, however, you already have a little muffin top, you might have to buy slightly larger pants to accommodate an IWB holster comfortably. This is aggravating, but having a gun dig into your belly is worse and will quickly lead to the gun being left at home. IWB and pocket holsters also tend to work best with slim pistols, because the cylinder of a revolver adds more bulk.

You will also need a cover garment to conceal the exposed grip of the handgun. Here women's styles can be more forgiving, because untucked shirts and blouses as well as light jackets are common and stylish. You should avoid clothing that's too form-fitting, which will make it more difficult to conceal the gun and make accessing it more difficult. Light-colored fabrics also require due caution, because a dark-colored gun is more likely to show through the garment.

POCKET CARRY

Men's pants tend to be baggier than women's, and having larger thighs and hips doesn't help either in terms of carrying a gun in a pants pocket. Women who want to pocket carry need pants that are baggy enough to disguise the outline of the gun and provide fast access to it. Cargo pants or cargo shorts with at least one pocket large enough to hold a small handgun are a suitable option.

A good compromise that's not available to men is skirts with front pockets. A loose skirt can be very comfortable and stylish, and if it's made out of sturdy wool, cotton or linen, it will support the weight of the gun without sagging or bunching curiously on one side. Women's clothing also tends to have a lot more variety than clothing for men, so it gives women an opportunity to get creative with concealed-carry pockets. Light jackets and sweaters, as well as different styles of pants, suits and skirts, can be found with multiple pockets that fit the bill.

Of course, all pocket carry should be conducted in conjunction with a suitable pocket holster that protects the trigger of the gun and masks its outline. Summertime concealed carry is a challenge for everyone, but especially for women. It takes a certain amount of creativity and perseverance to carry on your person every day. Don't get discouraged.

ALTERNATIVE CARRY

Moving up the torso, shoulder holsters are a popular concealed-carry option. Since the gun is held under the armpit, the waist is free to bend and move unencumbered. While these holsters might look rather elaborate, they're actually very similar to wearing a bra, and will feel familiar to women. Unfortunately, shoulder holsters generally require a jacket or vest to hide them, so like OWB holsters, they are most appropriately used in cooler weather. They are also most comfortable with a slim gun that doesn't press into the upper arm too much.

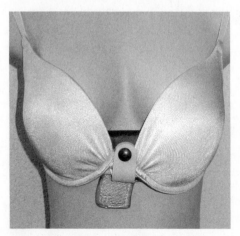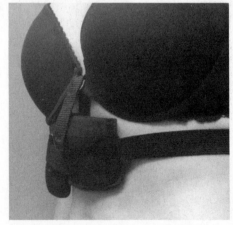

Attaching a holster or a small gun directly to a bra will keep them well-concealed. Flashbang (left) Deep Conceal (right)

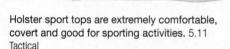

Flashbang makes a series of different bra holsters, but women must get used to a different draw style. Flashbang

A close relative of the shoulder holster is the bra holster, a relatively new innovation that exclusively benefits the female market. The bra holster takes advantage of a woman's natural curves to hide the outline of the gun and uses her bra to hold it up—no extra shoulder straps required. There are several models of bra holsters (with new ones constantly being developed), but the two general concepts place the gun in the front or on the side. In the former, the holster hangs from the front of the bra so the gun is concealed under the bust line. Women with larger busts find this particularly convenient, because they can easily hide a gun under this natural shelf.

The second type of bra holster hooks on to the side of the bra, with the gun held outside or inside the bra band or cup. Like with the shoulder holster, a slim gun will minimize bulk, but even so, you might find that this holster works only with certain bra styles or that you need to purchase a larger bra size if the gun needs to go inside the cup. Bra holsters are usually

Holster sport tops are extremely comfortable, covert and good for sporting activities. 5.11 Tactical accessed by reaching up from under the hem of the shirt, so they work best with an untucked shirt. If you have a top with a wide or low neck, you can access the gun from the top.

A comfortable alternative to bra and shoulder holsters is the concealment tank top. Also available in sleeved and cropped styles, it holds the gun in a built-in pocket with no straps or clips necessary. The gun pocket is usually located under the armpit, but some models put it at the waist or elsewhere. There are many colors and styles available to fit into your wardrobe as either a shirt or a camisole. 5.11 Tactical offers a women's holster shirt designed to fit the entire torso snugly—like sports attire—and features two underarm pockets ideal for small- and medium-sized handguns.

The advantage here is that the shirt will not shift position as you move, and the weight of the gun is evenly distributed. An inner neoprene and terry cloth layer cushions the gun and increases comfort. In general, you will need to add an outer garment that covers the pocket but still leaves it accessible—a jacket or shirt with an open front or a loose-fitting hem.

Another option for those who prize comfort while carrying is the belly band holster. This holster is excellent for everyday use, because it conceals the gun easily under any type of shirt that allows access to the waist. This is also one of the few holster types that can be worn reliably while exercising without it shifting out of place.

Underwraps from Galco offer great comfort and outstanding concealment. These elastic fabric bands are secured with hook and loop fasteners (Velcro) and are adjustable. They feature leather pockets that can hold firearms, extra ammunition and other accessories (knife, pepper spray, cell phone, etc.) and are ambidextrous. A simple T-shirt worn over them can serve as an excellent cover while exercising.

This Pistolwear belly band holster is designed for comfort and activities such as jogging. Pistolwear

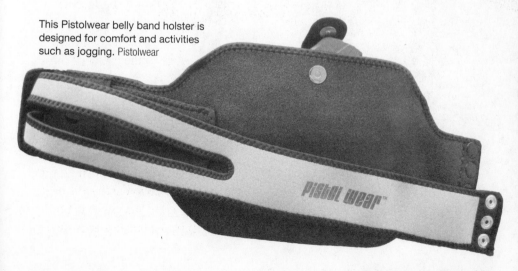

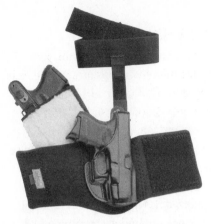

Ankle holsters for women can be used with flared-leg pants for easy access. Galco

Many women prefer ankle holsters, an option that can offer ideal concealment when wearing long pants with a boot cut or flared leg. These allow easy access to the gun and eliminate the aggravation of being poked in the ribs by the gun's grips. Ankle holsters require a very small gun and long, wide-legged pants, but they can easily be incorporated into a causal or business wardrobe. Galco's Ankle Glove features a wide elastic band with a sheepskin lining for comfort and an optional calf strap for added retention.

Women who love cowboy boots might also find a small clip holster in the boot to be the perfect method of carry. There are options to fit every style.

A dress presents one of the most challenging scenarios for concealed carry. With no room for a gun on

Unfortunately, Spandex workout gear doesn't work as well; it will allow a belly band to print as either an odd bulge on the waist or (worst case) as a clear outline of the gun. A looser top is recommended.

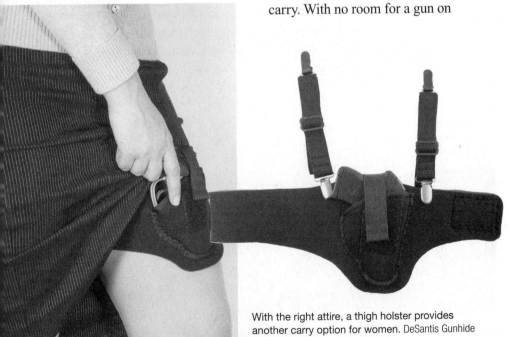

With the right attire, a thigh holster provides another carry option for women. DeSantis Gunhide

the waist or torso, the most common holster types are useless. However, the skirt provides ample concealment for a thigh holster. The various designs use different methods to hold the gun in place. Some have straps that loop around the waist; others rely on their own tight elasticity to stay up. Either way, test it first to ensure that it doesn't fall down or chafe against your legs.

A gun with a slim profile will allow you to walk naturally without it poking into your legs. DeSantis Gunhide produces the Thigh High Holster, which allows women wearing a skirt or dress to carry a small handgun concealed on the inner thigh. Neoprene construction offers comfort and twin garter straps ensure the gun and holster stay in place.

PURSE HOLSTERS

Arguably, the most comfortable way for many women to carry a gun is in a purse. This offers excellent concealment, is not affected by clothing choice, and can provide fast access. They require no change whatsoever to your routine; you're already carrying a bag anyway, so why not switch to a holster bag? It also eliminates many of the major concerns with on-body carry, particularly the weight of the gun and its visibility under clothing. A bag can also hold as big a gun as you want with complete discretion and comfort.

The major downside to off-body carry is the risk of losing the gun, by either forgetting your bag or having it stolen. A woman's purse is often a

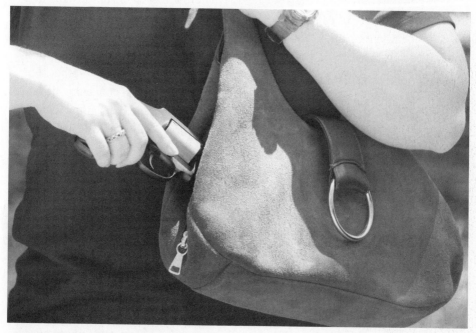

A purse holster will have a dedicated gun pocket with a zipper and lock for security. Jorge Amselle

There is a wide assortment of large, small and fashionable holster purses for women to choose from. Galco

primary target, and its loss leaves you defenseless and the criminal better armed. Even if a thief simply runs off with the purse, you now face reporting a stolen gun to the police in addition to the nightmare of calling all of your credit card companies. You must remain constantly aware of your purse to maintain quick access to it, as well as to prevent theft or access by unauthorized persons, especially curious children.

To help prevent these scenarios, there are special classes offered on gun and bag retention for those considering off-body carry. Taking a class is highly recommended if one is available in your area; look at it as an excellent investment in your own safety and well-being if you use a concealment bag.

The instructor will challenge you be more self-aware and to consider whether this method of concealed carry is right for you. If you are somewhat absent-minded and have a habit of forgetting your things, a holster purse might be nothing but trouble for you. If, on the other hand, you tend to treat your bag as almost an extension of your body, it can work well.

If you decide a holster purse is a good option, you will never need to worry about compromising style for the sake of safety. Concealment bags are available in literally every style and color imaginable. From slim clutches that can accommodate a subcompact gun and match the most elegant evening attire to large tote bags for those who would not dream of leaving the house without all their supplies, there's something for everyone.

There are even clever designs that imitate a briefcase, laptop case or smartphone holder. These are appropriate for men as well as women and blend well with business clothes. For hikers and athletes, concealment fanny packs and athletic bags allow hands-free security wherever you go.

The price point for these bags is equally wide-ranging. They start around $30-$40 and go up to sky's-the-limit designs in crocodile and ostrich leather (just like shopping for a regular purse). There are also inexpensive systems that allow you to convert any bag into a concealment purse by attaching a Velcro pad with an accompanying holster to one of the inside pockets. The Velcro attachment allows you to place the holster at the position and angle of your choosing, so it can be customized to fit well in any bag. This system is ideal for those who prefer high-end designer bags that might cost thousands but are not available in concealed-carry models, or for anyone else who is loath to give up a purse they already have and love.

The only caveat is that the holster should be given its own compartment in the purse. You don't want to reach for your gun in an emergency, only to find it entangled with your keys and a lipstick tube stuck in the barrel. Likewise, you don't want to reach into your bag for a pen and have it accidentally hook onto the gun. The gun needs its own private pocket, which means that a bag with only a single compart-ment is not going to make a good carry bag. Mixing loose items with your gun can also have tragic results if these items become entangled with the trigger and you end up firing a shot negligently.

Among the professionally designed concealment bags, there are two general types: those with fixed holsters and those with adjustable holsters. Fixed-holster bags have a small, dedicated pocket with the holster sewn permanently inside. This is particularly common in smaller bags, where there's only one way for the gun to fit. The pocket usually has a lock and key, to be used at the carrier's discretion. This feature is very useful for parents whose children might go digging in their purse.

The Galco Carry Safe, with a fixed Velcro backing, converts almost any bag into a holster. Jorge Amselle

Adjustable holster bags have a dedicated pocket for the gun, but the holster can be moved and positioned as the user wishes, usually by means of Velcro. In a large tote bag, being able to customize the angle and depth of the gun within the bag is extremely helpful to avoid an uncomfortable reach.

Once you've chosen your carry purse, it's important to practice drawing from it, both to acquaint yourself with the movement and to find out if there are any zipper or holster issues that might occur. Although a shooting range would be the ideal place to practice, many do not allow drawing from purses, since the gun often faces backward or sideways in the bag and therefore might be unintentionally pointed at others on the range. (For the same reason, many ranges do not allow the use of cross-draw holsters.) Instead, you can practice drawing from your bag at home with an unloaded or dummy gun.

Concealed carriers also need to get in the habit of holding their bag in a manner that provides easy access

Be sure to practice drawing from a purse holster to gain confidence. DeSantis Gunhide

There's no excuse not to carry in style with high-quality leather purse holsters such as this one from Galco.
Galco

to the gun. Depending on the style of bag, this might mean consistently carrying it on the strong side for a straight draw or the support side for cross draws. The bag should also be held so the holster pocket faces forward. Some larger bags allow ambidextrous access, but smaller bags have only one direction the gun can be drawn from. Get in the habit of carrying the bag correctly so when trouble hits, your gun is within easy reach.

Galco offers 10 different models of purse holsters in various styles, colors and sizes. Full-grain, glove-tanned leather purses in black and brown feature a fairly standard main area with multiple compartments, but the real benefit is that a gun can be stored in a separate side-loading, zippered compartment with an internal holster and thumb break. With shoulder carry, this places the gun easily within reach for both right- and left-handed draw, and the zipper includes a key locking mechanism for added security. Just don't get too comfortable and forget the gun is in the purse, should you go into a firearms-restricted area.

Embracing concealed carry does not mean completely discarding style and wearing an oversized blazer every day. Loose jackets and pants make concealment easy, but holsters can be worn even under dresses and workout clothes. Ironically, the holster, once strictly a man's accessory, lends itself readily to concealment under skirts and natural curves.

CHAPTER 8

COVER GARMENTS

Proper concealed carry is not just about clipping a holster to your belt, stuffing a gun in it and walking out the door. Concealed means concealed, not some of the time, not most of the time, but all of the time. Making sure your gun stays out of view requires commitment, attention to detail and vigilance. What is concealed one minute might be revealed the next.

Some types of carry will require more or larger cover garments and some will get by with less. Some will require a buttoned-up exterior and some will significantly decrease the speed of your presentation. The key is to find the right balance that works for you and with your preferred method of carry. Over the past 20-plus years, I've carried concealed using just about every method, with all sorts of cover garments and different guns, and my tastes and preferences have changed during that time. Yours likely will as

well, once you get used to one method and then discover a different one that works better.

Generally speaking, it's best to always carry the same gun in the same manner whenever possible, without regard to weather or clothing. Think

It's generally best to always carry in the same manner to build muscle memory. Jorge Amselle

of muscle memory. You have used a fork to feed yourself enough times that you can do it without even thinking about it, blindfolded, and still find your mouth with the fork every time. It's the same with any routine. When I was commuting to an office job on a daily basis for several years, I had my route memorized. It was so ingrained that sometimes, even on the weekends when I left the house to run an errand, if I zoned out, I would actually start driving to work.

Carrying a gun for personal protection is not much different, with one exception: Your life might depend on your muscle memory. I almost always carry a .380 ACP pocket pistol in my right front pocket. I prefer this method not because it's the most powerful or effective gun and not because it is the fastest or most comfortable way to carry, but because I find it suits me best and is the most versatile for my needs. This method of carry works with pants or shorts, and in all types of weather.

On the occasions when I am forced to go someplace where I cannot carry my gun, I still find myself not placing anything in my right pocket (because it's dedicated for my gun in my mind). I also find myself checking to make sure I have the gun even when I know it isn't there. In an emergency situation, this instinctive muscle memory will help me go right for my gun without hesitation or conscious effort, assuming I don't panic and freeze.

It is fine to try out different guns and holsters, as well as various types of carry, to find one that suits you best. However, if you fall into the habit of constantly switching guns and methods of carry, you might not like the results. You run the very real risk of finding yourself ill prepared in an emergency situation, and instead of quickly and smoothly drawing your handgun, you will find yourself searching for it and trying to remember if this is the one with the thumb safety or without.

I bring this up in a discussion on cover garments because I generally don't like to have to wear cover garments. With pocket carry, I don't even need a shirt—just pants or shorts. I am making a decision that prioritizes my comfort over carrying a more power-

The author prefers a pocket pistol for consistency and comfort, and because it doesn't require cover garments. Uncle Mike's

ful handgun. I'm also making a decision that recognizes the importance of consistency. This is a very personal choice and one that each of us has to make.

When we talk about cover garments, it does not have to mean a heavy jacket or blazer. A cover garment is just that, a piece of clothing that conceals your gun. Of course, that's the whole idea behind concealed carry, and selecting the right cover garment can be just as important as selecting the right holster.

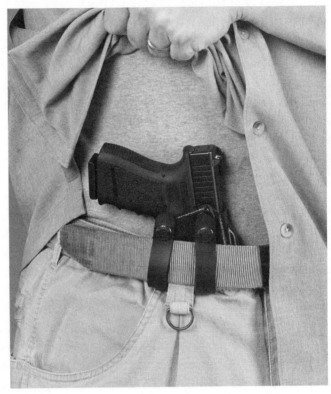

A cover garment should be loose enough to allow easy access to a gun. Galco

Make sure your garment does not interfere with your draw. It has to be loose enough so you can easily lift or sweep it out of the way. A tight jacket or one without any give that you have to unzip in order to reach your gun will seriously impede a fast draw. Likewise, a shirt, sweatshirt or sweater that's so tight you can't easily lift it away to reach your gun will hamper your draw.

You want a cover garment that's made from a material thick enough so the gun can't easily be seen through it (so get rid of your mesh tank tops). Clothing made from thin material can expose the outline of the gun when

pressed against it, although this is less of a concern with loose clothing. The cover garment that works best for you will depend on the type of carry you prefer.

There is one very important caveat with certain types of cover garments. We have all seen those fleece jackets and windbreakers that have the side drawstrings at the bottom of the jacket. These are designed for cinching the jacket tight against the body to maintain heat. I'm sure they work great for that. What they do not work great at doing is promoting safe concealed carry.

Side tabs on jackets can get caught in the trigger and fire a gun when returned to the holster. Cut them off ASAP. US CPSC

These elastic drawstrings and their plastic cinching devices have a very nasty tendency of getting caught up on guns and holsters carried on the waist. When you go to draw you might find that the drawstring traps your gun, slowing your draw or causing you to drop the gun. The worst part is that when you go to re-holster your gun the tab can actually get caught up in the trigger and cause the gun to fire, right into your leg. This has happened on several occasions, and there are plenty of videos online demonstrating this in graphic fashion, including one chief of police who

Weather will have the biggest impact on which cover garments are most appropriate. Sascha Kohlmann

has managed to shoot himself twice! If you have any drawstrings, tabs, doohickeys or other junk hanging off your coat right where you keep your gun, cut them off immediately.

DEALING WITH THE WEATHER

No matter where you live—except maybe Death Valley where it's always hot and it never rains—you will experience temperature changes and humidity in the form of rain or snow. Just as you dress to be comfortable with changing weather conditions, how you carry concealed will also require some adjustment.

In cold weather, you will likely be wearing a large, heavy jacket, which is a lot more forgiving for various types of carry. During the summer, this is less the case. You want to consider how you are carrying given the clothes you wear and how easy it is to

access your gun. A well-concealed gun that's hard to access is certainly better than no gun at all, but if you need it quickly, then maybe not. An easily accessed gun that routinely becomes exposed throughout the day defeats the purpose of concealed carry.

Where I live in the mid-Atlantic, we get all sorts of weather, and it's a good idea to check the weather reports regularly to make sure your cover garments and method of carry will be comfortable.

JACKET CARRY

A coat allows the same security as on-body carry with the added convenience that you can take the coat off and hang it nearby where you still have control and access but can dress more comfortably. Another advantage with coats is that their pockets offer you the flexibility of carrying a gun with no holster, although I highly recommend using a pocket holster.

Remember that the heavier the material the better. It's very easy to slip a small pistol or revolver into a jacket pocket, either the slash pockets on the front or sides, or an interior pocket for a quick cross draw. There are a few caveats to keep in mind. First, never place any extra items in the pocket where you keep your gun because these might interfere with your draw or worse, get caught in the trigger and cause the gun to fire.

The jacket should be made from heavy material so that it doesn't noticeably sag on the side with the gun or risk showing the outline of the gun. Too light of a jacket will cause the gun to bounce around as you move. Be sure the pockets are deep enough to keep the gun concealed and secure so it won't fall out. If the jacket pocket has a zipper, it will provide a more secure retention, but it will also slow your draw.

If the jacket pockets are too deep, it will be difficult to draw your pistol, and this applies especially to inside pockets during a cross draw. Depending on the type of handgun and the level of support in the pocket, as well as the size, shape and material of the pocket, your gun might shift around without a holster. You might find that

Concealing a gun in a coat pocket is a cross between on-body and off-body carry, because a coat can be easily removed. Rivers West

when you go to draw the gun, it's upside down or the grip is pointed away from you. Be sure to try out the jacket with this method of carry before relying on it.

If the gun weighs down one side of the jacket noticeably or uncomfortably, you can balance things out by placing a spare magazine or other items, such as your cell phone, keys, etc., in the opposite pocket. Keep in mind that an unholstered pistol in your pocket, depending on the design, can eventually wear a hole in your jacket. This happened to me when I spent one winter carrying a small revolver in a jacket pocket. Eventually, the sharp edge of the snub-nosed barrel wore a hole in the front of the pocket until the entire barrel was sticking out.

A good compromise that is not entirely holsterless can be found in dedicated concealed-carry jackets, many of which come with simple built-in holsters. The Olive Concealment Vest from Blue Stone Safety is a good option for warmer weather, although these types of vests tend to stick out, and the knowledgeable will recognize them for what they are. Regardless, this is a rugged

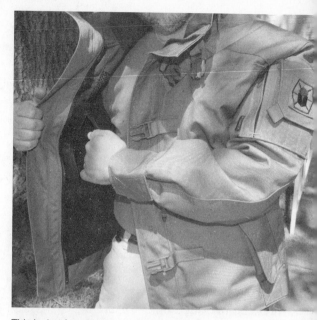

This jacket from Kitanica has several large, strong pockets for handgun carry. Jorge Amselle

photographer-style vest with lots of pockets. But rather than carrying film or extra lenses, they are designed to carry your gun and ancillary equipment and keep it easily accessible and organized. Usable by right- and left-handed shooters, the vest features 12 pockets, with space for up to six magazines and a special pocket for revolver ammunition.

Two roomy interior pockets are made from heavy 1050 Denier Cordura fabric, which prevents printing. Elastic bands keep your gun upright and handy for a fast draw. Outside loops near the shoul-

This fleece coat from Rivers West offers several carry options. Rivers West

der are convenient for hanging sunglasses and there's an American flag patch on the left breast. The external material is an 80/20 poly/cotton blend for durability and stain resistance. The vest is available in black or olive, and for the ultimate in self-defense, Blue Stone Safety also makes a version with removable ballistic panels.

Rivers West also makes a vest and several styles of dedicated concealed-carry jackets. Each of their four types of CCW jackets is made from their proprietary windproof and waterproof fleece for superior comfort in all types of weather. These coats and vest are available in a variety of colors and fit

in well with normal everyday activities, allowing the wearer to carry a concealed firearm without drawing unwanted attention.

The hidden interior and exterior zippers allow the wearer to easily access a concealed firearm on either the strong or support side. These coats also feature removable holsters with elastic to accommodate most handguns and are mounted onto a solid square surface, which hides the outline of the gun. They sit solidly inside the coat with a Velcro backing.

A double jacket liner keeps the gun suspended between the outer shell and the inner lining, and there's extra pad-

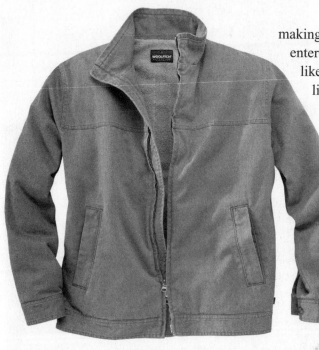

This Woolrich coat looks very normal, but has multiple carry options for conceal-carry use. Woolrich

making outerwear and recently entered the tactical market. I like it because their tactical line doesn't look tactical at all. The clothing is actually very casual and will raise no eyebrows. All the tactical features are completely concealed, as they should be.

The Discreet Carry Jacket has a heavy boulder-washed cotton twill outer layer and a warm polyester Sherpa liner. It includes many valuable features that concealed-carry permit holders and off-duty law enforcement officers will appreciate. The girth adjustable, hip-length jacket is long enough to cover up a high-ride, outside-the-waistband holster or any inside-the-waistband carry. The large side pockets will fit most mid-sized handguns and are reinforced for security, plus they feature accessory loops to lock down your gear and zippers for extra retention.

There are also large ambidextrous inside pockets with built-in holsters and Velcro retention for a secure cross draw. The back of the jacket even has a hidden accessory tunnel, good for storing plastic restraints or running wires for an ear bud/radio communication system. They really put a lot of thought into this design.

ding sewn into the jacket for improved concealability, whether the coat is open or closed. Most significantly, there's a built-in shoulder harness that supports the weight of the gun and distributes it evenly for improved comfort and no sag.

Their Pioneer coat has an attached hood and single holster cross-draw capability. The Full Metal Jacket features dual holsters for right- or left-hand use. The unused holster can carry spare magazines, and this coat has dual shoulder straps. There is also a CCW women's coat with various color options and a shapelier cut.

One of my personal favorites is the Woolrich Elite Discreet Carry jacket. This company has a lot of experience

WAISTBAND CARRY

If you are carrying your gun on the outside of your pants, you'll need to make sure your shirt or jacket is long enough to completely cover the gun for all of your movements. You can test this out with someone watching you from different angles as you bend over, jump, stretch and raise your arms. Doing this in front or a mirror is not good enough, because it's hard to see from behind.

You also want to make sure the cover garment will not sweep out of the way on its own or from a gust of wind and expose your firearm. A cover garment has to be thick enough so doesn't print the gun's outline through the material, and loose enough so you can quickly reach your gun and draw. Concealing a gun, especially a full-sized gun, with belt carry will be the most difficult of all types of carry, but it can be done.

On the rare occasions when I opt for this method of carry, I stick with smaller handguns in a high-ride belt holster and wear a coat that comes down at least to my wrists when my arms are hanging down. If I'm outside, I try to keep the coat zipped up. This will slow my draw, but it helps keep my gun concealed.

Wearing a heavy coat might not work year round, because you will be uncomfortable and stick out like a sore thumb. When I was in college, I worked as a security guard and we were always on the lookout for anyone wearing a large coat when the weather was hot. This often indicated a shoplifter. It's always best to avoid drawing attention to yourself.

A friend told me he likes loud Hawaiian shirts to use as cover garments, especially during the summer. It's not an especially fashionable look, but he has sound reasoning behind his poor taste. First of all, these types of

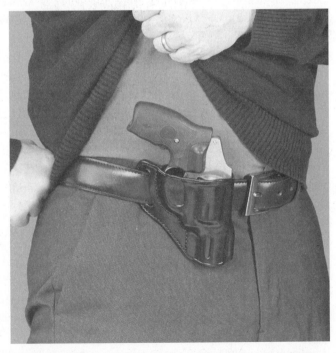

On-the-waistband carry is among the hardest to keep concealed. Galco

A loud shirt with lots of patterns can break up the outline of a gun and prevent printing.
Jorge Amselle

shirts tend to be fairly baggy and this provides him easy access to his gun, even with the shirt buttoned up in the front. Keeping the shirt buttoned also prevents a gust of wind from blowing it open and revealing his gun. The eccentric pattern of the shirt also acts as a sort of camouflage, so if his gun prints though the material, the outline is disguised by the patterns. Finally, the Hawaiian shirt is the polar opposite of the tactical guy look, and it helps shield you from additional scrutiny by people who know what to look for.

INSIDE-THE-WAISTBAND CARRY

Using a cover garment with IWB carry will be much easier, because your pants conceal most of the gun. The cover garment is only necessary to cover the grip of the gun. With some IWB holsters, you don't even have to do this, because they are designed so the gun is completely inside your pants and only a tab or other item sticks out for you to draw the gun.

The iTuck conceal-carry holster from TUFF Products is one example. This pistol holster is made from tough nylon with a Velcro adjustment system that makes it nearly universal for all types of handguns. This portion tucks completely inside the waistband, so it is not visible from the outside, even with a tucked-in shirt and no cover garment.

On the outside, there's a functional smartphone case that clips to your belt and includes a pocket for your ID, credit cards and cash. To draw the pistol, simply grasp the Velcro cover of the cell phone case and lift past the first tab all the way up so the holster and pistol come up above the waistline, offering a very quick and easy draw.

For most IWB holsters, however, you need a cover garment. Depending on the size of your handgun, this could be a longer T-shirt or polo shirt. You don't want it too long, though, or it will interfere with your draw. As mentioned above, it only has to be long enough to cover the grip of the

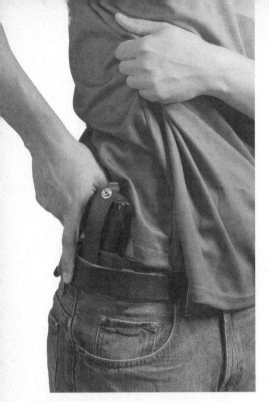

Inside-the-waistband carry means only the portion of the gun that's exposed needs to be concealed. Uncle Mike's

gun. The color and thickness of the material are also factors in terms of printing, so be aware of that.

There are several IWB holsters, such as those from CrossBreed, that allow you to tuck your shirt into your pants around the holster and gun. I would be cautious of using this with a white dress shirt, for example, because a dark-colored gun might show through. Also be aware that it will slow down your draw because you must first untuck your shirt to get to the gun. It will, however, provide a very high level of concealment with no obvious cover garment.

I find this type of carry is very comfortable, especially when I want to carry a slightly larger gun. I can easily keep it concealed with a blazer or casual polo or sport shirt.

CROSS DRAW AND APPENDIX CARRY

For cross draw or appendix carry, you'll need a loose-fitting T-shirt, or polo or button shirt. If it's cold, a sweater or sweatshirt works well, too. I find that with cross draw, the butt of the gun has a tendency to protrude a bit more. This might be gut-related because the gut pushes anything positioned in front of it outward, including a gun.

With appendix carry, where the pistol is carried with the grip to the rear, the effect is actually the opposite, so the gut helps keep the grip against the body with less chance of printing or exposure.

This quick-access shirt from Deep Conceal allows the wearer to carry cross draw in a belly band or shoulder holster. Deep Conceal

SHOULDER CARRY

Shoulder carry, or specifically carrying a gun in a shoulder holster, is a tough one to keep concealed. On TV and in movies, you often see police detectives carrying this way, but they also keep their badge prominently displayed on their belt in the front or just below the gun. This isn't to show off, but rather a response to the realization that their gun is almost certainly going to become exposed as they go about their day. In order to avoid startling onlookers, they want to make sure their status as a police officer is plain to see.

Because the gun is hanging from underneath your arm, every time you move it's going to swing around. Even if the holster is attached to your belt at the bottom, there's no way of eliminating all movement. This makes the gun more obvious under a cover garment, which needs to be a good-sized coat or at least a blazer. Even then, there will be a noticeable bulge on one side of your body. If you are trying to even out the weight by adding extra magazines to the opposite side, it can make you look even bulkier.

As I mentioned earlier, when I worked as a security guard, we received a call regarding someone carrying a gun in a shoulder holster. It turned out to be just some silly wallet rig, but he had a cover garment and *still* the shoulder holster was visible

A shoulder holster requires extra attention to prevent exposure. Diamond Custom

enough to alarm someone enough to call security. Keep in mind that this wallet was a lot smaller and thinner than most guns you are likely to carry in a shoulder holster.

Well, what if I just zip up my coat so it doesn't come open and expose the gun, you ask? That is certainly better, but still not ideal. I used to carry a full-sized pistol in a leather shoulder holster during the winter. I wore a bomber jacket as a cover garment because it was baggy and naturally padded so the bulge would be less noticeable. I also kept it at least halfway zipped up most of the time. Nevertheless, a police officer friend I ran into could tell right away that I was carrying in a shoulder holster, even though the gun was not visible.

I recommend large coats that add bulk to both sides of your torso and to keep them buttoned or zippered at least partway if possible—even though it could slow down your draw. But be aware that carrying in this fashion might be illegal in areas where the open carry of handguns is restricted. It might be legal for you to carry concealed, but if your gun becomes exposed (even unintentionally), you might have to answer some uncomfortable questions.

There are some shoulder holsters that offer a much higher level on concealment, especially for smaller handguns. These blur the line between a traditional shoulder holster and a belly band. Deep Conceal makes an excellent example of this concept that's meant to be worn as an undergarment.

The company's Ultra Carry Double Strap Concealed Carry Holster is made from a soft cotton fabric and features dual elastic straps in the front with Velcro adjustable loops as well as dual suspenders, which also have Velcro adjustable straps. Available in different sizes, the unit can provide a custom fit and offers significant comfort even against bare skin.

The Deep Conceal holster allows men or women to securely carry almost any size handgun tucked high underneath the armpit and can be completely hidden even under a light T-shirt. It is available in black or white to better match clothing choices and in

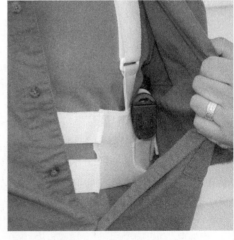

Close-fitting belly bands or shoulder holsters offer good concealability. Jorge Amselle

both left- and right-handed models. It also features dual magazine pouches on the side opposite the gun for semi-autos. This holster is a near perfect answer for anyone who wears a tucked-in dress shirt and needs complete discretion and quick access.

BACK CARRY

Carrying a gun in the small of the back is very comfortable for a lot of people, included me. I assume this is because most people don't develop a lot of back fat, so the gun isn't jabbing you in the gut or in the ribs as it is with front carry options.

However, since you can't see the gun or how it looks from behind you, it's important to be conscientious of the types of cover garments you choose with this type of carry.

If you're standing straight or sitting down, the gun will remain concealed with just about any cover garment that conceals the grip of the gun for IWB carry. Many small-of-the-back holsters are sharply angled to keep the barrel of the gun from poking out of the bottom of your cover garment and to allow for an easier draw when you reach behind, by positioning the grip closer to your hand. This is essentially a sort of upside-down carry that places the grip oriented upward.

The problem comes when you move. Assuming you don't work as one of those human statue street performers, you will find yourself moving a good deal throughout the day. With small-of-the-back carry, the biggest problem is when you have to bend over. If you are carrying in the small of the back, try to avoid bending over and instead bend at the knees if you need to (you're supposed to lift with your knees anyway).

Choose a cover garment that will not ride up in the back when you sit down or bend

Carrying closer to the back risks exposure when bending over. The gun grip will stick out and show as a bulge under the cover garment.
DeSantis Gunhide

over, otherwise your gun will be exposed without you even realizing it. This might be a bit off topic, but a friend once told me how he was on a crowded escalator during rush hour on his way to work when he noticed that the woman standing in front of him had part of her skirt stuck into her underwear, leaving her partially exposed. He was left with the uncomfortable choice of saying nothing or intervening. Don't let that be you.

You want a cover garment made of heavy enough material so printing is reduced. With small-of-the-back carry, printing can be a more serious concern. The garment has to be long enough to conceal the gun and loose enough to provide access when you need it. During the summer, you might be able to get by with just a T-shirt as long as you remain conscious of printing.

POCKET CARRY

My personal favorite is a carry gun in my strong side front pocket. The only cover garment you need is pants, shorts or some other type of bottom with a pocket. Whatever you choose, the pocket must be baggy enough so you can easily and comfortably reach into it to grasp the gun. But printing is a concern, especially when you sit. A good rule of thumb is that the gun should not be visible at all when you are standing. Place the gun in a holster in your pocket and have a friend walk around you to see if they can spot which pocket contains the gun. There should be no noticeable bulge.

Don't get pants or pockets that are too baggy, however, because this will cause the gun to swing about in an uncomfortable and possibly noticeable manner. Baggy pockets could also cause the gun to shift, so that when you reach for it you could find it in the muzzle-up position instead of the grip-

Some pocket holsters, such as this one from DeSantis, hide the outline of the gun and stay attached when drawn. DeSantis Gunhide

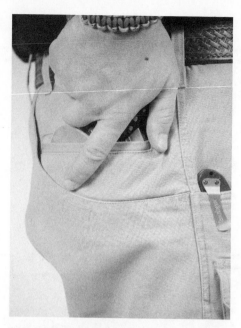

Pocket holsters can fit in front or back pockets depending on preference. Crossbreed

Pants with large, loose pockets keep guns concealed and allow for a fast draw. Jorge Amselle

up position. When you sit, the material of you pants will naturally stretch against your leg. If you have baggy pants, this will not be a factor. If the pants were barely concealing the gun in the standing position, sitting will really make it stick out and print through the fabric.

If you want to carry a small revolver in your pocket instead of a semi-automatic pistol, keep in mind that the overall shape is less square and the grip tends to stick out more, so you might need a baggier pocket than you would with a pistol.

Printing and gun orientation are the big reasons why using a proper pocket holster is paramount and should be considered part of your cover garment. It also protects the gun from dust and debris and protects the trigger from anything getting caught in it and causing a negligent discharge. A proper pocket holster will keep the gun oriented in the right direction, so that when you reach into the pocket the gun will be ready to be grasped. They also hide the outline of your gun to prevent printing, or at least mask it.

With most of my pants, the pocket pistol will not print even when I'm sitting down. However, I refuse to wear loose or baggy jeans and here I do have an issue. When I'm standing, there is a barely noticeable bulge where I carry my gun, but when I sit, it becomes a very protuberant rectangular projection. If anyone asks, I just tell him or her it's my wallet, which a lot of people like to carry in the front pocket anyway.

If baggy pants are not your style, you could do without the holster. The pocket holster, no matter how thin, adds extra girth to the gun. By carrying the gun alone in your pocket, you get the thinnest possible exposure. If you are going to do this, make sure you are carrying nothing besides the gun in that pocket.

My personal pocket pistol has a TR1 laser unit from Arma-Laser mounted in front of the trigger guard and underneath the dust cover. This square laser fills in part of the profile of the gun, and in the pocket, it gives it a more wallet-shaped look, even without the holster. It also helps to elongate the front so the gun stays properly oriented in the pocket. If you are going to pocket carry without a holster, this might be a worthwhile accessory.

ANKLE CARRY

Carrying a gun on your ankle has a secret agent vibe for a lot of people, and many wear one for a backup gun. If you want to keep your ankle holster and gun concealed, you'll need the right cover garment, and it isn't shorts. Pants will need to be long enough to keep the gun concealed when you

To keep an ankle holster covered and accessible, wide-legged pants that are cut a bit longer are advised. Galco

walk and especially when you sit down. This is not that easy, but there are some ankle holsters available that ride a bit higher on your leg and this can help.

Your pants leg will ride up when you sit down no matter what you do, and my advice is to wear socks that match the color of your ankle holster and gun to at least help camouflage it. Make sure the pants leg is wide and loose enough so you can easily pull it up and reach your gun. Polyester bell bottom disco pants are ideal, and it seems that clothing styles come around again every few years anyway.

Of course, as one of the lines from a popular movie goes, "Men don't have style; men wear clothes."

I have a friend who always carries a small revolver in an ankle holster, likely a habit from his many years as a law enforcement officer. Every time he sits down, you can see the bottom of the holster and gun, and if he crosses his legs, you see pretty much the whole gun. He is aware but unconcerned (again, as retired law enforcement, he's completely legal). I cannot recommend this level of comfort for the rest of us, and keeping your ankle gun concealed should be a top priority.

Straight-legged pants, especially dress pants that have a lighter fabric, work well for most everyone. Here we have the opposite issue from other types of cover garments. There are very few pants (especially for men) that use material so light that the gun will easily print or be seen though them, even if you wear Miami Vice white pants.

Dark-colored dress pants are about the perfect material thickness. Khakis are as thick as I would go. Most jeans are made from denim that's too thick and heavy to easily lift out of the way quickly to access your holster. Also, don't cross your legs with ankle carry unless you feel like you might need very quick access to your gun.

BELLY BANDS

Probably the manliest girdle you can wear is a belly band holster. I like them because they offer deep concealment under almost any cover garment. These bands are typically available in white but sometimes also in a flesh tone, which I prefer, especially if I'm wearing it against my bare skin. Belly bands are generally more comfortable against an undershirt, in which case get a white one.

Since belly bands are adjustable—a nice feature because none of us is perfectly round—you can wear it anywhere from under your armpits to below your belly button. Assuming you are not using a belly band as an IWB

With ankle carry, the gun might rub against the ankle. The author finds wearing boots makes it more comfortable. Galco

holster, cover garments can still be pretty basic. The belly band keeps the gun close to the body, which makes it much easier to conceal, especially smaller guns. It can be covered up easily with a T-shirt, polo shirt or button shirt.

Make sure the shirt material is not so light in color that the gun shows through it. You also want to make sure the garment is loose enough so that you can easily reach up underneath it or lift it up to access your gun. Keep in mind that the higher up your torso you have placed the belly band the baggier the shirt you will need to reach your gun. I suppose if you're wearing a deep V-neck shirt you might be able to reach in from the top to access your gun, but some might question your sense of style if you're a male.

With a button shirt, you can tuck it in so it looks even less like you are carrying. To access the gun, open up

some of the buttons (in an emergency, rip the shirt open Hulk Hogan style). I suppose you could also walk around with a few buttons undone and your hand in your shirt like Napoleon, but people might think you're weird.

If you want to carry in a belly band with a button shirt tucked in, I highly recommend the CCW shirt from Deep Conceal. This looks like a standard long sleeve dress shirt and you can wear it with a tie or roll up the sleeves for a more casual look. It's available in three colors and features a simple quick-opening system.

Basically, the buttons are sewn only to one side of the shirt so it looks like it's buttoned but it really isn't. Behind each button and on the opposite side of the shirt there are Velcro tabs that keep it closed. From the outside, it looks like a normal shirt, but when you need your gun fast, you just rip the Velcro open with your support

Belly bands require minimal cover garments, because they keep the gun so close to the body.
Jorge Amselle

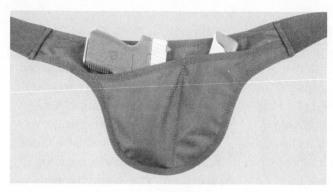

This belly band holster from DeSantis is designed to ride below the beltline in front. All that's needed to cover it are pants.
DeSantis Gunhide

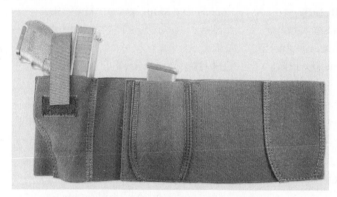

Some belly band holsters keep the gun in place using only tension, while some have retention. DeSantis Gunhide

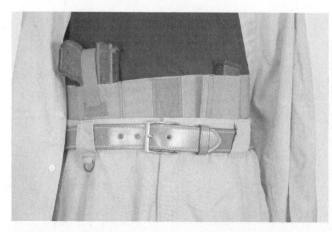

For increased levels of activity, some degree of retention is recommended. DeSantis Gunhide

hand (not Superman style) and reach in for your gun. It's also available in right- and left-handed models so the support hand can always get a good grip on the side of the shirt with the opening.

Those who use belly band holsters need to be mindful that many of them feature extra pockets, either on the strong side, the support side or both. These can be used for carrying spare magazines, ammunition or other essential items. It might not be a priority to reach these, but your cover garment should provide easy access to them. You might also need to access other items on your belly band with your support hand if your strong hand is occupied with holding your gun.

There is also the issue of retention. Many belly band holsters utilize nothing more than the elastic. This is fine for normal activities such as sitting and walking about. If you're involved in anything much more active—say you're attacked—this retention might not keep the gun where it needs to be for you to reach it. You might lose the gun altogether or worse, it fall into the hands of your assailant. At least with a tucked-in shirt the gun won't go flying, even if it comes loose from the holster. You might not be able to reach it, but neither will anyone else.

If you get a belly band holster with additional retention, make sure to keep that in mind when you select a cover garment. You might need to be able to reach inside or under your shirt to a greater extent to release the retention strap before you can access your gun.

FANNY PACKS

The great thing about a fanny pack is that the holster becomes its own cover garment. You don't need to do anything special other than strap on the pack. Of course, most fanny packs are going to look fairly obvious and they don't really fit in with some clothing choices (such as a business suit).

If you are carrying a small handgun, a belt-pouch holster might be a better option. The Sneaky Pete Holsters "Cell Phone" case is ideal. It looks like a leather cell phone case, albeit a large one, but provides instant access to a small pistol. They also make a less expensive model in nylon.

OFF-BODY CARRY

Cover garments are also not an issue with off-body carry, except to the extent that if your off-body holster doesn't really match your clothing, you will stand out and undermine the whole idea. A backpack that looks like it holds your Fallujah invasion-ready skateboard is not going to fit in with your business suit. Likewise, your briefcase won't work well with your Ramones T-shirt and Doc Martens. Most women don't carry a purse when they go for a jog, either, so keep that in mind.

With off-body carry, your holster is your cover garment and if this is your preferred method of carry, you will need to

With fanny packs there's no need for a cover garment. DeSantis Gunhide

adjust accordingly. Just like you have different clothes for different occasions, you will need to have different off-body carry holsters to fit various situations.

WOMEN'S CLOTHING
By Megan Amselle

Hiding a concealed weapon's outline might seem difficult under anything but a baggy jacket, but there are other options. Here are some tips for women on maintaining quick access to their gun while keeping it invisible to others.

The classic, outside-the-waistband holster is relatively difficult to hide. Women, in particular, find the added bulge to be an unwelcome addition to their waistline. Few holsters are slim enough to hide under a T-shirt or blouse without their shape being obviously visible. For the most part, OWB holsters require clothing that's best suited for cooler weather. Jackets, blazers, coats and loose sweaters all do a fine job of concealing the shape while still allowing access to the waist and gun. Summer clothes are more challenging, but a loose, short-sleeved cardigan can work well for covering a belt holster.

The belt itself is another issue. Many women are not in the habit of wearing a thick, sturdy belt capable of holding a holster. Luckily, there's a vast array of gorgeous belts available in all colors and styles to suit your fancy. Belts work great with jeans, but women sometimes run into problems with dress pants. Unlike men's pants, some women's pants lack belt loops on the waist or are made of delicate

Carrying off body eliminates the need for cover garments. Galco

This concealed-carry hoody from Blackhawk is perfect for casual wear or jogging. Jorge Amselle

Undergarment and bra holsters, such as this one from Undertech, keep a gun close to the body and concealed.
Jorge Amselle

blouses and button-down shirts can all work as long as they are left untucked, as can sweaters and tunics. Belly bands are also an excellent carry option while exercising. A T-shirt or sweatshirt is all the cover you need. Those who prefer spandex might encounter more difficulty, but a T-shirt worn over a spandex top is a feasible compromise. Be sure to check that your gun does not print on the outside of your shirt when you move or run.

When wearing a shoulder holster or tank top with holster pockets, you will need a second layer to act as a cover up. Jackets, coats, blazers and cardigans are all excellent options, because they all have the open front needed to maintain access to the weapon. Again, in hot weather the choices are more limited. A vest or a loose, open-front blouse will work well and can be dressy or casual as needed.

material that can't handle a leather belt. Keep this in mind when selecting pants if you plan to wear an OWB holster.

Pocket holsters and inside-the-waistband holsters are much easier to conceal, because the material of the clothing shrouds their outline. Any T-shirt or blouse that's not overly tight will suffice to cover the holster's shape. Of course, looser tops such as jackets or tunics work wonderfully. Pocket holsters, in particular, are less likely to attract attention, because their slim shape resembles an ordinary wallet or cell phone in the pocket.

Belly band holsters are easily concealed under any loose-fitting top that allows access to the waist. T-shirts,

Special concealment jackets for women from Rivers West offer comfort and quick access to a handgun.
Rivers West

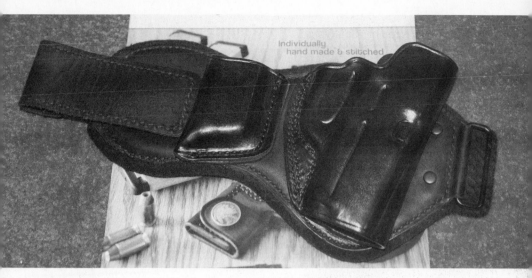

With the right pants, an ankle holster can be very comfortable. Jorge Amselle

Bra holsters eliminate the need for a belt or loose clothing around the waist. While care must still be taken to ensure that the holster does not print, the bust line creates natural hollows that can hide a gun under all but the tightest shirts. Most bra holsters require that you be able to reach up under your shirt from the bottom, so tucking it in is not an option. Some designs allow you to also reach down through the neck of the shirt, as long as the neckline is not too high. This is one of the few options that can be worn with a dress, because access to the waist is not necessary.

The other option when wearing a dress or skirt is the thigh holster. Depending on the size of the gun, a fuller skirt might conceal better than a pencil skirt (unless you are slim enough to have space for the holster between your thighs). Also ensure

that the skirt is long enough to fully cover the holster when sitting and walking. Miniskirts might not be up to the challenge.

Ankle holsters are a comfortable and convenient choice when wearing pants, but they work only with certain types of pants. The pant legs must be loose at the bottom—either boot cut or wide leg—to provide access to the firearm. And the hem must be long enough to always cover the holster, even when walking or sitting cross-legged. Test these actions before going out in public.

Of course, the easiest holsters to dress around are the concealment purses and the holsters that masquerade as cell phone cases. They don't require any clothing considerations. On the downside, they might become targets for thieves who don't even realize their true contents.

Regardless of the holster system you choose, you should be able to incorporate it into your daily wardrobe with little difficulty. However, keep in mind that very few holsters work in all situations, particularly when it comes to women's clothing. Most people prefer to keep two or three different types of holsters on hand to wear with various clothing types.

CHAPTER 9

AMMUNITION SELECTION

The general rule on caliber selection is to choose the most powerful cartridge you can comfortably shoot. This is good advice, but when it comes to concealed carry, it is incomplete. There are a vast multitude of calibers for handguns available and selecting the right one can be a daunting task. As a general rule, however, select nothing less powerful than .38 Special or .380 ACP for your defensive needs. That said, if all you can handle were a .22-caliber pistol, you would still be able to defend yourself.

Typically, the larger the caliber you select—especially in small concealed-carry handguns—the stronger the recoil. In pistols, a larger caliber will also mean reduced magazine capacity. Larger calibers can be more effective against an assailant, but not as much as you might imagine. Just because you're able to comfortably handle a .44 Mag. in a short-barreled revolver doesn't mean it's your best choice for concealed carry.

It's worth your time and money to try out as many different guns in as many different calibers as you can before buying a concealed-carry

handgun. Many ranges rent handguns and sell ammunition. You can also reach out to friends or instructors who have access to a variety of suitable handguns.

Once you have made your choice regarding the right CCW handgun and caliber that fits your needs, you will

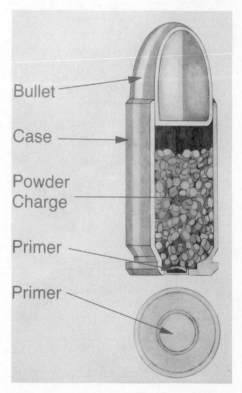

Bullet

Case

Powder Charge

Primer

Primer

The basic components of all modern defensive ammunition. NRA

need to select the best personal protection round and train with your handgun on a routine basis. For the inexperienced shooter, going to a gun shop or discount sporting goods store to buy ammunition can be just as confusing as buying the gun itself, because you'll be swamped with options.

Buy the right ammunition for your gun. A lot of different calibers sound the same but are not, while a lot of the exact same cartridges carry different names. Some guns can actually use multiple types of ammunition. A revolver chambered for the longer .357 Mag. can accommodate the shorter .38 Special, but the inverse is not true (or safe).

Consider the common 9mm cartridge. Standard 9mm ammunition can go by several different names such as Parabellum or Luger. But there are other types of 9mm ammunition that have different names or a designation

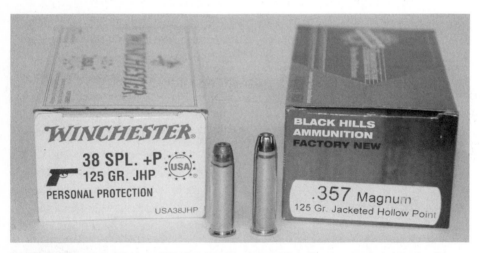

It's OK to shoot .38 Special in a .357 Mag. handgun but not the other way around. Jorge Amselle

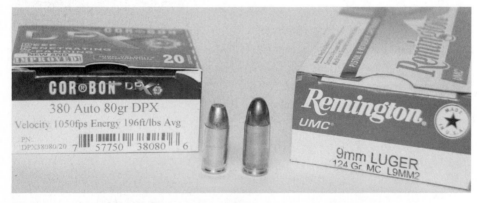

Standard 9mm and .380 ACP (also called 9mm Short) are not the same ammo and are not interchangeable. Jorge Amselle

listing the diameter and length of the cartridge. Just because it says 9mm on the box does not mean it is the correct ammunition for your gun. The different types of 9mm cartridges meant for different guns are not interchangeable and bad things will happen if you mix your ammo. When in doubt be sure to ask.

If you end up buying the wrong ammunition, it might physically fit into your gun, and it might even fire when you squeeze the trigger. But each time you do this, you are taking a huge gamble with your safety. A wrong-sized cartridge could cause huge jumps in pressure, which could damage or destroy the gun and severely injure you. Anyone who's worked at a shooting range will have plenty of stories of shooters who showed up with the wrong ammunition and tried to shoot it with unfortunate results.

When in doubt, ask someone knowledgeable, read the owner's manual and look at the gun. Almost all modern guns have the proper caliber marked on the barrel. Check the box of ammunition you are buying. It will say what caliber and style of ammunition it contains. Don't be shy about asking questions.

At a gun show a few years ago, I ran into a friend who had met a father and son who had purchased a rifle but were novices to guns. The rifle was chambered in 7.62x39mm, but they noticed only the 7.62mm part and bought a large amount of 7.62mm ammunition from a dealer. What they got was 7.62x51mm ammo. Fortunately, my friend explained their mistake before any harm was done.

RANGE AMMUNITION

Assuming you know the right type of ammunition for your gun, there will still be wide price disparities and different types of the same caliber

Cheaper range ammo will typically use a full-metal-jacketed bullet, such as the 9mm second from left. The others are more expensive expanding bullets designed for self defense. Jorge Amselle

ammunition to choose from. For the sake of simplicity, I divide them into two categories: range ammunition and self-defense ammunition.

For range use, buy whatever you can find that's the cheapest. But be aware that many manufacturers specifically warn against using reloaded ammunition, which is ammunition that has been shot one or more times and someone used the empty brass case to load it again.

There is nothing inherently wrong with reloaded ammunition, and many people save a lot of money reloading their own empty cases. A case that stays in good condi-

tion can usually be reloaded as many as five times before the brass becomes too weak. There are also some commercial ammunition reloaders who sell ammo at a discount. The danger is you have no idea how many times the brass has been loaded or what precautions have been taken.

For an individual reloader, it's easy to get distracted and load a double charge of powder in a cartridge, or no powder at all. A friend of mine had taken up reloading as a hobby and to save money. He was careful and conscientious, but one day when we were out shooting some of his reloads, one shot rang distinctly different. We immediately stopped shooting to inspect the gun and found a bullet lodged halfway down the barrel. The cause was a "squib" load—an under-powered round that contained a live primer but no gunpowder. If we had kept fir-

Winchester makes specific range ammo for training that matches the ballistics of their self-defense rounds. Winchester

ing with the blockage in the barrel, the best thing that could have happened was ruining the gun.

I would also avoid solid lead, uncoated or unjacketed ammunition, at least in semi-automatic handguns. Lead ball ammunition can work well, but it requires extra care in cleaning, because the soft lead can build up in the barrel's rifling. With some types of barrels, the manufacturer will warn specifically against using solid lead ammunition with no jacket. Solid lead bullets are cheaper because they don't have a copper jacket, but saving every last penny should not always be the priority.

Standard full-metal-jacket (FMJ) ammunition— whether it's made in the United States or a foreign country—is perfectly suitable for range use and training. In fact, I prefer it. This ammunition will be cheaper, allowing you to train and shoot more. It will typically kick less, increasing your comfort on the range and extending your training sessions by avoiding fatigue. It is both more reliable and less reliable at the same time. It's more reliable because the bullet shape is a solid conical form with nothing to get caught up and stop the gun from cycling.

It is less reliable because it's loaded faster and with less special attention than defensive ammunition. If you get a malfunction, you want it to happen on the range, not in a defensive encounter. The occasional range malfunction can actually help you train for clearing jams quickly. It helps you identify a problem by feel and sight, and if one occurs during an actual incident, you will be better prepared to handle it.

DEFENSIVE AMMUNITION

Ammunition specifically designed for personal protection is far different from what you will find for normal

Defensive ammunition is designed to expand and cause maximum damage. Federal Premium Ammunition

FBI protocol requires that defensive ammunition penetrates barriers such car windows, and also penetrates sufficiently in soft tissue and expands reliably. Jorge Amselle

range use. This ammunition will cost one dollar or more per round on average, and is loaded with a much higher degree of precision. Much of this ammunition started out being designed for law enforcement use and has found its way to the civilian self-defense market.

When you buy defensive ammunition, it often comes in smaller boxes of 20 or 25 rounds. The boxes will also feature a lot more graphics and verbiage to advertise what the cartridge does. Defensive ammunition is also called expanding ammunition, designed to expand once it hits a soft target. It has a lead core (although some can be solid copper) surrounded by a copper or other material jacket and topped off with a deep cavity.

On TV and in the movies, we often see people flying backward after they have been shot. This is, of course, pure fantasy because the laws of Newtonian physics show that any gun powerful enough to do that would have the same effect on the shooter. Nevertheless, in any self-defense situation it's vitally important to understand what your ammo can and can't do.

In Miami, during the spring of 1986, eight FBI agents cornered two bank robbers, and the shootout that ensued sparked an intense debate and adjustment of how law enforcement officers were armed and trained nationwide. Early in the gun battle, one suspect was shot with a 9mm round that went through his arm and into his chest. That wound (the first of several) proved fatal, but not before he was able to kill two FBI agents and wound several more. The entire gun battle lasted less than 5 minutes with almost 150 rounds fired.

Following this tragic incident, the FBI spent considerable effort studying wound ballistics and ammunition. How was it that despite numerous wounds the two suspects were able to continue fighting? The key is in understanding what types of wounds can stop a person—damage caused by blood loss or trauma to the central nervous system. The most important factors in this regard are shot placement, size of the wound cavity and penetration.

BULLET WEIGHT

It's important to understand that ammunition is not just sold by caliber and bullet style; it's also sold by bullet weight. Clearly marked on a box of ammunition is the weight of each bullet in grains. One ounce of lead weighs 437.5 grains. Why such an odd number? I don't know, it's probably a British thing. When you buy .45 ACP ammunition, and it says on the box that it's 230-grain ammo, that means each bullet is slightly more than a half-ounce of lead and copper.

Why does any of this matter? It actually matters a lot. Returning to our Newtonian physics lesson, we know that force is mass times acceleration. The bigger the bullet, the more mass

A lightweight bullet traveling very quickly can have as much or more force than a large bullet traveling slower. Federal

it has and the more force it produces. In my experience of testing a lot of different weight bullets, there's a reduction in velocity with heavier bullets, but it's a small enough reduction that you still get greater force from a heavier bullet.

Again, a heavier bullet will also produce more force forward and backward, which you will feel as slightly increased recoil. The biggest issue with bullet weight, however, is in handgun performance. With a revolver, it doesn't really matter except in some rare cases. With a semi-automatic pistol, it can make a big difference. If you select ammunition that's too light, it might not produce sufficient force to reliably cycle the action. I've seen this with 9mm pistols firing ammunition that weighs less than 115 grains.

Some manufacturers make lightweight ammunition that will func-

tion reliably in a semi-auto, because they've dramatically increased velocity to compensate. One example is Liberty Ammunition, which produces a very accurate 50-grain +P 9mm round designed to fragment on impact. This round travels at a very high velocity, close to twice that of a standard 9mm round, but its fragmenting design helps stop a threat and prevent overpenetration. It does produce a great deal of muzzle blast, however.

So when you buy ammunition, read the label and fully understand what it is you're buying. You might be using it to save your life and you might not get a second chance.

EXPANDING AMMUNITION

Shot placement is a factor of accuracy and comes from practice, but bullet effectiveness is a function of its design. For personal protection

Defensive ammunition should expand reliably and retain as much of its weight as possible.
Jorge Amselle

and maximum effectiveness, a larger wound cavity is better, which is why expanding or hollow-point ammunition is preferred. The FBI determined in their testing that at a minimum, a bullet must be able to penetrate at least 12 inches in ballistic gelatin (and up to 18 inches is preferable) in order to hit and damage vital organs and blood vessels.

When the bullet expands, it can reach double its normal diameter. This causes far greater damage to the target, and it also helps to slow down the bullet in its travel. You do not want a bullet that hits your target and just keeps going through it and on into a wall, a room, the next wall, another room, outside and across the street (this is over-penetration). With some FMJ bullets this is exactly what can happen. The hard bullet with no expansion just keeps going until it hits something hard enough to stop it. By expanding and slowing down, defensive ammunition avoids over-penetration and reduces the risk to anyone behind your target.

I once attended a ballistics seminar hosted by ATK, the

Federal Guard Dog ammo will expand no matter what the barrier is and has no hollow point to clog up.
Federal

world's largest producer of ammunition, including Federal and CCI/Speer, where we were given in-depth demonstrations of bullet performance through various barriers and into ballistic gelatin. We all know that the force of the bullet is a factor of its mass or weight multiplied by its velocity. Velocity does have a higher multiplier effect on force, but faster bullets don't necessarily perform better when it comes to penetration. Adequate expansion and penetration are factors of bullet design and weight more than anything else.

SHOOTING THROUGH BARRIERS

In terms of bullet design for expanding ammunition, one factor is shooting through heavy clothing. The fibers of the material, or even drywall, can clog the opening of some hollow-point bullets, preventing them from expanding and resulting in over-penetration. Also, some hollow-point

Bullets have a tendency to tumble when they impact windshield glass, but they still expand and penetrate sufficiently. SIG Sauer Academy

This ammunition was fired through glass, sheet rock, car door steel and heavy clothing, but still expanded and penetrated 15 inches into ballistic gelatin. Jorge Amselle

bullets experience jacket separation when going through barriers. This fragmentation of the bullet divides its forward momentum among the individual fragments, slowing each down and possibly failing to deliver sufficient penetration for any of them to cause threat-ending damage.

In the demonstration, we tested various types of Federal ammunition through several layers of denim and through windshield glass, and then measured the expansion and penetration of each round. All the rounds performed extremely well and achieved expansion of 1.5 times their original diameter or greater. Through windshield glass, given that it's an angled surface, bullets had a tendency to tumble, but they still expanded and

penetrated sufficiently.

None of the bullets tested from Federal experienced any fragmentation thanks to their bonded design, which bonds the lead core to the copper jacket. The bullets tested were designed for law enforcement use, but in the civilian market, Federal's Hydra-Shok is an excellent choice, providing 100 percent weight retention, and good penetration and expansion in a reduced-recoil load available in a variety of personal-defense calibers.

Another outstanding round is Winchester's Supreme Elite Bonded PDX1. The FBI selected this round as their standard service ammunition based on its performance in their ballistics testing. A bonding process ensures that the bullet will retain all

Bonded ammo, such as this load from Remington, keeps the copper jacket and lead core together for better performance. Jorge Amselle

of its weight, while the hollow-point design ensures reliable expansion across a wide range of velocities and distances. The shell cases are nickel-plated for reliable pistol chambering and ejection.

One round I have tested that does not require any bonding is Cor-Bon's DPX, a solid-copper hollow-point bullet. I fired this round in .40 S&W through a ¾-inch pine board, and it penetrated the board completely, expanding reliably with zero fragmentation. According to Cor-Bon, this round will produce a consistent 12 to 17 inches of soft tissue penetration, even through barriers such as clothing and glass, and will expand to as much as 200 percent of its original diameter.

I do have a note of caution on this whole business of shooting through barriers. Most of this testing has to do with meeting the needs of law enforcement officers, which are very different than those of home or personal defense for civilians. For obvious reasons, you do not want to shoot at a target you cannot see. However, if an assailant has taken cover behind a door, for example, and is using it as a shield from which to attack you, it's nice to know you can fire through the door.

RELIABILITY

One concern with self-defense ammunition has to do with reliability in semi-automatic handguns. Most modern semi-autos are designed to reliably function with all types of hollow-point ammunition, but in reality this is not always the case. All semi-auto pistols must strip cartridges out of a magazine and lift and feed them into a chamber. The rounder and smoother the bullet, the easier this is, but when a bullet has a big flat hole in the front, this can get trickier.

In my experience, there are few guns that will not reliably cycle and function with hollow-point ammunition, but you never know. My advice has always been to find a defensive round you like and test fire it in your

Ammo should always be tested to ensure reliability and to break-in a new gun. Jorge Amselle

gun before settling on it as your ammunition of choice.

This serves several functions. First, it will tell you if it will reliably cycle in your handgun. The last thing you want is high-quality ammunition that causes your gun to malfunction when you need it most. Second, it allows you to experience the recoil, muzzle blast and noise of the full-power loads. Self-defense ammunition is usually loaded to higher pressures than range ammunition, and it's important to get used to the difference.

NON-EXPANDING DEFENSIVE AMMUNITION

In certain states (New Jersey) and localities, it's unlawful to use hollow-point ammunition against a person. In Detroit, the police aren't allowed to use these types of rounds either. The politicians in these jurisdictions do not view it as humane. It seems odd that criminals and assailants should only be shot "gently," but it's far from a new position.

The Hague Convention of 1899 established the principle against using expanding ammunition in warfare, which some seem to have taken to heart, despite the fact that to kill animals "humanely" expanding ammunition is preferred.

In response, Federal Premium Ammunition created a full-metal-jacketed round, the Guard Dog Home Defense, that expands reliably in soft tissue like a hollow point and stays together. This round is especially useful for guns that have trouble feeding standard hollow-point ammunition.

I attended a ballistics demonstration by Federal in Bozeman, Montana, and witnessed firsthand the efficacy of this round as it consistently produced 12 to 13 inches of penetration in gelatin. With no hollow point to get clogged, expansion of .40 S&W ammunition to .65 inches occurred equally well through heavy clothing as in plain gelatin. The silver-colored bullet appears solid but internally it features a special blue-colored polymer. The ammunition tends to have slightly lighter overall weight, higher velocities and lower recoil as well. It is available in 9mm, .40 S&W and .45 ACP.

PLUS-P AMMUNITION

Some defensive ammunition will be marked +P or sometimes even +P+. You will see this on boxes sometimes marked "for law enforcement use" and think to yourself, "It must be good, then." The fact is that it depends on your gun.

All ammunition is supposed to be loaded to a standard pressure for each caliber, according to the Sporting Arms and Ammunition Manufacturers' Institute (SAAMI). It's their job to set "industry standards for safety, interchangeability, reliability and quality" for all ammunition.

Using 9mm as an example, the standard pressure is 35,000 PSI and for +P 9mm ammunition it's 38,500 PSI.

Your gun might not be rated to handle the higher pressures of +P ammunition, and the owner's manual should be consulted. Using higher-pressure ammunition might damage the gun and cause injury. Ammunition that is rated +P+ is even worse, because there's no standard pressure for this.

So why would anyone buy +P ammunition? Remember that force equals mass times acceleration, and the same-size bullet traveling at a higher speed will produce more force. However, this is not necessarily a good thing. For every action there is an equal and opposite reaction, and a bullet fired forward with greater force will also produce greater recoil. In a small CCW handgun, you will certainly feel the difference, and it will likely not be pleasant. The +P ammunition also has a louder report and produces more muzzle flash, which could affect your night vision in a low-light encounter.

Ammunition that's rated +P produces higher velocities and more force, but will not necessarily penetrate or perform better. Modern defensive ammunition is designed to utilize the bullet's velocity to maximize performance. It will expand reliably at the standard pressure for which it was designed. There is no advantage in sending the bullet flying faster, and for some of these bullets it might actually hinder their performance.

From a practical application, the only real reason for using +P ammunition is in firearm performance and reliability. Some guns might prefer the higher-pressure rounds and perform more reliably with them.

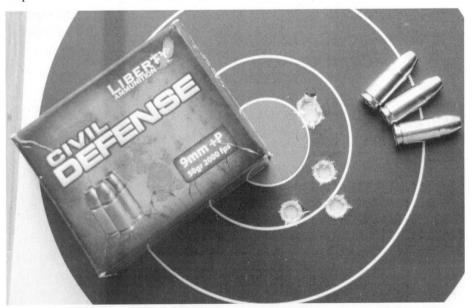

Ammunition labeled +P is loaded for higher velocities. It kicks more and produces more muzzle flash. Jorge Amselle

Modern defensive ammunition is specifically designed for short-barreled concealed-carry handguns. Jorge Amselle

CCW AMMUNITION

For a long time, ammunition manufacturers produced defensive ammunition with an eye toward law enforcement needs, and this meant optimizing bullets and cartridges for performance in full-sized duty handguns. Government customers clearly buy ammunition in very large quantities, and it was thought that if it's good enough for cops, it's good enough for civilians.

But then a funny thing happened. Manufacturers began to notice that civilian defensive shooting needs were a major force in the market on their own. They noticed that millions of people were now carrying sub-compact and micro handguns for self defense, and they noticed that many of these new customers were women. Extensive testing though ballistic gelatin and barriers also revealed that bullets designed for full-sized handguns perform differently out of the short barrels popular for CCW use.

The short-barreled handguns we use for concealed carry do come with a cost. With a shorter barrel, the gunpowder in the cartridge case has less time to burn. The force imparted to the bullet from the burning powder increases as the powder burns. To maximize that energy, you want all of the powder to burn before the bullet exits the barrel. This takes about 20 inches of barrel in many cases to impart the maximum velocity and force onto the bullet.

Of course, none of us is going to carry a handgun with a 20-inch barrel, but there's still a significant difference between a 5-inch barrel and a 2-inch barrel. With the shorter barrel, a large portion of the unburned powder ignites outside the barrel in front of you after the bullet has already "left the building," so to speak. All this does is make a lot of flash and noise and does nothing to improve bullet performance.

Manufacturers have developed cartridges with different powder mixes to maximize bullet performance out of short barrels. Now you can buy ammunition that is almost micro-tailored to your particular gun. Hornady Ammunition offers two distinct loads.

Critical Duty is designed for law enforcement agents and civilians using full-sized duty handguns. This ammunition offers better barrier penetration and terminal performance. Critical Defense ammunition, on the other hand, is designed to meet the specific

needs of short-barreled handguns popular for concealed carry. This CCW ammunition produces less recoil and less barrier penetration, but still expands reliably for good terminal performance.

In fact, the key element for all custom-designed CCW ammunition is to both reduce recoil and muzzle flash. SIG Sauer, known more as a handgun manufacturer, has also introduced a line of premium self-defense ammunition designed to function in both compact and full-sized handguns. The SIG Elite Performance centerfire pistol ammunition is custom-made and uses a unique bullet design that goes beyond the usual jacketed hollow-point configuration.

SIG ammunition uses a V-crown hollow-point design that features a hidden hollow cavity behind the main V-shaped hollow point with preset cuts to ensure uniform and controlled bul-

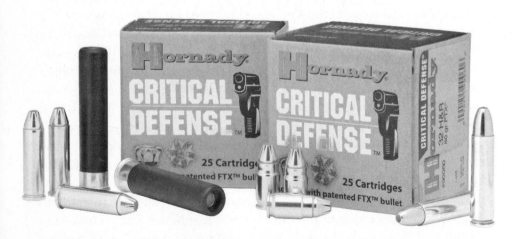

Hornady produces two types of defensive ammunition: one for full-sized handguns (Critical Duty) and one for compact handguns (Critical Defense). Hornady

let expansion. The ammunition was tested in ballistic gelatin through various barriers including heavy clothing, plywood and Sheetrock, and its expansion and penetration remained consistent.

The jacket and lead-alloy bullet remain locked together through a toothed channel along the length of the bullet. This effectively prevents bullet separation and ensures full weight retention for proper penetration, expansion and terminal effectiveness. The nickel-plated brass case has been engineered with a low flash powder to save your night vision in low-light conditions and coated for corrosion resistance, lubricity and reliable feeding and extraction.

Firearms manufacturers, such as SIG Sauer, also make defensive ammunition for their guns. SIG Sauer

AMMUNITION FOR WOMEN

Having personally trained hundreds of men and women shooters—novices and experienced shooters alike—I've seen that women shooters can often outshoot their male counterparts and handle recoil just as well. However, they also disproportionally tend to dislike it, my wife included. Apparently, I am not the only person to notice this, because ammunition manufacturers have developed defensive loads specifically for women (or anyone else who is recoil sensitive).

Hornady introduced a reduced recoil revolver cartridge that still has the knockdown power to be loaded into a carry gun—the 90-grain .38 Special FTX Critical Defense LITE. Designed specifically for lightweight, short-barreled revolvers, this ammunition reliably expands through different barriers and offers solid penetration. It comes in a pink package, has a pink polymer tip and a portion of the proceeds go to breast cancer research. In addition to reduced recoil, it produces less muzzle flash out of short barrels.

My wife carries an S&W 340PD revolver, which weighs only 11.5 ounces. Although it's easy to carry, it can be quite painful to shoot, especially with her usual load of 125-grain Remington Golden Saber .38 +P cartridges. While this is certainly a very effective load, it doesn't improve her marksmanship as she grits her teeth and flinches her eyes. Hornady's .38 Special FTX Critical Defense LITE,

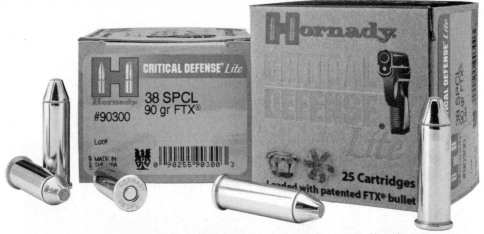

Hornady has developed special low recoil defensive ammunition for women. Hornady

Low-recoil ammunition makes lightweight revolvers much more comfortable to shoot. Hornady

however, is the only self-defense load that did not make her hand hurt afterward. Instead of anticipating the shot and the recoil, she was able to focus on her aim, resulting in better shot placement. According to Hornady, this round gets an average penetration of 9 inches and expands to more than a half-inch.

Winchester has developed a very interesting ammo combination in their Train and Defend product line. Called W Train & Defend, this consists of two distinct types of ammunition mar-

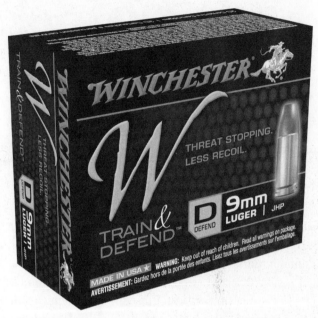

Winchester makes low-recoil defensive ammunition for women. Winchester

keted specifically for women and new shooters. The ammunition is identified by either a "T" for training purposes, or a "D" for self-defense purposes on the box to easily differentiate between the two.

Both types of ammunition feature low recoil for comfort and are ballistically matched. That means both types of ammunition have the same recoil and point of impact. Shooters can train with the cheaper full-metal jacket range ammunition that matches the feel and accuracy of their self-defense ammunition. This represents a huge training advantage and an incredible cost savings for the average consumer. The training

ammunition comes in 50-round boxes and features lead-free primers for safer use in indoor ranges, brass shell cases and full-metal-jacketed bullets.

The "D" self-defense ammunition has nickel-plated cases, so they can be easily distinguished from the training rounds. The Winchester bonded jacketed hollow-point bullets are specially designed for maximum expansion and penetration to stop a threat, while reducing recoil for quicker follow-up shots.

STORAGE AND MAINTENANCE

All ammunition should be stored in a cool, dry place away from moisture and humidity. Modern ammunition is

Store ammunition in its original box in a cool, dry place with no moisture or humidity. Jorge Amselle

made with sealants to protect against the elements, but nothing lasts forever. If ammunition is properly stored, it will remain effective for decades, but if it isn't stored properly, its lifespan can be reduced.

Ammunition you carry on a daily basis is subject to being knocked about, exposed to dust, debris, lint and sweat as well as temperature changes, etc. My recommendation is to replace your carry ammunition at least annually. Just shoot the old stuff and get a new box of the ammunition you like to carry.

If ammunition looks old or corroded, don't use it for carry purposes. There are plenty of gun owners who will gladly take old ammunition off your hands if you feel uncomfortable using it. If your ammunition gets dusty or dirty, you can clean in by wiping it down with a clean cloth. Do not use any solvents or oils on your ammuni-

tion, because this is much more likely to damage it. Even if you can't see it, solvents and lubricants can get into your ammunition and compromise the chemicals that make up the powder and primer.

MALFUNCTIONS

Just as your gun can malfunction, so can your ammunition, especially if it has not been properly stored. There are three basic types of ammunition malfunctions. Misfire is when the round simply does not go off. On the range, always keep the gun pointed in a safe direction (downrange) and wait 30 seconds before you clear the objecting round. It could be that a round simply did not exit the magazine, so there was nothing in the chamber. It could also just be a hard or bad primer.

Wait 30 seconds with the gun pointed in a safe direction in case you have

With a misfire, wait 30 seconds before clearing it and keep the gun pointed in a safe direction.
Gunsite Academy

the second type of malfunction, a hang fire. A hang fire is a perceptible delay in the ignition of the cartridge. It might be a function of corrupted powder and the round does not go off right away. It might take as much as 8 seconds for the round to detonate and fire.

You don't want to be waving the gun around or looking down the barrel when that happens. You also don't want the cartridge detonating while you're opening the chamber, because that will create shrapnel and possibly injure you. Fortunately, hang fires are very rare. I have experienced it only once, and that was with some 50-year-old French military surplus rifle ammunition, and the delay was only a split second (but still noticeable).

The last basic type of malfunction is a squib load. This is the result of an underpowered cartridge. The cartridge fires, but it will sound and feel noticeably different from a normal round. The gun will kick a lot less, and it will sound much quieter. It could be that only some of the gunpowder ignited or that there was no gunpowder in the cartridge—only the live primer.

If you experience this, cease firing immediately and inspect the barrel for any obstructions, because the cartridge might have had enough force to send a bullet halfway down the barrel and left it lodged there. If the barrel is clear, you can continue to shoot. You should

Bad ammo can cause all types of malfunctions, including this stove pipe. Jorge Amselle

never fire a gun with an obstruction in the barrel because this will damage or destroy the gun and likely cause injury to you.

Here's another warning when it comes to ammunition. Most people who carry concealed do so with a round in the chamber. Occasionally, you will have to unload your gun—when storing or cleaning it, for example. When you reload and re-chamber a round, be conscientious of which round you are chambering. If you continually chamber the same round over and over again, the bullet will gradually and almost imperceptibly become seated deeper and deeper into the cartridge case. The result of this powder packing is that when the bullet is fired, it will generate a much higher and possibly unsafe chamber pressure. This is only a problem with

semi-automatic handguns. I would not re-chamber the same round more than a couple of times. After that, use a different round.

If you find yourself in a life-threatening situation, where you have to use your concealed-carry handgun, some of these rules are significantly relaxed. If you experience a misfire under these circumstances, immediately clear the recalcitrant round and load a fresh one. With a revolver, this is much easier because all you have to do is squeeze the trigger again to rotate the cylinder and bring a fresh round in line with the barrel.

RECOMMENDATION

There is no surer way to start an hours-long, friendship-ending argument among gun owners than to ask the question: Which is the best car-

Caliber selection is less important than using high-quality ammunition. SIG Sauer Academy

tridge. You would be better off bringing up religion or politics. The .45 ACP and the 9mm cartridges are each over 100 years old. They have been and continue to be used by militaries around the globe with great effect. But since their inception, gun owners have been arguing angrily over which one is better.

Here's the secret: It doesn't matter. It makes virtually no difference which defensive cartridge you choose; they will all get the job done. Select the pistol and cartridge that best suit your needs and preferences. Any cartridge in the .380 ACP or .38 Special ranges or above will serve you well. For decades, European and American police departments predominantly issued handguns to their officers in these two chamberings, and this was before the advent of modern expanding ammunition. If they were ineffective or weak, they would have been replaced from the start instead of being used for 50-plus years.

With modern defensive ammunition

and the accompanying technological improvements in gunpowder, primers and bullet design, the difference in terminal effectiveness between these cartridges has radically decreased. A 10th or a 20th of an inch greater expansion isn't likely to make the difference between life and death. Penetration will make a bigger difference, but that's a factor of bullet design more than cartridge selection. Whether your bullet penetrates 9 inches or 18 inches into soft tissue matters much less than your accuracy and shot placement.

With all of these caveats, my personal recommendation for the best all-around concealed-carry handgun cartridge is the 9mm. Any well-designed modern defensive round in 9mm will give you all the expansion and penetration you are likely to need. It's among the easiest cartridges to find on store shelves because it's so popular, so you are unlikely to find yourself out of ammo. It is probably the cheapest (or close to it) non-rimfire handgun ammunition you will find, especially if you buy in bulk. It has very moderate recoil in all but the smallest handguns. It lets you accommodate more rounds in the same-size gun, giving you greater firepower. It's available in just about every type of handgun, including some revolvers. All of these reasons make it easy to train with and is appropriate for different members of your family.

Are the .40-caliber and the .45 ACP cartridges more powerful and larger?

Sure, but if terminal effectiveness is your only criteria, you should carry a bazooka. I don't really follow my own advice on this issue. Because I prefer to carry a pocket pistol, I use the .380 ACP most often. There are pocket pistols chambered in 9mm, but I find these to be slightly larger and with harsh recoil (which discourages practice and training). Of course in an actual lethal encounter, the recoil will be a very distant thought.

CHAPTER 10

ACCESSORIES

You have your concealed-carry gun. You've picked out the best holster for your needs and the best defensive ammunition. That could be all you need, but there's no reason it can't be better. There are lots of accessories that can help you be more effective and improve your odds against an assailant, each of which deserves careful consideration.

At the same time, you don't want to overdo it. I had a friend who was very passionate about being prepared for anything, a Boy Scout mentality that should be commended. He routinely carried a full-sized 9mm pistol on a belt holster on one side and two spare magazines on the other (that's 62 rounds of ammunition). He also carried a cell phone, a large folding knife,

Gun shops are a great place to get all the accessories needed for concealed carry. Colonial Shooting Academy

pepper spray and a high-lumen tactical flashlight. In addition, he had a backup handgun and ammunition for it. All he needed was a grappling hook, some rope and a cape and he could be Batman. I seriously wondered how he kept his pants up.

When selecting accessories, keep in mind the realm of the possible versus the realm of the probable. Is it a good idea to have a fire extinguisher? Of course. Is it reasonable to carry it with you everywhere you go? Probably not. Anything is possible, but not everything is probable. It makes no sense to prepare for every possibility, but it does to prepare for likely probabilities.

SPARE MAGAZINE/AMMUNITION

For a long time, I was not a fan of carrying a spare magazine or spare ammunition. I figured it was unlikely I'd ever even need my concealed-carry gun and even if I did, I'd have five to seven shots (depending on what I was carrying) loaded in the gun. I wasn't planning on repelling Al Qaida, just dealing with one, possibly two, assailants. I figured that if I needed extra ammunition, I was probably in over my head anyway. But this is short-sighted, and there are legitimate reasons for carrying at least a few spare rounds.

One of the things that convinced me of the error of my ways was when I noticed that with pocket carry (my preferred method), there were a few times when the magazine release button got depressed enough to release the magazine. I routinely check to make sure the magazine is always seated but still, if I were to draw my pocket pistol with the magazine loose, I would have only the one round in the chamber. Looking around for a magazine you dropped in the middle of a fight is not ideal. It's far better to

While more is usually better, one spare magazine should do for most concealed-carry applications.
Jorge Amselle

have a spare magazine right where you know where to find it on your person.

The other issue is that with most small concealed-carry handguns, you are somewhat limited in terms of ammunition capacity. My pocket .380 pistol has a six-round magazine, so I get seven rounds with one in the chamber. Most concealed-carry revolvers have a five-shot cylinder. Consider this fact: New York City police officers involved in shootings score hits with only 30 percent of their shots, and if the suspect is shooting back at them, the hit ratio drops down to 18 percent. In Baltimore County, Maryland, officers perform better, with a hit ratio of 64 percent, but in low-light conditions this drops to 45 percent. These are trained and experienced police officers, well-prepared for such situations. What will your hit ratio be with your level of training if you're caught entirely by surprise in a low-light confrontation?

If you have seven shots and miss with 70 percent or more, you will be lucky to get two hits. That might not be enough to stop an assailant, and if he has accomplices you are in big trouble. Given this consideration, carrying a spare magazine or extra ammunition all of a sudden makes a lot more sense.

Some guns are sold with only one magazine, especially concealed-carry pocket pistols, and revolvers, of course, have no magazines. Buy a spare maga-

A speed strip is an effective way to carry extra ammo for a revolver. Jorge Amselle

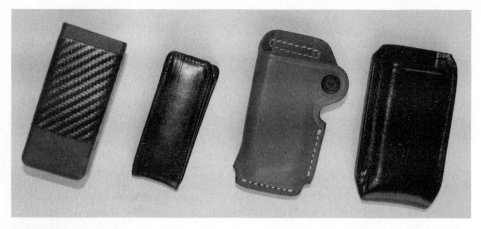

Don't just stick a spare magazine in a pocket and hope for the best. Use a proper magazine holster.
Jorge Amselle

zine for your concealed-carry pistol. For revolvers, get a speed strip—a long piece of rubber with holes for five or six spare rounds of ammunition. These speed strips make loading the revolver faster and easier, because you can load two rounds at a time.

Both magazines and speed strips are very flat and can be easily carried in a pocket. I recommend always carrying your spare ammunition in the same manner and in the same place on your body. That way, you won't be hunting around for it in a stressful situation, but will know right where to find it.

Keep your spare ammunition in its own pocket and don't mix it with your keys or spare change. If a pocket isn't convenient, there are small and inconspicuous magazine belt pouches and IWB pouches available. If you have to place your magazine or ammo in a pocket with other items, you can use a special magazine holster that will protect the ammo.

Since a spare magazine is so much smaller than the gun itself, you can sometimes find those that have a bit higher capacity. Compact versions of full-sized guns usually accommodate the larger magazines. If I'm carrying my Glock 19 with a 15-round magazine, my spare magazine will be the larger 17-round magazine. For my pocket pistol, I buy the extended spare magazine that gives me one extra round and a small rest for my pinky, so I can also get a better grip on the gun when I change magazines. Finally, remember that just as you rotate the ammunition in your carry gun on a regular basis, you should also periodically replace the ammunition in your spare magazine.

WEAPON LIGHTS

The biggest problem with mounting anything extra onto your gun is getting it to fit into a holster. The issue is that for each gun there are dozens of

Weapon lights are effective for identifying a target in low-light conditions. Viridian

different holsters, and each gun might accommodate any of a dozen different mounted accessories. That means holster makers have to come up with an exponentially increasing number of holsters for each gun/accessory combination. The most obvious solution is for the accessory makers to design matching holsters, and that's what many of them have done.

Weapon lights for handguns are not particularly new, but what has changed is that they have become much more powerful and smaller. Smaller is good because it makes them far more compatible with concealed carry.

Having a high-output flashlight on your handgun makes sense for a variety of reasons. Bad guys love the dark; it makes it easier for them to surprise you and more difficult for you to identify them. A weapon light helps you identify your target before you shoot. It also helps you orient your shot and silhouette your sights for better aiming. And, finally, the light itself can be used as a weapon to blind and disorient your assailant.

Some people believe it's a bad idea to have a light mounted on your gun because it shows the bad guys where you are. But they seem to forget that we are talking about civilian personal protection, not Seal Team Six going in after Osama. The bad guys by definition initiated the attack on you, so they've already seen you and know where you are. They might be using low-light conditions to their advantage by hiding in the shadows. The benefits of a weapon-mounted light far outweigh any possible tactical disadvantages in this scenario.

I always keep a light mounted on my home defense gun. That way, I have only to reach for my gun, and I already have a defensive light handy. It is vitally important to remember one thing: A weapon-mounted light is a weapon, and it should not be used as a flashlight. Do not use it to search around your house, outside or anywhere else, because you will invariably end up pointing a loaded gun at things and people you don't want to shoot.

Viridian Green Laser Sights has developed a very interesting tactical light for pocket pistols. Its Radiance light features a proprietary filter that reshapes the usual round light beam into a wide, oval shape, narrowing the beam top to bottom and allowing a much wider field of view—more than twice the width of a normal tactical light. This reduces the amount of time it takes to identify threats and also helps avoid tunnel vision, which is especially good if you are dealing with multiple threats.

This technology is available on Viridian's compact Reactor Tactical Light for pocket pistols. Currently, these are being produced for the Ruger LCP and LC9, and are being offered with Viridian's Enhanced Combat Readiness (ECR) holster. The unit attaches to the front of the trigger guard and produces a 100 lumens constant and 140 lumens strobe light. A strobe light is especially useful for disorienting an assailant.

The ECR holster is designed so that as soon as you draw your gun, the light/laser turns on at whatever setting you have selected, using an electronic sensor inside the holster to activate the laser unit rather than a mechanical system. Will you remember to activate your light/laser in a high-stress, self-defense situation, where quick access might be needed? With the ECR, you don't need to think about it. All you have to do is draw your pistol. Viridian also sells a larger light—green or red laser combination unit—that installs on the accessory rail of larger handguns and a matching ECR belt holster.

A simpler weapon-mounted light can be purchased from ArmaLaser. The Stingray SRX LED TAC-Light

Special filters can provide wide-angle illumination for faster identification of hostiles. Viridian

ArmaLaser makes the smallest LED tactical light available for handguns. ArmaLaser

can be easily installed onto any mid- to full-sized pistol accessory rail using a small Phillips screwdriver and will fit into many non-molded holsters. The unit is very small and has a rear ambidextrous on/off switch and a single LED 25-lumen bulb, which will illuminate an area out to about 40 feet. According to ArmaLaser, this is "the smallest, lightest, slimmest weapon-mounted tactical light on the planet."

HANDHELD LIGHTS

Another option, which I pretty much always carry, is a separate flashlight. I have several, in fact, from super-high-output penlights to a small keychain light. Unlike a weapon-mounted light, these can be used for searching and scanning without endangering anyone. The other advantage is that you don't have to worry about holster fit because the light is

Handheld lights can be found in a variety of sizes, which means there's never an excuse not to pack one. Terra LUX

separate from the gun, but can still be used in combination.

I took a class at Gunsite Academy in Arizona that included the use of a handheld flashlight in conjunction with a handgun. There are two primary ways to use a flashlight with a handgun. In the first, you place your hands together back-to-back. The arm holding the light is bent and you are pushing the back of that hand against the back of the hand holding the gun. The gun arm is outstretched. The two hands brace each other, and the light beam goes wherever you point the muzzle of the gun.

In the second method, you hold the arm with the flashlight away from your body and above your head with the beam oriented toward the threat. This makes it so the bad guy cannot pinpoint your exact location should he fire at you, but it makes it harder to keep the beam and the muzzle aligned. Reloading can also be a challenge, and instructors recommended tucking the light under your arm with the beam oriented toward the threat. This frees up your hands to reload or perform any malfunction drills. However, in a high-speed situation, you might be better off just dropping the flashlight.

I'm a big fan of the Bright Strike EPLI penlight, which is made from aluminum, is only 5 inches long and is powered by easy-to-find AAA batteries. It has simple push-button activation in the back with three settings: high at

A handheld light held away from the body makes it difficult for the bad guy to pinpoint his target's exact location. Jorge Amselle

Using a handheld light in conjunction with a handgun keeps the muzzle and light beam aligned.
Jorge Amselle

160 lumens, low at 80 lumens and a high-strobe. The pocket clip makes it easy to carry, so you can always have it with you. Plus, you can take it places where guns are not allowed.

A tactical flashlight can be a lifesaver all on its own, and there are countless scenarios where it might come in handy. If you are walking to your car in a dark parking lot or garage, you can use the light to scan the area for anyone who might be hiding in wait or even under your car. The beam on these lights is nothing like the old flashlights I grew up with, but is more like a car headlight. You can easily spot and identify people and objects 100 yards away.

If you're in a building during a power outage or, God forbid, a fire, a tactical light will help you find your way out. If you go for a walk at night, you will be able to identify the source of any noise. If you are assaulted, the light can be used to temporarily blind the bad guy while you run for cover. I consider the tactical light among my most important and valuable pieces of everyday gear.

KNIVES

A pocket knife is another important piece of gear. Not necessarily for self defense, but rather just for everyday use. I use my pocket knife more than I use my keys or wallet. However, they can also be an essential component of your self-defense preparedness.

Ideally, a pocket knife will have a quick-opening feature that allows you

These Hoffner knives make excellent defensive tools. Jorge Amselle

to open it one-handed. It should have a belt clip so you can keep it easily accessible in a pants or jacket pocket. And finally, it's best to carry your knife so you can access it with either hand; barring that, place the knife so you can access it with your support hand.

If you should ever get into a situation where your gun hand is compromised (say in a struggle over your gun). You can access your knife with your support hand and use the blade to cut the arm or hand of your assailant to regain control of your gun. This involves a high level if skill and training, so you should seek out an expert in unarmed and knife combat to help you train. Otherwise you risk cutting yourself.

In some cases, self defense using a knife might be the only option. Jorge Amselle

If you're in an area where you cannot carry a gun, your knife might be your primary defensive tool. In this case, you still want to keep it where it can be reached by either hand, or at least on your strong side.

Be aware that the laws on knife carry are usually very dated and have not kept pace with concealed-carry laws for handguns. In many areas, knife carry is restricted, even if you have a concealed-carry permit for your handgun. Like the general rule for handguns, it's best to keep your carry knife concealed as much as possible and always follow the local laws.

One excellent knife defense course that's offered around the country is Safer Faster Defense taught by Alessandro Padovani, a life-long martial artist and personal-defense instructor. This one-day course can be fairly advanced, and there are distinct classes taught for civilians and law enforcement personnel. Elements of the class typically include knife defense fundamentals, extreme close-quarter knife defense, defending against multiple assailants and defending against a gun grab. A comprehensive 2-day course covers all of the topics.

Brian Hoffner is another expert who has more than 30 years of law enforcement experience as a patrol officer and firearms and defensive tactics instructor. He offers a DVD course for

those who cannot attend his class in person and has also designed his own combat folding knife with extra features that add to its versatility as a defensive tool.

Hoffner has added a flat bolster at the front with sharp and very aggressive

Where it is not legal to carry a gun, a knife might be the best option for personal defense. Hoffner

serrations. With the blade closed, these offer a less-lethal striking surface, which also provides the operator with the option of using the knife as a defensive tool without having to deploy the blade. The pommel end is similarly serrated but instead of being flat, it comes to a distinct point, which provides additional striking capabilities and can be used as a compliance tool when applied to pressure points on an assailant.

A knife is a lethal weapon and using one in self defense involves the same criteria as using a gun. Using a knife for self defense can also get ugly very quickly. Slashing and stabbing an attacker is a gory, messy, bloody act that few civilians are prepared for. Of course, if someone is attacking you, it might come easier, but it's still better to be mentally prepared for such an encounter.

WEAPON LASERS

More common and certainly more useful than a weapon-mounted flashlight is a weapon-mounted laser. Weapon-mounted laser technology has come a long way from the giant red laser Arnold Schwarzenegger had mounted on his AMT Long Slide 1911 .45 ACP in the first Terminator movie. Not only are today's lasers miniscule by comparison; improved technology has also delivered green lasers.

The use of laser sights on personal-defense handguns has dramatically increased over the years with the expansion of concealed carry and the improvements in laser units, making them both smaller and more affordable. They provide the tactical advantage of being able to engage threats from various angles and positions much more easily and quickly, especially in low-light conditions.

An increasing number of lasers—available in red and green—are available for compact concealed-carry handguns. LaserMax

Most pocket pistols are not designed to be target guns, and their sights are usually small and rudimentary. A laser puts a bright red or green dot right on the target, showing you where your bullet is going to go. In a stressful situation, fine motor skills are compromised, so using your gun's sights can become more difficult. You also become threat focused. The laser allows you to keep your eyes on the target and easily see where your shots will go. Plus, there are few ways to better communicate to a bad guy that he's in trouble than putting a bright red dot on his chest.

Green lasers are more expensive, but can now be found in the same models as red lasers. The advantage is that green light is far more visible to the human eye, especially in bright sunlight. I've tested both red and green lasers extensively and can certainly attest to this. In sunlight, a red laser works well out to no more than 15 feet. A green laser remains bright and easily seen at 50 feet or more.

Lasers are typically smaller than tactical flashlights, so you have a variety of options for installing a laser on your gun without having to switch to a special holster. Crimson Trace is a leader in this field, and their grip-mounted lasers feature instant activation when you grip them, while still remaining small and unobtrusive and allowing the use of standard holsters.

The company has both red and green lasers available to suit every

Viridian is a leader in green laser technology, which is more visible to the eye than red lasers. Viridian

need. These are especially well-suited for revolvers and makes attaching a laser to almost any gun very easy. They also have "grip" lasers for guns that don't have separate grips, such as Glocks. Crimson Trace teamed up with Gunsite Academy to offer a specific gun laser course that trains participants in the best use of a laser-equipped handgun for personal protection.

For pocket pistols, Armalaser teamed up with holster manufacturers DeSantis and Don Hume to offer shooters a complete laser and carry package. With the laser, you get a free DeSantis Nemesis pocket holster designed to hold your gun with the laser attached, or you can upgrade to a

Crimson Trace's grip-mounted lasers are adaptable to most guns with no need for a new holster. Crimson Trace

A laser/light combination makes target acquisition much easier and faster in low-light situations.
Crimson Trace

leather Don Hume holster. Laser units are available to fit eight different pistol models from KEL-TEC, Glock, Taurus, Springfield, KAHR and Ruger.

The most distinctive feature of the ArmaLaser unit is that it automatically turns on when you need it and turns off when you don't—no buttons, levers or switches needed. It uses an electric strip to activate the laser as soon as your hand makes contact with it. The system adds only 1.2 ounces to the gun and adds no discernible width or height. In fact, the extra block in front of the trigger guard is almost flush with the front of the gun and actually helps prevent printing by disguising the silhouette of the pocket gun.

LaserMax is another very innovative company—the only manufacturer of fully internal guide rod laser units that need no adjustment. They are eas-ily installed by replacing the factory guide rod on most semi-auto pistols, and don't interfere with holster use or rail-mounted accessories. LaserMax also offers pulsating lasers, green lasers and infrared units for increased visibility, even in bright daylight.

The company also offers lasers that are rail-mounted, frame-mounted and side-plate mounted (for revolvers). In addition to the CenterFire units specifically designed for the Ruger LCP and LC9 pistols, the company has several other new items, including its Genesis rechargeable green-laser rail unit and its new guide rod lasers for sub-compact Glocks. Two other rail-mounted lasers include the Uni-Max, which has its own rail and can be combined with a light, and the Micro, designed for rail-equipped sub-compact pistols.

In green laser technology, Viridian Green Laser Sights might be the leader and offers a unit specifically for pocket pistols, which includes their ECR holster that automatically turns the unit on when you draw your gun. They also have larger red and green laser units that mount to a pistol's accessory rail.

Lasers are not going away anytime soon; they are simply too effective for self defense, and many gun manufacturers offer their products with lasers already installed. Most of my carry guns are equipped with lasers, and I prefer the kind that activate automatically, either by grip activation, touch activation or holster activation.

SIGHTS

Precise shooting requires using sights. There are trainers who emphasize a more natural shooting style in close contact shooting situations, where focusing on the sights is not a priority. There are situations where speed and "combat accuracy" are all you need, but there might also be times when greater precision is

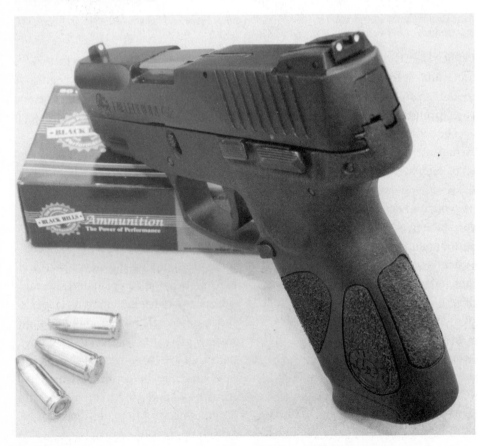

Standard sights with three white dots make target acquisition simple. Jorge Amselle

Most pocket pistols have virtually no sights. The Diamondback DB380 is an exception. Jorge Amselle

needed, and you should train for both. However, if you can't see your sights, you will not achieve much accuracy.

Low-light conditions (which bad guys prefer) are the biggest culprit in making it difficult to see your sights, but very bright sunlight can also cause them to wash out. Even a dark background can make it hard to see your sights, because the black sights can blend in. Fortunately, there are plenty of accessory manufacturers that make sights designed to enhance the sight picture and help you achieve hits easier and faster.

In the concealed-carry market, many smaller guns tend to have proportionally smaller sights. This is especially the case with pocket pistols, where some of them hardly seem to

have sights at all. Most often what you get is a black front sight post and a black rear sight notch. Many larger guns have three white dot sights or a front white dot and a white square notch for the rear sights. However, you can also get upgraded sights that offer excellent visibility in low-light situations.

Replacing the sights on your gun might or might not be easy. Some guns do not have removable sights, and even the ones that do often require a special tool. If you're looking to replace your sights, it's generally well worth the money to have a professional gunsmith do it.

Hi-Viz and TruGlo offer high-quality fiber-optic front and rear sights. Since focusing on the front sight is

A large, bright front sight is a great improvement to any defensive handgun. XS Sights

more important in defensive shooting, many people opt for just the fiber-optic front sight. These are available in several colors and, if preferred, you can install one color on the front and a different color on the rear for more contrast. Fiber-optic sights are longer than standard sights because the material needs to gather the maximum amount of ambient light possible and focus it at the end.

Fiber-optic sights work very well in both bright-light and low-light conditions, and they never wear out. They can be a bit more fragile than standard iron sights, however, but if they're well-designed, this is not an issue. Also be aware that in very low light, the fiber optic does not work very well because there is too little light to amplify.

For very low-light conditions, night sights are the best way to go and are extremely popular. These are sturdy steel sights with radioactive material inside called tritium. This material can be found on high-end diving watches and will glow brightly for more than 12 years. Tritium is an isotope of hydrogen and exists as a gas. In gun sights, it's stored inside glass tubes, which are coated with a luminescent material. The radioactivity of the tritium causes the material to glow. There is not sufficient radiation to be harmful, and the glass tubes are designed so they won't break.

The leading company making tritium sights is Trijicon, and it has front and rear sights available for just about every handgun. These sights also feature a white circle around the exposed tritium tube to enhance visibility in daylight conditions and act like a three-white-dot sight. Again, you could just replace the front sight with tritium for a more cost-effective option. Trijicon sights are popular with law enforcement personnel and are often included as a standard upgrade direct from many handgun manufacturers.

Another company that has a good reputation for innovative tritium sights is XS Sight Systems. XS sights use large white dot and tritium front sights, which can be used on their own, and a V-shaped rear sight with a central tritium post. The sight picture for XS sights is a bit different from the traditional notch and post. Instead, XS uses a post and ball, so when you align the sights, it almost looks like a golf ball sitting on top of a tee. This is designed to provide a much faster and more effective combat sight picture and there are more than a few experts who swear by them. A note of caution here: Just because you can see your sights doesn't mean you should shoot at a target you have not identified.

Another much easier and cheaper option for low-light sights is either bright-colored paint or glow-in-the-dark luminescent paint. If you've ever had an inexpensive timepiece, then you have seen this sort of paint, which will glow when exposed to light for some period of time afterward.

One manufacturer that offers simple DIY paint kits is Bright Sights, and there are a variety of colors to suit your tastes or whatever color you feel you can see best. On occasion, I've taken a bit of white paint to the odd front sight or two with good effect. The nice thing about paint is that it's very easy to apply and can also be easily removed if you change your mind.

Finally, you have different-shaped sights designed for faster targeting and sight picture acquisition in low light and stressful situations. Most of these are not especially well-suited for precision target shooting, but they will get you combat accurate hits faster when you need them.

Sure Sight offers an interesting concept here: a pyramid-shaped sight. The rear sight forms the bottom half of the pyramid (or triangle) and the front sight is the top half. There's no mistaking when the two are aligned, because each has a bright yellow outline to help in low-light conditions. The size of the triangle is significantly larger than traditional sights, so it's easier to see as well.

Another company called Speed Sights uses a traditional three-dot-sight pattern, but instead of dots, it uses much larger diamonds with two in the rear being one color and the one in the front a different color. These sights can also be purchased with tritium inserts to greatly enhance visibility.

Ameriglo offers traditional dot sights, black sights, fiber-optic sights and tritium sights, but most interesting is their rear ghost ring night sight. This works almost like a military rifle peep sight and consists of a large circular hole with tritium inserts at the 3 and 9 o'clock positions. They are very well-suited for older people or those wearing bifocals and provide very fast front-sight acquisition.

GRIPS

To many folks, grips seem more like an affectation or a way to personalize a firearm than a true accessory, but that depends on which grips your get. Certainly, a set of laser grips from Crimson Trace qualifies as a legitimate and useful accessory, but what about a set of fancy ivory or pearl grips, or those made from some exotic wood? I've seen grips made from animal bones and even fossilized mammoth teeth. All of these look great, but they seem like a waste on a gun you are supposed to keep concealed.

There are practical grips designed not so much for looks but to provide you with an advantage in a defensive

situation. The best of these are designed to actually do what their name implies: grip. You want grips that are textured so they grab your hand and stay there. You want a grip that won't rotate and change position every time you fire a round. Good defensive grips will help you keep a firm hold on your gun if your hands get sweaty, wet or muddy. But depending on your method of carry, you don't want a grip that catches on your clothing and makes the gun harder to draw.

God'A Grip offers a universal solution in a rubberized pistol grip enhancement that also provides some recoil absorption. These rubber panels fit on the front of the pistol's grip and are available with or without finger grooves. They install easily and are secured under the existing grips by an adhesive strip. They are made from Sorbothane, which is a shock- and vibration-absorbing elastic polymer,

Replacement grips can personalize a gun, reduce recoil, increase comfort and provide a better fit to the hand. Pachmayr

Revolver grips have the advantage of more size adjustments. VZ Grips

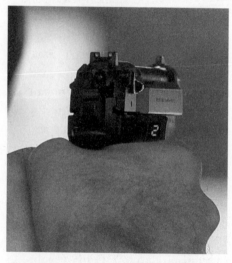

These Radetec grips actually indicate how much ammo is left in the magazine. Radetec

Hogue grips have long been known for producing high-quality rubber replacement grips, but they also make wood grips and even hybrid grips that combine the beauty of wood with the resilience of rubber. They have a truly expansive selection of grips available, and I'm a big fan of their soft rubber material. It grips the hand very well and provides good recoil absorption. The rubber material might be too soft for some shooters and does have a tendency to stick to fabric. If this is the case for you, they have grips in several other materials.

Pachmayr is another well-known grip company, having been in the recoil reduction business since the 1940s with their first recoil pad and later on rubber handgun grips. They have a large selection of grips and styles, and I've found that the rubber material they use is less soft and less sticky.

For fans of the 1911 (both full-sized and compact models), the American Legend Grips from Pachmayr combine wood laminate and rubber, offering a very high degree of versatility and style. They combine the recoil-absorbing rubber side panels with aggressive

and help prevent muscle fatigue from over-gripping. You can also trim them to fit. The advantage here is that you get a better gripping surface at the front of the frame where you need it most without adding any bulk.

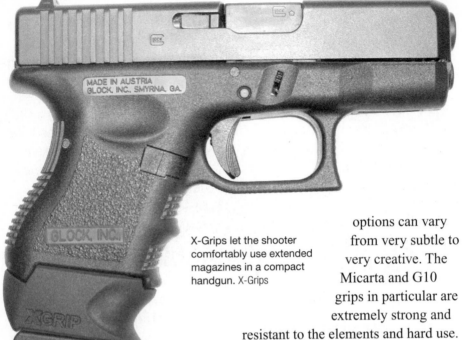

X-Grips let the shooter comfortably use extended magazines in a compact handgun. *X-Grips*

molded checkering for a superior grip. The wrap-around style of these grips also includes deep finger grooves in the front, which aid significantly in weapon retention and controllability as well as comfort.

VZ Grips is a Florida-based company that makes dozens of different custom grips for all types of handguns and revolvers using wood, carbon fiber, G10, Micarta and other materials. The laminate grips can be found in a wide variety of colors and styles, with different textures to provide either aggressive gripping surfaces or smoothed surfaces for improved comfort. The laminate grips really show off the different color patterns and are extremely appealing. Checkering

options can vary from very subtle to very creative. The Micarta and G10 grips in particular are extremely strong and resistant to the elements and hard use.

If you want grips that really stand out, look to Radetec Ammo Counter. These are black polymer grips made for full-sized pistols and feature a digital display that lets you know how many rounds you have left in your magazine or alerts you when you are running low. Just don't get all enthralled with the digital display and stop paying attention to the threat in front of you.

Another grip that does a good job of multi-tasking is X-Grips, specifically made for compact concealed-carry pistols. With many micro and sub-compact pistols, the size of the grip is very small, and you are lucky if you can get two fingers on the grip. This can be uncomfortable and makes the gun more difficult to shoot. It also limits the magazine capacity. Many compact pistols, however, accept higher-capacity magazines.

X-Grips is a polymer grip extender that fits over these longer magazines and provides a uniform and continuous grip on your compact handgun. This essentially provides the ergonomics of a full-sized grip that can be easily removed, because it's only attached to the magazine. You can carry a standard compact magazine in your CCW gun for superior concealment and a backup larger-capacity magazine with the X-Grip for added firepower and comfort. This can also make range time more comfortable, because the larger grip is more ergonomic.

GUN BELT

We spend a lot of money on a carry gun, as well as on a good-quality holster and ammunition, but how many of us give much thought to the belt we use for our gun and holster? When you carry, your belt is supposed to do more than just hold your pants up; it is an essential component of your concealed-carry gear. If you don't want to make a cheap belt the weak link in your kit, then you need to invest in high-quality gun leather. A good-quality gun belt won't sag and will stay in place when you draw your gun.

So why do you need a stiff belt? Holsters are designed to provide some give to both retain the gun and to allow you to draw it. If you combine this natural give with a weak belt, you end up with too much motion when you draw, which can make it more difficult to draw your gun in a hurry.

A weak, ill-fitting and saggy belt also allows the holster to move around too freely on your waist and bounce as you walk or run, especially with heavier guns. A lot of us also carry spare magazines, a knife, cell phone, tactical light and pepper spray, and all that needs to be on a tough belt.

Daltech Force offers a high-quality gun belt at a reasonable cost, and they even include shipping. Their Super-Stiff Gun Belt, part of the popular BullBelt brand, is made from two strips of high-quality leather with an interior bendable metal strip that literally allows the belt to stick straight out with no sag. Another advantage to this belt is that it looks normal and won't draw unwanted attention. The Daltech SuperStiff BullBelt is indeed very attractive, with brown or black leather

A strong, well-built gun belt makes sure gear doesn't sag or come loose. Daltech Force

High-quality gun belts come in a variety of styles to fit any taste. Jorge Amselle

and a variety of buckle choices.

Another high-quality custom leather gun belt maker is Disse Outdoor Gear, which makes its belts in the United States by hand one at a time to your specific measurements and tastes. Using a process the company calls Disse Amerihide, they produce a belt that's attractive, extremely sturdy and will hold up to rough use.

Disse glues and stiches together two pieces of thick, top-grain leather, which results in a ¼-inch-thick belt that provides enough flexibility to remain very comfortable. The outer layer is drum-dyed in black or brown, while the inner layer remains natural in order to avoid any chance of staining your clothing. Nylon threading provides an attractive and strong bind.

There are a variety of duty and dress styles, colors, widths and buckle options to choose from. I use its AnyDay belt, and it's comfortable and sturdy for a full day of holster wear.

If you're looking for something more outdoorsy or tactical, there's the Bushido Tactical Operator Belt designed for civilians, military and law enforcement. The key is in the special buckle, which is manufactured in Austria specifically for mountain climbing and heavy industrial use. The patented Cobra buckle features a very quick two-finger release that will not release under pressure or with only one tab depressed. It will also withstand more than 4,000 pounds of force—or one Thanksgiving dinner.

The buckle design also prevents it

from slipping through the belt loops when unfastened, which helps ensure that your gear stays where it belongs. Trust me, when you have a lot of heavy things on your belt and have to use the restroom, there's a distinct tendency for your gear to try to escape. This belt will stop that from happening. The buckle turns 90 degrees in order to allow it to go through the belt loops, and the Velcro strap allows the user to set the belt to a specified length. Adjustments on the fly are a bit difficult, however, so it's best to avoid large meals. Bushido Tactical manufactures the belts in-house using mil-spec nylon webbing. The belt also includes a sturdy polymer insert, which strengthens it for heavy holster use.

CLEANING KITS

A cleaning kit doesn't seem like much of an accessory, but you would be surprised just how much you need one. Of course, you should clean your gun after every time you shoot it but with concealed carry, you need to clean it even when you don't shoot.

The gun you carry every day gets exposed to sweat, humidity, dust, debris and a lot of pocket and clothing lint. Even with a holster, your gun gets exposed to these elements. I carry a pocket pistol, and it basically operates like a lint trap in a clothes dryer. The lint doesn't just get on the gun; it gets in the gun—inside the action, inside the hammer mechanism, inside the magazine, etc.

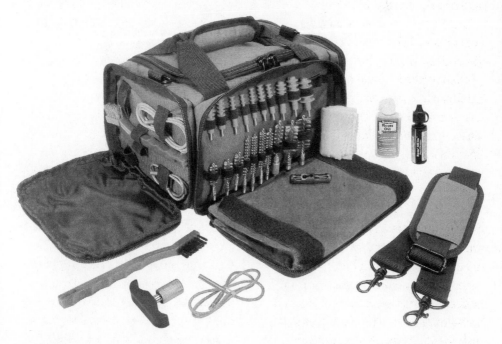

Concealed-carry guns are exposed to sweat, humidity, dust, debris and a lot of pocket and clothing lint. They benefit from regular cleaning. Remington

I've gone to the range to train with my CCW gun and found that it was malfunctioning way more than I would like, considering that it's a tool I depend on to possibly save my life. The problems were entirely the result of pocket lint, which was gumming up the works and causing misfeeds. You do not want this to happen when you actually need your gun.

As a matter of routine, your concealed-carry gun should be cleaned monthly. Unload and disassemble the gun, and wipe off all the dust and debris (you might need a gun brush for this). It's very important to disassemble the magazine and clean it out thoroughly. Run a patch though the barrel and clean the action. You do not need to do a full cleaning with a bore brush or solvent, but make sure to apply a very light coat of oil when you are done and function check your gun to make sure everything is working as it should.

CHAPTER 11

TRAINING

Having the best and most expensive gear and equipment is of little benefit if you don't know how to use it. Regular and proper training should be a routine part of your self-defense preparedness. I am not talking about joining a militia or become a doomsday prepper, but rather be willing to spend a few minutes each week and a couple of hours every few months on some basic and easy training.

I know there never seems to be enough hours in the day between work, family and other obligations. I'm extremely lazy when it comes to exercise or my own training, and if I weren't in the gun business, I would do a lot less of it. You just have to get creative and if done right, your training can be a lot of fun.

Training on a regular basis is the only way to be sure your gear will work when you need it. Just as you

Good gear is not a substitute for good training. Jorge Amselle

check the batteries in your home smoke alarms on a routine basis, so should you check the batteries in your tactical flashlight, gun laser, optical sights, etc.

In preparing for your training, never forget the first rule of concealed carry: Always have a gun with you. I'm fortunate to have never been involved in an incident where I needed my gun, and I hope I never am, but there have been times when I did not have my gun on me and I wished I had. When I was in college and worked part time as a security guard, a very

The first rule of concealed carry is to carry a gun at all times.
Jorge Amselle

irate person charged at me with what appeared to be intent to do me harm. All I had was a radio to call for help (which thankfully arrived in time).

Another time when I was new to concealed carry, I was not used to carrying every day. I stopped at a local convenience store and while I was shopping, a customer began yelling at the clerk. The argument concerned the receipt and what he thought was insufficient change, and the clerk demurely disagreed. The customer become more and more irate, finally issuing a serious threat and telling the clerk to wait while he got something from his car. At this point, I was concerned that my

only avenue of escape was the front door and I didn't want to exit while a possibly armed and extremely angry man was headed back into the store. Fortunately, the man simply decided to leave and did not return.

On another occasion, I had a job in a city that does not allow concealed carry. As I was buying a subway pass, a homeless man started asking me for money and telling me a long and obviously fake story about his car breaking down. I politely refused, but he became more and more insistent. Finally, I told him to get lost, and it was at this point that he became extremely belligerent and threatening. Fortunately, he thought better of actually assaulting me in the middle of a crowded subway station. Just to be clear, I would not have used my gun in either of these situations, because neither of them escalated to the point of being life threatening, but I did not know that at the time.

SAFETY

Safety should be the first and last thing on your mind when you're training. Safety is not something you do once and then forget about, like checking off items on a list. Other than during live-fire training on the range, you should never have any ammunition in your training area. Ammunition should be kept in a separate room from where you're training. If you are interrupted during your training, you have to go through all of your safety procedures from the beginning before you go back to your training.

It is very easy to get used to your firearm when you carry every day and to start treating it like just another item you keep in your pocket. This can lead to a lackadaisical attitude that can be dangerous. There are plenty of examples on the Internet of police officers standing in front of a classroom explaining how guns are dangerous and how they are trained experts—with the end result being the "trained expert" shooting himself in the leg by accident.

Jeff Cooper, one of the most well-known firearms trainers and founder of the Gunsite Academy, used to say that there are no accidental discharges of firearms. All such instances are the result of negligence and that is what he insisted they be called: negligent discharges.

One area where a lot of people make safety mistakes is in the restroom. A gun on your belt is heavy and uncomfortable when you are trying to take care of business. It's a lot easier to remove the gun from its holster and set it down someplace in the stall. It's

GUNSITE FIREARMS SAFETY RULES

1. *All* guns are *always* loaded.
2. *Never* let the muzzle cover anything which you are not willing to destroy.
3. Keep your finger *OFF* the trigger until your sights are *on the target.*
4. *Always* be sure of your target.

Gunsite Academy, Inc.
www.gunsite.com

These are important gun safety rules to keep in mind for concealed carry. Gunsite just as easy to forget you removed your gun and leave it behind when you are done. This happens more often than you would think. It happened to a friend of mine, and when he remembered that he'd left his gun behind and went to retrieve it, the gun was gone. That's not a good feeling, and he had to call the police and report it stolen.

DRY FIRE AT HOME

Dry-fire training is the practice of firing your gun with no ammunition. This builds muscle memory for the trigger feel and helps you avoid flinching or anticipating the shot. It is great practice that can drastically improve your accuracy and best of all; it's free and can easily be done at home.

Before you start, remove all ammunition from your gun and place it in a separate room from where you practice. Identify a safe direction to aim your gun, such as a solid masonry

Dry-fire training helps with trigger control and sight alignment. Jorge Amselle

wall. You want something that could stop a shot in the worst-case scenario. It's probably a good idea to stay away from any windows as well; you don't want to frighten the neighbors.

Place a target on the wall and practice consistently squeezing the trigger without moving your sights. Spend no more than 15 minutes a few times a week on this skill-building exercise. Once you start getting tired, the benefits of further training go out the window for the most part. If you are interrupted during your training, it's best to call it quits for the day. You don't want there to be any chance that you reload, forget and go back to "dry-fire" training.

There are those who focus exclusively on defensive firearms use and scoff at the benefits of dry-fire training. It's true that in a defensive situation your instincts take over, and there's not much time for careful sight alignment and trigger squeeze. However, that does not mean that in a defensive situation, you will not be called upon to make a careful, deliberate and accurate shot. In that case, your dry-fire training will pay off.

DRAWING AND PRESENTATION PRACTICE

Before you commit to one type of carry or another, it is very important to get a feel for it and learn its advantages and limitations. Here's where your training in drawing and presentation counts. The fact is, if you never

Practice drawing slowly at first until it becomes second nature. Jorge Amselle

practice drawing and pointing your concealed-carry handgun, you are more likely to panic in a stressful situation, search for your gun and have a much slower draw.

Again, this is training that can be done easily and safely at home for a few minutes at a time a few days per week. The safety criteria are the same as with dry-fire practice. Make sure there's no ammunition in the room where you train. Don't train for more than 15 minutes per session. If interrupted, stop your training for the day. Something as simple as a phone call can be enough of a distraction to lead to a negligent discharge.

When practicing your draw and presentation, make it as realistic as possible, which includes wearing your cover garments so you get used to sweeping or lifting them out of the way. It's best to start slow and practice a good, smooth draw that avoids sweeping any part of your body. If you're carrying in a cross-draw position, lift your support arm up so that it's not in front of the muzzle once you lift your cover garment. A good tactic is to place your support hand against your head and lift your elbow up toward your assailant. This keeps your arm out of the way of the muzzle and provides protection from strikes to your head.

If drawing from the strong side, lift or sweep your cover garment and lift the gun out of the holster straight up so your elbow is behind you. Move your support hand to your chest and rotate your strong-side elbow down, bringing the gun inline with the target. If the assailant is very close and you cannot extend your arm for fear he might try to grab your gun, you may fire from this position. Make sure to rotate your strong hand so that the slide of the gun is at a slight angle away from your body. This will prevent your body or clothing from interfering with the action of the slide and causing a malfunction.

If you are going to full extension, push the gun forward and bring your support hand forward to get a solid two-handed grip. Continue driving forward with both hands until you are at full extension toward the target. Doing this slowly at first helps ensure proper technique. As you get used to it, you can speed up your motions. Again, doing this for 10 to 15 minutes a few times per week will help you develop muscle memory so you will be able to perform the necessary functions under stress. A final tip is to have someone observe you and offer pointers for things you might have missed.

What about re-holstering your weapon? Everyone wants to achieve a fast draw and presentation and many shooters tend to quickly re-holster their gun as well. This is a mistake; your draw should be fast, but your re-holstering should be slow and deliberate. It is while re-holstering that negligent discharges often occur.

People in a rush to holster their guns might forget they have their finger on the trigger, or part of their cover garments can get caught up in the trigger. Remember that when you are ready to re-holster, the trouble should be over and there is no need to rush.

RELOADS

If you carry spare ammunition (which you should), practicing rapid tactical reloads should be part of your training routine. This is something you can easily do at home with dummy ammunition or laser inserts, or at the range as part of your live-fire training. A speed reload occurs when you have fired your gun until it's empty and then you reload. With a semi-automatic pistol, this means hitting the magazine release and either letting the magazine drop free or manually removing it and letting it drop to the ground while retrieving a full spare magazine and inserting it.

The key to doing this quickly is consistency. Always keep your spare magazine in the same place on your body, with your bullets always oriented in the same direction. Experts disagree on whether you should carry your magazines with the bullets oriented forward or backward, and I have heard of advantages for each. Whichever you select, do it consistently or you might end up trying to insert your magazine backward.

For revolvers, if you shoot until you are empty, first place the revolver frame and cylinder in your support hand and then open the cylinder latch with your strong hand and push the cylinder open with your support hand's two middle fingers. With your support hand thumb or the palm of your strong hand, hit/ flick the ejector rod while pointing the

Reload Step 1: Don't look at the gun, look for threats.

Reload Step 2: Index finger on the front of the bullet for proper orientation.

Reload Step 3: Using the index finger, lead the magazine to the pistol.

Reload Step 4: Firmly and fully seat the magazine.

Reload Step 5: Overhand slide rack to get back in action. Jorge Amselle

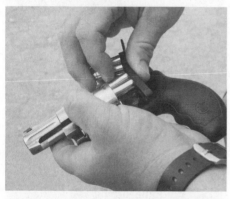

Reloading a revolver means switching hands, but with practice it can be done quickly. Jorge Amselle

gun upward. Any empty cartridges that do not fall out on their own will need to be manually removed. Then point the open gun down and reload, closing the cylinder and placing the gun back in your strong hand.

A tactical reload occurs when you find you have the time to "top off" your handgun during a stop or lull in an altercation. For a semi-automatic handgun, remove the partial magazine and replace it with a full magazine. Hold onto the partial magazine in case you need it later, and place it in the same spot where the full magazine was previously stored.

For revolvers, the move is a bit trickier. Follow the same procedures as for a speed reload, but instead of pointing the gun upward to empty it, point it downward. When you press and release the ejector rod, the live rounds will go back down and the empty expanded cases will stick up. You can then simply grab and pull those out and discard them, and load fresh rounds to top off the cylinder.

You will want to minimize the time you spend looking at your gun while you reload, especially if you're facing an active threat. Ideally, you will be able to complete your reloads without looking at the gun and instead focus on the threat or scan for additional threats. Practice your reloads slowly and deliberately at first and build up your speed over time as you build muscle memory.

Join a range and train with a concealed handgun on a regular basis. Jorge Amselle

LIVE FIRE RANGE TRAINING

When it comes to concealed carry, establishing a training regimen is essential and includes regular visits to the range. For safety reasons, some ranges restrict your ability to practice drawing from concealment and firing, or they might restrict the types of holsters you can use for such practice. Some ranges might allow holster work but require you to stick with strong-side holsters only—no cross draws. The reason for this is that during a cross draw you basically have a loaded gun pointed at other people on the range.

It might also be difficult to find a range that allows you to practice firing while moving or firing from cover. Most ranges do not have the facilities to allow you to practice live fire room clearing drills either. For this level of training, you should work with a qualified instructor, at least when starting out and for safety reasons. You will also need to call around to

area ranges to ask about their safety guidelines and to find one that allows you to do what you need to do. I find it is best to go during the middle of a weekday when ranges are typically less crowded.

A good range exercise, if you can arrange it, is to have two or three targets set up at slightly different distances and angles with different numbers and letters painted on them. Have a friend call out letters and numbers at random, forcing you to identify your target and then draw and shoot. Your friend can also call out additional numbers or letters after you have engaged the first target to simulate a multiple assailant encounter.

If the range allows it, engage targets from odd positions, such as lying on your back or on your side, crouched down, sitting and on one or both knees. In a real situation, you might get knocked down and have to defend yourself from a disadvantaged position.

Make sure that if you are shooting from a prone position, your shots hit the backstop and don't go off into space.

All live fire training doesn't need to be tactical. Just plain target shooting on a regular basis will help you improve your sight alignment, breath control, grip, and most importantly, trigger squeeze. You can also incorporate dry-fire training into your live-fire sessions. When I'm helping students on the range who have trouble with flinching or anticipation, I ask them to alternate between five rounds of live fire and five rounds of dry fire. The improvement in just one session can be dramatic.

Another helpful training tool is the ball and dummy technique. Have a friend load your magazine or revolver and randomly include one dummy round. When you hit the dummy round, the gun should not move; if it does, you know you are flinching and have poor trigger control. This technique is also a great way to help you train for and deal with malfunctions.

Look for a range that allows tactical shooting from different positions, but be aware of your backstop. Jorge Amselle

Every time after you confront a threat in a live-fire or dry-fire situation, scan the area to each side and behind you while keeping your gun oriented toward the original threat. This breaks your tunnel vision and makes you look for any additional threats. You might be facing more than one assailant, and do not want to be so focused on the initial threat that someone else can sneak up on you.

Looking around also allows you to identify avenues of escape or retreat. Don't get into the habit of just scanning the area without really looking. Going through the motions won't help you in a real situation. Force yourself to identify something different in your area of observation each time you scan so that you are actually paying attention and not just moving your head around.

After engaging a target, scan the area for more threats. Jorge Amselle

Training with a friend or family member is a great idea, because you can observe and help each other—and it's safer. You should avoid shooting alone at an informal range where there's no one to call for help should you become injured. Be sure to have a cell phone handy, know the address of the location where you are shooting and have a suitable first aid kit with you. I always carry a Trauma Pak with QuikClot from Adventure Medical Kits in my car and in my range bag. If the worst happened, this kit would keep me or another person from losing too much blood before emergency help arrived. Make sure you understand how to use the first aid kit ahead of time.

PROFESSIONAL INSTRUCTION

If you are new to firearms, you absolutely need to get professional training. For casual plinking, learning from a friend is fine but not for serious self-defense shooting and concealed-carry purposes. If you are an expert, you also need professional training. No matter how much experience you have, you don't know anywhere near as much as you think you do.

I've been shooting for over 30

Professional instruction, especially with regard to higher-skill defensive tactics, is essential.
Jorge Amselle

years, served in the military, worked in security and am an NRA certified instructor. I've taught hundreds of people, have been carrying concealed for 20 years, have attended a dozen different training and defensive courses and have been a gun writer for more than 4 years. And I'm still routinely learning new things. Every class I take opens my eyes to things I never even considered before. No matter how much I think I know, every instructor I speak with manages to teach me something worthwhile.

There are many different firearms instructors and training schools out there. I list a few of the best known here, but feel free to shop around in your area and don't be afraid to ask questions. Being comfortable with the instructor you choose is very important, and you should never do anything that feels wrong or unsafe.

One great place to start is with the courses offered by the National Rifle Association. NRA courses are taught locally by independent NRA Certified Instructors following a specific course guideline. The NRA offers defensive courses for pistols, including Personal Protection Inside the Home as well as Personal Protection Outside the Home. This second class is geared toward the needs of those who carry concealed and is divided into two parts: a basic class and a more advanced course with more range time. Both personal protection courses also include a section on self defense and the law, which

must be taught by either an attorney or a police officer.

Gunsite Academy, founded by Lt. Col. Jeff Cooper in 1976, might be the most widely recognized name in formal firearms training. Cooper developed many modern pistol techniques and his facility, located in Paulden, Arizona, continues his work with pistols, as well as rifles and shotguns. The primary class is Pistol 250, an intensive 5-day combat pistol course developed by Cooper himself, and emphasizes marksmanship, gun handling and a combat mindset. Over a 5-day period, students focus on building these skills through a series of live-fire drills utilizing 1,000 rounds of ammunition.

Thunder Ranch is home to Clint Smith's training school, which offers many specialized and standard firearms courses. For concealed carry, the best course might be the "Home and Vehicle Defense with Trauma Block" class that addresses self defense at home or from inside a vehicle. In addition to discussing and practicing various handgun techniques for use in these environments, students learn how to deal with emergency medical care as a result of ballistic trauma.

Smith also offers a specific "Defensive Revolver" course. Despite a preference for more modern designs among today's shooters, the efficacy and reliability of the revolver cannot be discounted, and it remains a favorite among many shooters, especially beginners. This course covers handling

Gunsite Academy in Arizona offers intensive training that emphasizes marksmanship, gun handling and combat mindset. Gunsite Academy

a revolver, dealing with malfunctions, drawing and low-light tactics.

Massad Ayoob Group (MAG) offers a different perspective that goes beyond how to use lethal force for self defense and gets into the *when* to use lethal force issue, which is equally important. Ayoob has had a long career in law enforcement and is a nationally recognized expert in lawful self defense.

Ayoob's "Armed Citizens' Rules of Engagement" class is a great place to start and covers legal issues, tactical issues and dealing with the aftermath of a self-defense shooting, all in an

intensive 2-day course. MAG also offers a 2-day live-fire pistol course that covers the tactical realities of self defense, including drawing from concealment, use of cover, firing from the weak hand, as well as speed and accuracy under pressure.

For those living in the Northeast, the Smith & Wesson Academy in Springfield, Massachusetts, has a great list of courses for all levels of shooters. "Defensive Handgun Techniques in Close Quarters" in particular addresses the real-world issue of self defense inside one's home, which typically involves a lot of corners and short firing distances. In recognition of the high stress involved in such situations, this course focuses on instinctive shooting, rather than a front-sight focused approach, although both are covered.

SIG Sauer Academy encompasses a vast, state-of-the-art facility adjacent to its Epping, New Hampshire, factory and

SIG Sauer Academy in New Hampshire offers courses for all skill levels. SIG Sauer Academy

offers courses from beginner introductory shooting to specialized advanced courses for military and police. There are also several armorer schools focusing on the complete line of SIG Sauer firearms.

The 1- and 2-day home protection courses are the most popular for civilian shooters and include handgun, rifle and shotgun training, as well as dealing with low-light self-defense situations and even a reality-based course that uses non-lethal Simunitions.

More intensive civilian courses address issues such terrorism, unarmed combat and close-quarters combat with a knife, pistol or rifle.

Gander Mountain Academy offers a unique wrinkle in their civilian firearms training. They are the only training center that has police-style, fully immersive video simulators available to the general public. These offer various scenarios designed to

test accuracy and judgment with shoot/don't shoot situations have been around for some time, but until now were limited to law enforcement and military use. Gander Mountain utilizes 300- and 180-degree simulators, as well as a virtual video range with instructors who can review your reaction to different scenarios and help you improve. They also offer free firearms safety classes, hunter education and concealed-carry courses. Many courses are offered to only ladies to provide a more comfortable learning environment.

Front Sight, located close to Las Vegas, Nevada, offers intensive training for civilians, including an automatic weapons course. Most appealing to those seeking to carry concealed in the greatest number of states is its 5-day "Armed Citizen Corps" training, which consists of an advanced 4-day defensive handgun course and a

Several Gander Mountain stores feature virtual-reality based scenario training. Gander Mountain

Reality-based training with safety munitions prepares students for real-world defensive shooting situations. Jorge Amselle

full day for a 30-state concealed-carry license (or more depending on your state of residence).

Students learn to quickly and accurately draw from concealment and to engage targets under stress. Realistic training scenarios include shoot/don't shoot, target engagement at contact distances, shooting while moving and effective use of cover.

Rob Pincus founded I.C.E. Firearm Training Services and developed the "Combat Focus Shooting" course to deal with reality-based defensive shooting situations. This course primarily emphasizes developing intuitive shooting skills, not just marksmanship. The training is based on an analysis of real defensive shootings. Despite the name, this is not an offensive shooting class, but rather is designed to quickly deal with a threat in the most efficient manner possible.

TRAINING AIDES

There are many products available that can make practice more fun and interesting and help you get the most from your training time. One simple and handy training tool is a Blue Gun, which replicates the size, look and feel of an actual firearm, while providing complete safety.

These plastic molds, available for many of the most popular handguns and long guns, mirror all of the same controls of your firearm, albeit in non-functional form, to further aid in training.

Blue guns fit in a standard holster and can be used to practice drawing a concealed-carry pistol. The bright blue color makes it clear to everyone that

Training aides and laser devices, such as the SIRT Pistol, are great for practicing at home. Next Level Training

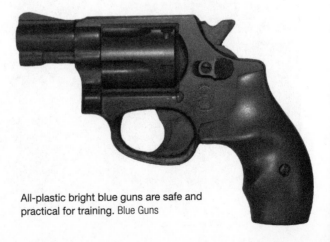

All-plastic bright blue guns are safe and practical for training. Blue Guns

it is not an actual firearm. At more advanced levels, these guns can be used to practice close-quarter combat and disarming techniques, while avoiding any chance of negligent discharge or damage to your actual firearm.

Another simple yet indispensable tool for training is the use of dummy rounds. These clearly marked rounds allow new shooters to safely practice weapon-handling skills, such as loading and unloading, as well as clearing malfunctions. There are many types of dummy rounds available, but I prefer those that use actual brass cases and bright orange-colored plastic bullets.

These function best with little chance of the cartridge rim breaking. They also last the longest and provide clear visual safety, even from the back where the bright plastic can be seen through the empty primer hole.

If there's a drawback with dry-fire training, it's that there's no visual cue to indicate hits or misses. However, there are many laser devices that address this issue, including the SIRT (Shot Indicating Resetting Trigger) training pistol from Next Level Training. This well-built steel and polymer mock pistol mimics the size and feel of a full-sized Glock 17/22 and features a resettable trigger, allowing more time and focus on trigger control and less on racking the slide.

The key advantage with the SIRT Training Pistol is its dual laser system, which provides immediate visual feedback of trigger mechanics. When the user begins to squeeze the trigger a red laser comes on, and when the shot breaks a green laser activates. It can take as many as 10,000 trigger squeezes to build the muscle memory necessary to achieve good trigger control.

Another popular laser training device, the

The SIRT training pistol fires a laser and replicates actual trigger feel. Next Level Training

Dummy rounds with no primers and bright plastic tips are great training tools. Jorge Amselle

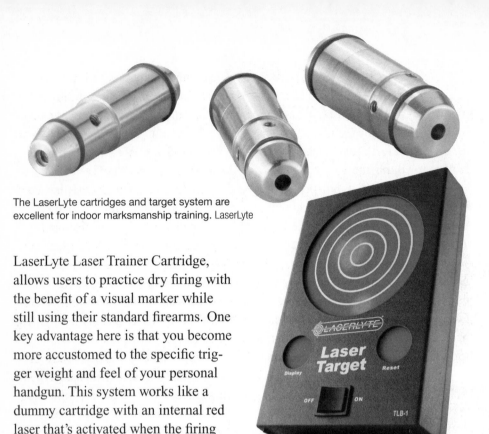

The LaserLyte cartridges and target system are excellent for indoor marksmanship training. LaserLyte

LaserLyte Laser Trainer Cartridge, allows users to practice dry firing with the benefit of a visual marker while still using their standard firearms. One key advantage here is that you become more accustomed to the specific trigger weight and feel of your personal handgun. This system works like a dummy cartridge with an internal red laser that's activated when the firing pin strikes the "primer."

LaserLyte cartridges are available in 9mm, .40 S&W, .45 ACP and, just recently announced, .380 ACP. The rounds must be inserted directly into the chamber and remain there until removed using a pencil. This allows the user to rack the slide to reset the trigger if necessary without having to reinstall the device. Since it isn't weapon specific, you can also use the same cartridge to train on any firearm that's chambered for it. Users can practice drawing from concealment and quickly engaging targets at home or anywhere safely. The batteries will last for 3,000 or more trigger squeezes.

LaserLyte also makes a portable laser target, the Laser Trainer Target system (TLB-1). This unit provides a bull's-eye target approximately 5 inches in diameter, which can register and store hits from up to 50 yards away. Smaller target areas at the bottom right and left of the bull's-eye will display all of your hits and reset the target for a new round of practice.

It cannot be overstated how much of an aid in improving marksmanships skills this unit provides by allowing shooters to visualize their shot groups easily, just like live fire produces holes on paper targets. It also allows the shooter to gauge his or her progress over time in an entertaining manner,

LaserLyte Reaction Tyme target forces shooters to speed up and shows laser hits. LaserLyte

shooters to practice with their own preferred firearms, including rifles.

The TR-700 target is portable, self-contained and works with both batteries and AC power. Available inserts can simulate increased distances without having to physically move the unit and are available in standard bull's-eye, silhouette and game targets. More advanced Beamhit units connect to your PC for increased versatility and feedback, as well as tracking your proficiency improvements over time.

One method I like to use in dry-fire training involves a weapon-mounted laser unit or standard red dot or holographic weapon sights for both pistols and rifles. With the laser on, I focus on my trigger squeeze while maintaining minimum movement on the target. It is especially instructive to watch your laser bounce around on the target while you dry fire and to train yourself to eliminate as much movement as possible throughout your trigger squeeze, as well as after the trigger breaks.

New training devices and methods are becoming available on a continuous basis to help shooters improve their skills more easily and conveniently, and at a lower cost. Focusing on the fundamentals and building muscle memory is the key to improving, no matter if the purpose is speed, accuracy, drawing your pistol or tactics. Keep training.

which encourages further practice. The unit is very compact, measuring only 9.5 by 6.25 inches and is thick enough to stand on its own for easy setup. Three AA batteries are conveniently included and are good for up to 6,000 shots.

Another popular laser targeting device is the Beamhit Laser System, which offers comprehensive kits for civilians, law enforcement and military use, and covers everything from basic marksmanship to full automatic belt-fed weapon systems. These units are sold as a comprehensive kit, with either a weapon-mounted laser or one that goes inside the barrel and laser-reading electronic targets, allowing

CHAPTER 12

LETHAL FORCE AND THE LAW

By John Frazer
Frazer is an attorney practicing firearms law in Fairfax, Virginia, and Washington D.C. (www.jfrazerlaw.com). The opinions in this chapter are his and are presented for general information only. For legal advice, contact a qualified attorney in your state.

Are you prepared to use deadly force? That's the question everyone who's thinking about owning or carrying a gun for self defense needs to answer. Other chapters in this book will help you answer this question when it comes to the hardware of self defense—the guns, holsters and other equipment you need, and some of the software, such as quality training and the never-say-die attitude you'll need if you're forced to fight for your life. But since this book is about self defense for law-abiding people, this chapter will tell you how to keep on being one—even in a life-threatening confrontation.

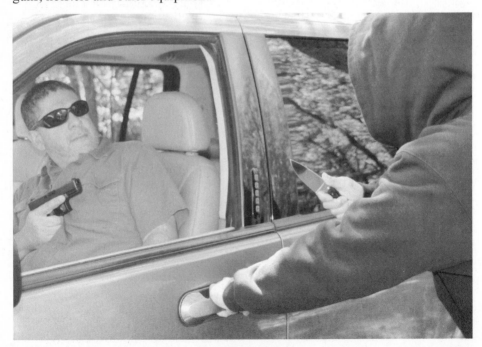

Lethal force should be used only as a last resort. Jorge Amselle

THREE BATTLES

Self-defense trainers often speak about three fights that happen in a self-defense situation:

1. The physical fight: surviving and prevailing in the incident itself.

2. The legal fight: surviving and prevailing in the criminal and civil proceedings that often follow a physical fight.

3. The moral fight: surviving and prevailing in terms of upholding the values you, your family and your community believe in.

The three fights are closely linked. Most importantly for this chapter, our country's laws express the values by which others will judge you. And your behavior during the physical fight will provide the facts by which you'll be judged.

JUSTIFIABLE USE OF LETHAL FORCE

The next question most people ask is, "When can I use deadly force?" But that's not really the right question. You'd be better off asking, "When *must* I use deadly force?"—a question that better expresses the way the law looks at self defense: a last-ditch option that's better than the alternatives, such as being killed or maimed. Always remember that self defense is one form of "necessity defense," the same kind of rule that might allow you to drive on a suspended license if it's the only way to get a loved one to the emergency room.

But whichever way you want to phrase the question, there's a bottom-line answer. Although state laws vary greatly, as a general rule: **You will be justified in using lethal force if you are an innocent person who reasonably fears an imminent threat of death or serious bodily injury and you use the necessary amount of force to protect against it.** Importantly, in some situations in some states, you must also retreat—but only to the extent that you can retreat safely. Now let's take that general rule apart piece by piece.

INNOCENCE

First, self defense is a right that belongs to innocent people. The law doesn't like people who go around starting fights. So logically enough, the law doesn't let you start a fight and then claim self defense when the person who you picked on fights back and you clobber him. There's a whole doctrine about turning the tables. An initial aggressor can become a lawful defender if he tries to withdraw from the fight, communicates that to his victim, and the victim uses force against him anyway. But do you really want to be the person trying to show all that in court? And what do you get out of it anyway, unless you really like picking fights and paying big legal bills afterward?

What does this mean for you as a lawfully armed citizen? The answer to that boils down to two concepts: avoidance and de-escalation.

Avoidance means adjusting your behavior so you're never in a fight to begin with if you can possibly help it. It includes awareness and physical avoidance. Sure, you can walk a few feet from the guy on the street who's wearing

Self defense is for innocent people. Jorge Amselle

nothing but a plastic garbage bag and blaming passers-by for the end of the world and all of his other problems. And you can be prepared to fight him if he decides to do something about all that. But wouldn't it be better if you were on the other side of the street?

De-escalation means that when you haven't completely avoided a situation, you're ready with verbal skills to calm a person down or (better yet) ready to just plain walk away, no matter how hard the guy is pushing your buttons.

Massachusetts lawyer Andrew Branca puts it well in his excellent book *The Law of Self Defense*, when he writes that, "Having a gun means you have to take guff from everybody. And maybe even be real polite and say 'yes sir' in the process." When someone cuts you off in traffic, catcalls your spouse or blows his stack at you for not wiping off the weight bench at the gym, you

can complain to your barber or your bartender, but don't get in the hothead's face and risk being seen as the aggressor if the situation escalates. (All of that goes double when there are already some bad feelings in the air—for example, if the person giving you guff is your ex-spouse, unfriendly neighbor or disgruntled business associate.)

Finally, even if a fight does happen despite your best efforts, you want everyone's roles to be clear to anyone who's watching. As instructor John Holschen of InSights Training Center puts it, you want witnesses to point to your attacker and say, "That guy attacked the other guy," not to point at both of you and say, "Those two guys were fighting." If you've tried to walk away, shouted, "Leave me alone!" when the person chased you, and otherwise obviously tried to avoid using force, you've improved the chances of that.

Is an aggressive panhandler a reasonable justification for the use of lethal force? Jorge Amselle

REASONABLENESS

The next concept in our general statement is reasonableness. If you use force, you're going to be judged by what's known as the "reasonable person" standard. In the older cases, this was the "reasonable man" standard. As my criminal law professor in college put it, "The reasonable man plays a reasonable game of tennis." A reasonable person is sane, sober and responsible. He pays his bills on time and wears his seat belt. (Some legal scholars have suggested that the reasonable person is impossibly perfect.)

But there's a twist. Because you'll be judged for what you actually did, the standard you'll be measured against is what a reasonable person would have done in your situation. Although state laws differ on degrees

and details of how they apply this, this means the reasonable person isn't just any reasonable person; it's a reasonable person who knew what you knew at the time of the incident.

In other words, you won't be held to the standard of a reasonable person who doesn't know anything about guns, or tactics, or self-defense law, or who had no perception of the attack. Instead, to take a few hypothetical examples, you might be held to the standard of a reasonable man who has taken the basic concealed-carry class in the state, who saw and heard someone pull a gun and demand money. Or you might be held to the standard of a reasonable woman who shoots defensive pistol matches every month, and who was being approached by an angry ex-boyfriend with a knife that's nearly as long as his record of violent crime.

And as a final twist, there's this: The reasonable person standard is used to judge whether your actions were objectively reasonable. But your actions also have to be subjectively reasonable. In other words, even if a reasonable person would have done the same things you did, your actions won't be justified if you, yourself, didn't think they were reasonable.

Suppose, for example, someone is swinging a baseball bat at you from across a restaurant counter and you respond by shooting at him. A reasonable person might perceive that the would-be slugger posed an imminent threat. But you later tell a friend that you were sure you were far enough back from the counter that the attacker couldn't really have touched you. That statement is going to hurt your case, because it shows that you didn't actually reasonably believe you were in imminent danger.

IMMINENCE

And that brings us to imminence: the idea that you can only use force to stop a danger that's going to happen right now. Outside of the special cases involving battered woman syndrome, courts across the country are clear: You don't necessarily have to wait for an attacker to take the first swing, but you can't use force until danger is "immediate," "near at hand" or "pressing and urgent," as various courts and legislatures have said.

Suppose you have an enemy who's sworn he's going to kill you. But you aren't high on his list, so he tells you, "I'm going to find you on Tuesday, and when I see you I'm going to kill you."

Is this assailant too far away for the threat to be imminent? Jorge Amselle

You see him on the street on Monday and he just waves and says, "See you tomorrow." Would you be legally justified in using force? The answer is no. And if you see him on Tuesday and he just waves and says nothing, the answer is the same. No imminent threat, no justifiable force.

The flip side of this is that revenge is not self defense. If someone punches you on Super Bowl Sunday, you can't punch him back during the World Series. No matter how much you think he deserves it—and even if you're right—it's just not necessary in the eyes of the law.

So how do you know when an attack is imminent? One widely used way of answering that is the "Ability-Opportunity-Jeopardy" model, sometimes known as AOJ. This has three questions you must ask yourself:

Ability: Does this person have the physical means to hurt me? That might include a weapon such as a gun, knife or blunt object. Or—as we'll get to in a moment—it might include overwhelming physical strength or force of numbers, such as a rioting mob.

Opportunity: Can the person use those physical means to hurt me? A person holding a big rock, but standing 300 yards away from you, might want to hurt you very badly. But he can't do it right now.

On the other hand, in the demonstration now known as the "Tueller Drill," Utah police trainer Sgt. Dennis Tueller famously showed that, on aver-age, an attacker with a contact weapon such as a knife or club can cover 21 feet and inflict an injury all in the time it takes the average trained person to draw a handgun and fire a single shot.

Many people now refer to this as creating a "21-foot rule," allowing use of lethal force against anyone within that distance. But that's a misinterpretation. A person with a knife 21 feet away, but on the opposite side of a 10-foot chain-link fence, probably doesn't pose a lethal threat. But the same person on an unobstructed sidewalk could be a threat even farther away, if your pistol is hard to reach or you're weighed down carrying a child. (And remember that a single shot might not even hit the attacker, much less stop him.)

Jeopardy: Even if the person has the physical means to hurt you, and could use those means, are you in any real danger from him? Here's a classic example I've heard from several self-defense trainers: If you're in the kitchen when your spouse is chopping onions for dinner, your spouse has the ability to hurt you (a deadly 10-inch chef's knife) and the opportunity to hurt you (he or she is just a few feet away). But there hasn't been any threatening move or other indication that an attack is happening.

DEATH OR SERIOUS BODILY INJURY

The question of whether your potential attacker has the ability to hurt you leads to the issue of what constitutes deadly force. Although some states allow the use of deadly force in other circumstances, the only universal rule is that a defender's deadly force is justified by an attacker's deadly force.

So again, what is deadly force? The general rule is that it's force that could cause death or serious bodily injury. (Some states refer to "grave" or "grievous" bodily injury, but the concept is the same.) Generally speaking, serious bodily injury is an injury that's life-threatening, or that's likely to cause a permanent disfigurement or disability, such as the loss of a limb or an organ. Finally, rape is inherently considered a serious bodily injury.

PROPORTIONALITY: TYPE OF FORCE

Does a person have to be armed at the same level you are to threaten you with deadly force? No. You can use a gun to defend against an attacker with a knife, club or other weapon, or with no weapon at all, as long as all of the other points in our general rule are met. That's right—deadly force against unarmed attackers isn't automatically illegal. But legally, it's more challenging.

The key concept is "disparity of force." If you're 85 years old and weigh 105 pounds soaking wet and holding your walker, and find yourself suddenly knocked to the ground and beaten by the official Hell's Angels rugby team, lethal force might well be justified. If you're a rugby player being poked in the chest by the 105-pound senior citizen with the walker, then probably not. In either case, the question will be whether you reasonably feared that death or serious bodily injury were imminent, and whether the force you used was necessary to stop the attack.

But as Utah attorney and author Mitch Vilos points out, the use or threat of deadly force against an unarmed person is more likely to get you arrested, or even prosecuted, than if the other person was armed.

For example, Arizona hiker Harold Fish was convicted of second-degree murder after shooting a person who had confronted him with a crazed look on his face, cursing, swinging his arms and making punching motions—all while accompanied by two barking dogs that hemmed Fish in on the trail. Only after 3 years in prison and a half-million dollars in legal fees was Fish able to win on appeal, because the trial court had failed to tell the jury that unarmed acts (such as reckless endangerment, threatening or aggravated assault) can be the type of "unlawful physical force" that would justify self defense under Arizona law.

None of this, by the way, means you can't use a lesser degree of force than your attacker. No law says you can't wrestle a club-wielding attacker to the ground, or pepper spray an attacker who has a gun—as one brave and quick-thinking college student recently did to stop a killing spree in Seattle.

But if the attack isn't deadly, your response generally can't be either.

MORE PROPORTIONALITY: DURATION OF FORCE

Closely related to the idea that only a deadly attack justifies a deadly response is the concept that deadly force is only justified as long as a deadly attack continues. Factors making the duration excessive can include both the amount of force used and the movements—or lack of movement—of the person against whom the force is used.

We don't need to come up with a hypothetical when a real case will prove the point, so here's one cited by Vilos. In *U.S. ex rel. Davis v. Gramley*, the defendant claimed self defense after shooting his brother 26 times (including a pause to reload) after they argued over adjusting the thermostat in the house. The prosecutor didn't buy it. Neither did the jury or the appellate courts. The fact that the defendant couldn't remember if his brother was coming after him didn't help him a bit either.

As a bottom-line rule, any use of force against a person who's already down, seriously injured and not moving is going to be, as Vilos puts it, a "thumbs-down factor."

ALTERNATIVES TO LETHAL FORCE

How do you ensure that your acts can be proportional to the threat you face? One way is to make sure you have alternatives to lethal force. A Vietnam veteran once told me his rule for dealing with the constant fatigue of life in a combat zone: "Never stand

Pepper spray can be used as an alternative to lethal force. Jorge Amselle

when you can sit, and never sit when you can lie down." The self-defense equivalent might be, "Never shoot when you can use pepper spray; never spray when you can shout, 'No!'"

But that doesn't mean you have to use alternatives in every situation. Police instructors and other trainers sometimes talk about "escalation of force"—implying that you have to climb every step of the ladder—but that's not quite right. While it's safe to say that the less force you have to use, the better, the legal standard is whether the force you actually used was justified at the time you used it.

An aggressive drunk poking you in the chest might merit only a loud, "Back off!" or a dose of pepper spray; but if the first sign you're under attack is the sound of gunfire and a spray of dust as bullets hit the cinderblock wall next to your head, you're under no obligation to use anything less than deadly force to protect yourself.

DUTY TO RETREAT VS. STAND YOUR GROUND AND THE CASTLE DOCTRINE

If you've been paying attention to the news for the past couple of years, it shouldn't be any surprise that one of the most controversial alternatives to lethal force is running away. During the past 10 years, many states have passed so-called "Stand Your Ground" or "Castle Doctrine" laws that abolished the duty to retreat before using deadly force in self defense, as long

as you're in a place where you have a legal right to be. (In some states, you have to retreat before using even non-lethal force.) Unfortunately but not surprisingly, the recent glaring media spotlight on this trend has hidden the media's glaring errors about the legal issue involved.

First—and most important for defense-minded citizens to remember—is that just because you don't have to retreat, doesn't mean you can't retreat. Let's be clear: No law-abiding person should ever have to give up his freedom of movement and action to a criminal attacker. And no one forced to defend himself against a criminal attacker should be second-guessed in the comfort of an air-conditioned courtroom for not finding a way out.

But retreating will often make sense. Retreating might allow you to use less force, or no force at all—resulting in less risk of injury in the "first fight," less legal risk (and lower defense fees) in the "second fight," and fewer moral or psychological consequences in the "third fight."

Retreating also helps establish that you were the innocent victim in the incident. The fact that you retreated might be proven by physical evidence, by eyewitnesses or surveillance cameras, or by your own statements. But all other things being equal, it's better to be the person who was trying to avoid the fight, not to cause or escalate it. As Branca points out, retreating when possible helps establish that your

In some situations safe retreat is not possible. Jorge Amselle

choose to retreat, but if retreating will put you in more danger, don't do it.

2. In some states you don't have to retreat when you're in your own home. This is the "Castle Doctrine," based on the idea that your home is your castle and you're not required to risk leaving it under deadly attack. Some states extend the same protection to the area outside the home, or to businesses, occupied vehicles, or both.

3. In many "Stand-Your-Ground" states, the protection of the law is limited to people

use of force was reasonable and necessary, because you tried to avoid using force at all.

Second—and closely related—is that even in states that still require defenders to retreat before using deadly force, there are often important limitations:

1. You never have to retreat if you can't do so safely. That's worth remembering even when you're in a "duty-to-retreat" state. You might

who are in a place where they have a right to be and who aren't engaged in illegal activity. So a person trespassing or violating a restraining order might have to retreat even if he's unlawfully attacked. And a person who's dealing heroin might have the right to be on the street, but he might still have to run away before resorting to force when his rival dealer opens fire.

The bottom line to all of this is that there's no substitute for knowing your state's laws. If you're traveling or don't know the state's laws, the legally safest option is to retreat if it's safe.

DEFENSE OF OTHERS

So far, we've talked about only self defense. But most of us don't just want to defend ourselves. We have spouses or romantic partners, children, elderly relatives, friends and other good people we spend time with. We want those people to be safe and protected from crime, too. Fortunately, the law allows for this. Generally speaking, you're justified in using force to defend another as long as that person would be justified in using force herself.

Be sure of a situation before you intervene. Jorge Amselle

That sounds simple, and it might be—if the situation is clear. But as Branca points out, things get dicey fast when you intervene in a situation that's not 100 percent clear. The person you think you're rescuing might see things differently and could even be the original aggressor in the fight.

A friend of mine learned this the hard way on shore leave in San Francisco and ended up being assaulted by the woman he thought he was saving from a criminal beating. Police officers learn the same lesson every day in domestic violence cases, and similar situations sometimes even lead to tragic "blue-on-blue" shootings of undercover officers.

There's no easy blanket answer on when you should intervene. If it's your spouse, child or another loved one that's being attacked, nothing can or should stop you from trying to stop the attack. And if you're in the middle of a clear-cut crime where you and others are being targeted at random by madmen, the legal odds are probably in your favor, too. But if that little voice in the back of your head says "domestic dispute" or "drug deal" or "barroom brawl," you're way better off looking for a phone instead of a pistol.

DEFENSE OF PROPERTY

Even more risky than defense of others is defense of property— whether it's real property, such as your

Property can be replaced, human life cannot. Jorge Amselle

house, or personal property, such as your wallet or bicycle. There's probably no greater variation in state deadly force laws than there is in this area.

As a general rule, the law doesn't favor use of deadly force in defense of the property itself. Most of the exceptions to that are rules that allow for the protection of homes, but which really exist to protect the people who live in the home. Some of these laws go back to ancient times, when you might well have died if you were forced out of your hut in the winter, or when enemies might try to burn down your home to force you into the open.

To dig a little deeper, though, there are different rules between states when it comes to defending homes and defending other buildings, such as businesses. And there are different rules within states between defending the structure itself and sometimes the immediate area around it (known as the curtilage) versus defending against trespassers on open land. The law can also be different for forcible and non-forcible entries, and for intrusions during the nighttime versus the daytime.

Also, some states have created legal presumptions that protect those defending against intruders in certain places. In Florida, for example, the law presumes that if you use or threaten defensive force against what you knew was an "unlawful or forcible entry" into a home or occupied vehicle, you'll be presumed to have had "a reasonable fear of imminent peril of death or great bodily harm." (The presumption doesn't apply if you use force against someone else who has a right to be there, or against a known law enforcement officer performing official duties, or if you're engaged in some unlawful activity yourself.) Essentially, laws like these bring clear-cut home-defense situations under the same general rules that govern defense of oneself or others.

But with all these variations, it's simply impossible to state any general rule about defending your property. The answer is to know your state's law, and if in doubt, look at every possible use of force under the general rule for personal defense: Is this intruder or trespasser putting me in reasonable fear of imminent death or serious bodily injury?

When it comes to personal property, the laws generally provide even less protection for defenders. But for the sake of this chapter, let's keep it simple. Even if your state does legally allow the use of force (deadly or otherwise) to keep someone from stealing your iPad or your '57 Chevy, ask yourself a few questions:

• "Am I willing to spend six figures on legal fees over this?"

• "Am I willing to be known for the rest of my life as 'the person who shot the kid stealing a TV?'"

• "Will I be able to sleep at night if I take a human life to defend something I can get at the store or go on Amazon or eBay to replace?"

Not many people will answer, "Yes" to all three.

BRANDISHING AND OTHER CHARGES

When most people think about the legal consequences of using lethal force, they naturally think of homicide charges, such as murder or manslaughter. That's natural enough, because those are the most serious charges you can face. But "lethal force" doesn't automatically result in death, so any number of other charges could apply. Depending on state law, those might include:

• Attempted murder.

• Simple assault (a threat of force) or battery (a use of force).

• Aggravated assault or battery (generally, an assault or battery involving deadly weapons or a higher risk of serious injury).

• Malicious wounding.

• Unlawfully discharging a firearm.

• Brandishing or displaying a firearm or other weapon.

In general, if your actions were legally justifiable as self defense, defense of others or defense of property, that justification will carry over to lesser charges such as these.

One specific issue that a lot of people ask about is whether brandishing or displaying a firearm is considered a use of deadly force. In other words, would you have to be justified in actually using your gun before you'd be legally justified in showing it—for example, by pulling back your jacket to show that you're armed?

The answer depends on your state

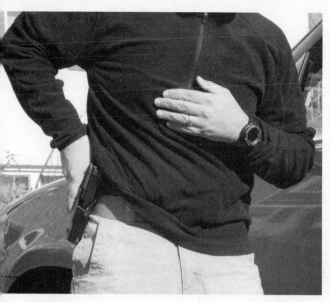

Displaying a firearm to ward off an assailant is a bad idea and can constitute lethal force in itself. Jorge Amselle

sary, does not constitute the use of deadly force." Other states—even New Jersey—have similar laws.

But be careful, because in some states, anything more than showing the person a gun will be considered a use of force, not just a threat. In a New York case, for example, the state's highest court found that drawing a pistol, "cocking it, holding it with two hands and arms extended and aiming it," was not just a threat, but also an actual use of force. Actually firing a gun will almost certainly be considered a use of force.

and on the specific charge that might be involved. The traditional rule is that if deadly force isn't justified, then threatening it isn't justified either. As the Missouri Supreme Court put it, "The brandishing of weapons in an angry or threatening manner ... creates a substantial risk of death or physical injury," so it can only be justified if the situation would justify the use of deadly force.

But that's not the law everywhere. Some state legislatures or courts have decided that just displaying a weapon isn't deadly force. In Texas, for example, the state law says that, "A threat to cause death or serious bodily injury by the production of a weapon or otherwise, as long as the actor's purpose is limited to creating an apprehension that he will use deadly force if neces-

Actually firing a gun will almost certainly be considered a use of force—a critical issue to bear in mind if you're wondering whether you should ever fire a warning shot. That's an issue on which state legislatures and courts are divided. Some hold that because any bullet that's fired might ricochet or fall on someone, a warning shot is always a use of deadly force that can only be justified if it's used reasonably and necessarily to prevent imminent death or great bodily harm. Others look more closely at details of the event; in those states, firing toward a person would generally be considered a use of deadly force, while firing into the air or ground might not be.

As always, the answer is to know

your state's laws. If you don't know for sure, or you're traveling, play it safe. Assume that any time you show someone your gun in self defense—let alone fire it—your action will be considered a use of deadly force, which will only be justifiable if it fits our general rule.

AFTERMATH OF A DEFENSIVE ENCOUNTER

Other than "9mm vs. .45," few topics divide gun owners and defensive trainers more than the subject of what to do after using defensive force. How to handle the tactical situation of a just-ended fight is outside the scope of this chapter, but the legal aspects are not.

Fortunately, the issue can be simplified when you realize that many of the right things to do are also things that will help establish you as innocent in the eyes of the law. And the wrong things to do are ones that will make you look guilty. That means:

• Do call the police.

• Do give first aid to those who need it if you can safely and effectively do so.

• Do tell the police any information that would help them make the scene safe, such as the location of any at-large attackers, dropped weapons or injured people.

• Don't run away—at least, not any farther than necessary to be safe. (Taking shelter in a nearby business is OK; catching a bus to Canada is not.)

• Don't lie to the police.

• Don't hide evidence.

A much more controversial topic is exactly how you should implement some of these. For example, you don't want to lie to the police, but you also don't want to say anything that you think is true, but turns out later to be a false impression that you got under severe, life-threatening stress.

False memory is a real problem. If you don't believe it, you owe it to yourself to try some realistic force-on-force training. A dozen years ago, I was videotaped in several self-defense scenarios using Simunition marking cartridges, and then debriefed before watching the tape a few weeks later. In one scenario, I vividly remembered—and would absolutely have testified under oath—that I barely entered a room and fired two or three shots at a dangerous attacker holding a hostage. But the tape told a different tale. Incontrovertibly, I went all the way into the room and circled all the way around the bad guy while firing six shots.

So, how do you avoid that situation when you've been in the real-life fight of your life? In the United States, we're lucky because our Constitution gives us an answer that everyone knows by heart from watching TV: Exercise your right to remain silent and to consult with an attorney.

But doesn't remaining silent mean that you shouldn't tell the police anything at all? The answer is no. Just tell them the few things that had better

There are lawyers and there are *good* lawyers. Brooke Novak

all fields. But there are also few, if any, self-defense specialists, because there just aren't enough self-defense cases for any one person to make a living on.

What you'll want is a skilled criminal-defense lawyer, with experience in cases beyond run-of-the-mill shoplifting or drunk driving. Ask around among other lawyers, and even among police officers, and you can get a fair idea of who's respected in your area. Then save that person's phone number where you or a loved one can find it when you need it.

One thing you don't really need to do is to pay a big fee to have a lawyer on retainer. Any practicing lawyer likes having plenty of clients, and most of us will want a fee advance when we're actually starting to do something for you, just to make sure we don't get stiffed later on. But most of us will also be happy to take your call, and your check, only when you really need us.

There are also various law firms and other organizations offering prepaid legal services or self-defense insurance plans to gun owners. I know some of the good people involved in those programs and they're worth checking out; just be sure you under-

be obviously true: "That guy attacked me and I was in fear for my life." And the facts they need to know right now" "The other guy ran that way past the Burger King, and I think there's someone else hurt over by that green car".

Then, politely and respectfully, tell them something else that's very true: that you'll be happy to answer questions and make a statement once you calm down, but that you'd like to have a lawyer present. Avoid any overly scripted responses or cutesy cards listing all the rights you want to invoke under the Constitution, Declaration of Independence, Magna Carta and Code of Hammurabi; they aren't legally necessary and might make you look like more than a little too prepared.

While we're talking about lawyers, the obvious question is which one you want to talk to. Today, there are very few general-practice lawyers, and even fewer who are really skilled in

stand what you are and aren't getting for your money.

CONCLUSION: LEARNING MORE AND LIVING RIGHT

This chapter has to be short, so it only gives you the bare outlines. Responsible people making serious decisions about the use of force owe it to themselves, their loved ones and their communities to be well-informed. Fortunately, there are plenty of places you can go to learn more.

The best source of law for your state is the law itself: the statutes and court decisions that you'll be judged by if you're forced to defend yourself. Many lawyers will be happy to give a free or cheap consultation to go over the basics.

If you want to do some work yourself, many county courthouses and law schools have libraries that are open to the public. Your starting point should be the state's model (or sometimes "pattern") jury instructions. These are the instructions that a judge would read to a jury if you were on trial for using force or for any other crime. The instructions will usually be footnoted with the state code provisions and key cases that define crimes and defenses, and from there you can backtrack your way through the statutes and case law.

Just remember that case law develops from closely decided cases. By and large, it's the marginal uses of force not the absolutely clearly justified ones that result in convictions and appeals. So while the facts of the cases might be filled with human drama, they're also filled with good examples of what not to do—a steady stream of road rage incidents, bar fights, lovers' quarrels and drug deals gone bad.

There's a lesson for you right there. If you live and act as an innocent person who only uses force when reasonably necessary to protect yourself against serious attacks, you'll go a long way toward avoiding that necessity in the first place, in surviving the legal aftermath and in living happily with yourself, your family and your neighbors for years to come.

Further Reading

For more general reading, here are a few popular or scholarly books that will help. All of them are easy to find online, in hard copy or e-book editions.

Massad F. Ayoob, *In The Gravest Extreme* (1980)

Andrew Branca, *The Law Of Self Defense* (2nd ed. 2013)

Joshua Dressler, *Understanding Criminal Law* (6th ed. 2012)

Mitch & Evan Vilos, *Self-Defense Laws Of All 50 States* (6th ed. 2013)

CHAPTER 13

WHAT TO CARRY WHEN YOU CAN'T CARRY

By Megan Amselle

A s a college student in Philadelphia, I always carried pepper spray with me. No matter if I was in class, at home studying or out jogging, I was always glad I had at least some form of self defense. Of course, personal safety and defense is important to everyone, but not everyone can or wants to carry a firearm for protection. For example, teenagers not yet old enough to carry a gun still need options to defend themselves when they're out alone. Teenage girls are particularly vulnerable and frequently targeted by criminals.

In some places it's illegal or impractical to carry a gun, but there still might be a need for a means of self defense. Ed Dunens

There are also (unfortunately) many facilities that ban firearms on their premises, including the vast majority of colleges and universities, many state and local government buildings, all federal buildings such as post offices, and even many private businesses. Not to mention that concealed carry is completely out of the question for practical purposes in many jurisdictions. In these situations, a less-lethal defense can be a lifesaver.

It is unfortunate, but criminals by their nature are cowards who prey on the weak and infirm. Young people, women and the elderly are often targeted. Even so, less lethal options are sometimes regulated and banned just as firearms are. There are many localities that ban stun guns as well as other defensive items such as batons. Be sure to check your local laws before you carry any defensive measure, because even pepper spray is illegal in certain cities (usually the places where you feel the greatest need to carry it).

It is very important to keep in mind that we use the term *less* lethal rather than nonlethal because, as one can gather from the news, tasers and stun guns can sometimes cause heart attacks and death. Pepper spray can cause a severe reaction in an asthmatic person and any impact weapon could be lethal. For these reasons, less-lethal defenses should be reserved for true emergencies only and never used casually (regardless of the prank videos seen on the Internet).

PEPPER SPRAYS

Pepper spray is an extremely common defensive device, particularly popular among teenage girls and women who are uncomfortable with guns. I recommend it for everyone as a good personal defense tool. Anyone could get into a situation where they feel threatened—say by a drunk or an angry dog—but not enough to warrant the use of lethal force. Although pepper spray should not be used casually, it's good to have it as an option.

But don't expect someone to just collapse and give up when sprayed. These chemicals cause only an intense burning sensation in the eyes, nostrils, lungs and skin. How severe it is depends on how well the target got sprayed. Likely, an attacker will become angered after you spray him. The best strategy might be to run away immediately after you spray an attacker and call for help. It's probably not a good idea to hang around and admire your handiwork.

Pepper spray has many advantages: it's lightweight, inexpensive and easy to use. There are, however, some disadvantages as well. Some people do not seem to be greatly deterred by sprays (particularly criminals who are high on drugs), and wind can blow the pepper spray back into the face of its carrier. For this reason, practicing with the spray is essential.

Look for extended-range sprays—at least 15 feet is good. Be aware that the longer-range sprays also tend to come

Get to know the distance that pepper spray will work. It has to hit the assailant in the face to be effective. U.S. Navy

in larger canisters. Also, these sprays can lose some effectiveness at longer ranges. If you're using a spray in a real encounter, you have to use it up close for maximum effectiveness. Try to keep it inside 7 to 10 feet, especially if wind and other environmental conditions are a factor.

Testing your pepper spray dispenser can help you visualize its range and confirm how many sprays you get per canister. Usually, you get only a few seconds total spray time for the smaller devices, so you might get one or two chances. Remember, you have to hit an assailant in the face for maximum effectiveness. You will want to observe the spray pattern as well. Some sprays are more of an aerosol,

while others are much narrower, like a water gun. Others actually foam up and stick to their target.

Practice outdoors in an area where others will not be affected and check the wind direction before you start. However, if you do experience a little blowback, it's not the end of the world, and it will help you appreciate the effects of the spray. This will also help you deal with the very real possibility of getting some blowback in a real-life situation.

Professionals who are trained to use pepper spray get sprayed as part of their training in order to understand and appreciate its effects. I don't recommend intentionally spraying yourself, but if you get a little taste by chance that might be a good thing.

It might seem like a waste of money to use your pepper spray against a tree, but just like you train with a handgun, you need to understand exactly how your pepper spray works to use it well. Even the most expensive units usually cost less than a box of defensive ammunition. It's worthwhile to buy two or three of the style and brand of pepper spray you like and use one for training. Many spray manufacturers also offer cheaper training units, which are basically identical to their standard pepper spray but filled with water instead. This makes it easier to practice without fear of causing discomfort to yourself or a willing volunteer.

New formulations, such as pepper gel and pepper foam, have been developed to minimize the risk of blowback and are excellent options when indoor use is a possibility (college dorms and apartments come to mind). Aerosols, by contrast, have a greater tendency to stay airborne and affect everyone in a given area. This might be better if the danger comes from multiple assailants, but dispersal also dilutes their effectiveness.

In recent years, manufacturers of pepper spray containers have designed them to be more discreet and concealable. While the classic spray canister

It's important to train with pepper spray to become proficient with its use. Ruger

is still the most popular, there are also models designed to look like a pen or a lipstick tube for maximum subtlety. Small canisters with a clip or wristband are a great choice for joggers (even those carrying guns), because they can be used against aggressive dogs without causing permanent harm. There are even sprays that fit on key chains and can go everywhere with you.

Ruger has developed an excellent line of pepper spays. Their standard model is sold as both the Tornado 3-in-1 and the Ruger Stealth (stealth in the sense that it doesn't flash or make noise). This is a law-enforcement-strength pepper spray that rates at 2 million Scoville heat units—about a thousand times hotter than Sriracha sauce. It has a 15-foot spray range and includes a convenient belt clip for easy carrying.

Some pepper sprays are cleverly disguised for discreet carry. Ruger

This model comes in a unique safety holder designed to reduce the chance of an accidental discharge. To access the spray, you slide the safety door down and push a release button. The sprayer then pops free in your hand, already in firing position. This mechanism becomes second nature after a bit of practice, but you will definitely need to familiarize yourself with it to avoid fumbling in a true emergency situation. If you prefer a simple point-and-spray model, Ruger's Armor Case should fit the bill. It has the same potent liquid but in a classic pepper-spray container.

Moving one step up from its standard model, Ruger has introduced the Tornado 5-in-1, also sold as the Ruger Ultra. This has the same setup as the 3-in-1, but also includes a strobe light and 125-decibel alarm, which activate simultaneously and automatically whenever the safety is released. The strobe is designed to spook or confuse an attacker, and the alarm draws the attention of anyone else in the area, making this a great option for joggers and anyone out after dark. There are instructions for deactivating the alarm to allow you to practice drawing the spray.

Ruger also makes convenient spray holders if you want to keep your pepper spray at home or in the car rather than on your person. The Home Defense wall unit attaches to any surface (for example, the wall next to your bed) and acts as a holster for your spray. In an emer-

Manufacturers make defensive sprays in a variety of sizes. Smaller sprays might be good for only one shot, however. Jorge Amselle

gency, this can save precious seconds spent searching and fumbling around in the dark. The similar Vehicle Defense unit mounts on the power outlet of your car, holding your spray at the ready.

For those seeking an extra-discreet option, Ruger created the lipstick pepper spray. This clever design looks just like a tube of lipstick and even comes in a variety of colors including red, pink, black, silver and blue. Even when opened, the spray nozzle looks just like a perfume spritzer. This should be carried in every woman's evening bag in case of attack or (God help you) a very aggressive date.

For more casual carry, the Ruger key chain pepper spray dispenser is extremely convenient. This is great for those who often forget their spray in a bag or jacket pocket. With this key chain, you always have a defense as long as you have your keys on you. It even comes in a discreet pouch so its function is not obvious.

Mace, a company that's practically synonymous with defensive sprays, has introduced an excellent new training kit. It includes two pepper-spray canisters: one containing the real thing and one filled only with water. They are different colors so you don't mix them up: a blue trainer and a red live canister. The kit also includes a target to practice on and an instructional DVD.

Once your skills are ready for the real world, the red canister contains Mace's powerful spray plus an added ultraviolet dye for marking an attacker. This is a great benefit because your assailant won't know he has been tagged, but police will be able to easily identify him. The canister is good for about 20 very short bursts, making it a dependable addition to your self-defense arsenal.

Sabre, another well-established defensive products company, offers a pepper spray in a gel formula. The gel, which contains the same powerful ingredients as Sabre's regular pepper spray, is not as easily dispersed by the wind, making it much less likely to affect bystanders or yourself.

The PepperBlaster II uses a gel that sticks to the target better and is less affected by wind. Kimber

The company also has an all-in-one system for women called the Safety Chick kit, which should be a popular product for college-bound women. There are two versions of this system. The "At Home" kit includes pepper spray, a personal alarm, a door stop alarm and possibly most important of all, a set of coasters reminding party-goers to keep an eye on their own drinks. The "Travel" kit drops the pepper spray (which may be illegal in some places) and adds peephole covers for a hotel room door. This kit is a one-stop personal safety arsenal.

The Kimber Pepperblaster II is another innovative self-defense spray. It's about the size of a pack of playing cards, with a slight pistol grip and a trigger. It offers two blasts of very high-powered pepper spray. Since it's a gel and not an aerosol, it's not affected by wind or rain and has an effective distance of at least 13 feet. Kimber claims it is three times more effective than other sprays, but finding a volunteer to test this might be difficult.

Each pull of the trigger empties the entire contents of one of the two capsules the system contains. It even has sights on top, so you can effectively aim for an assailant's face. It promises a 3-year shelf life (longer than other sprays) and can disable an attacker for up to 45 minutes.

This brings up an important point. Pepper sprays don't last forever. Especially ones you carry around and are exposed to shaking, sweat, heat, humidity and cold. Any pepper spray should be replaced at least yearly. Use this as an opportunity to train with your old unit.

STUN GUNS

Stun guns have gained popularity in recent years, particularly Taser products that do not require physical contact with the attacker. Most stun guns must touch skin when discharged to be effective, but civilian Tasers can be fired from up to 15 feet away (police Tasers have a range of 45 feet). A Taser fires two steel darts con-

The civilian Taser fires two darts that shock an assailant from up to 15 feet away. Taser

Stun guns generally pack a punch somewhere between 200,000 and 2 million volts and render an attacker disoriented and immobile with just a few seconds' discharge. However, they are not likely to render an assailant unconscious, contrary to what popular TV shows and movies show. In fact, they only immobilize a person for as long as the current is running. As soon as you stop pressing the button, the person can move and might be angry as well.

nected by wires back to the unit and both have to penetrate the skin to be effective. The Taser has a single-use cartridge that fires the darts and must then be replaced. As long at the darts are in contact with the person's skin, you can keep shocking him.

Criminals, having nothing better to do, have figured out that if they drop and roll when they are hit with a Taser, they can sometimes break the wires. Even if this happens, the Taser can still be used as a standard direct contact stun gun. Breaking the wires and forcing yourself to roll as you fall is a lot easier said than done, however. When you are hit with a stun gun or Taser, your muscles lock up and you lose control of them. You immediately fall to the ground. Sometimes people get injured from the fall if they hit their head on hard pavement or something else.

At police and firearms security trade shows, you can occasionally see demonstrations of people getting stunned. They will ask for volunteers and typically have no shortage of them. I heard of one case where volunteers were being offered a free hat, and guys were lining up for it. Regardless if it was simple bravado or a really nice hat, apparently getting half-electrocuted was bearable to more than a few.

Regardless, it is important to not have a cavalier attitude. Stun guns also sometimes cause serious damage and even fatalities from falls or heart attacks, and are therefore not to be used casually. The laws regarding their use are constantly evolving, so research is required before carrying one.

Although there are gun-shaped models available, the most concealable designs are small and pocket-sized; some actually double as cell phone cases. There are also models that are rod-shaped and perfect for late night dog walkers, because they usually include a built-in flashlight. Other interesting designs include a keychain model and a stun gun walking stick, which is ideal for hikers. There are even bejeweled stun guns meant to appeal to teenage girls who might be intimidated or put off by the utilitarian appearance of most designs.

Small stun guns can be handy and very powerful, but skin contact must be made. Ruger

Ruger also produces stun guns in three levels of size and strength. The Ruger 650V (which fires at 650,000 volts) is the smallest model, a square unit that fits in your hand and can be easily carried in a pocket or purse. It features a soft rubber outer coating and a finger-contoured grip. The safety switch, which prevents accidental discharge, has an LED light so it can be easily located in the dark. The unit comes with a carrying case and batteries included.

The Ruger 800V (800,000 volts) has many of the same features as its smaller sibling. However, it's longer and shaped more like a flashlight, so it's not as easily carried in a pocket. Instead, it comes with a wrist strap so it can be carried like one of those collapsible umbrellas, either on your wrist or belt, or in a bag. Both the 650V and 800V are available in black or pink, which makes them look even more like an umbrella or personal flashlight. The 800V also features electrodes that are pointed so they can pierce through clothes to reach skin, which is a handy feature when an attacker's bare skin is out of reach.

The ultimate Ruger stun gun is the 1MV Flashlight (that's 1 million volts). As the name suggests, it is an ultra-bright LED flashlight that also happens to have a built-in stun gun. Its electrodes are pointed like those on the 800V for maximum effectiveness through clothing. It comes with a carrying case, rechargeable battery and wrist strap if you want to take it out and about, as well as a wall charger for when you're at home. Any mugger foolish enough to mistake this for just another flashlight will quickly find himself incapacitated.

Personal Security Products (PSP) makes many innovative devices for personal protection. Their Zap Dazzle stun gun resembles a blinged-out cell phone case, but this palm-sized stun gun delivers 950,000 volts of protection. PSP also offers a stun gun in the form of a walking stick, which can be carried either collapsed into a baton or lengthened for hiking. It features both a built-in stun gun and flashlight— perfect for dog walkers or anyone who goes out walking alone.

Guard Dog Security offers several stun guns that are disguised as everyday items, such as cell phones and flashlights. The flashlight stun guns have the added benefit of being fully functional as high-lumen-output tactical flashlights in a very compact design. You get the benefit of two great defensive and practical tools in one.

IMPACT DEVICES

In areas where stun guns and pepper sprays are outlawed, defensive options become fewer and less effective. But there are still many choices on the market: collapsible batons, loud personal alarms, heavy-duty flashlights, key chains and shoe laces with sharp plastic spikes. International travelers

Impact devices used against sensitive areas can dissuade an attacker. This Hoffner folding knife has a strike face when closed. Jorge Amselle

might find that a sap filled with coins or weights is their only choice for getting through customs.

However, all these options require hand-to-hand fighting, which is not intuitive for an unprepared civilian. A good self-defense course is therefore an essential companion to whichever of these defensive measures you choose.

Classes with a physical component or martial arts training can prepare you to be both mentally and physically ready to defend yourself. In fact, even those who carry firearms would benefit from regular training of this sort, because there's no guarantee that your gun will be accessible in every emergency.

Collapsible batons should be carried with caution, because their use is restricted in many localities and strikes to the head can be lethal. A smaller category of strike weapons includes tactical pens. These functional pens are typically made from aluminum and feature a pointed end that can be used for stabbing and a serrated flat end that can be used against pressure points or bone. The serrated end also has the advantage that it can be used to capture DNA (skin and blood) from an assailant. Don't try taking these with you when you fly, though, because they will be confiscated.

Personal Security Products makes an interesting-looking polymer key chain that has two pointed ends and room for your fingers to hold it, basically a type of brass knuckles. PSP also has an aluminum disk with sharp points that can be easily placed on the back of a ball cap or on your watch wristband. You can then use your hat to strike with this weighted device, while the device on your wrist makes it very unpleasant for anyone to try and grab you there.

In the ball cap category, FAB Defense's GOTCHA Cap disguises a hard polymer self-defense weapon underneath the brim of the hat. Designed by a martial arts expert, this tool is easily grasped with the hand and instantly deployed when you need it. It features two sharp points in the front and dull strike points at the ends. This company offers several other innovative strike tools as well.

Finally, one item I really like is the Kubba Kickz from Fury Tactical, hard plastic sharp points that you can lace right into your shoe or boot, giving you a significant advantage in a fight. They are especially well-suited for joggers who don't want to carry a lot of other gear. They can provide protection, even in areas where guns and sprays are illegal or impractical.

With all of these options, there is never an excuse to be unprepared. Your safety and well-being are ultimately your responsibility. Have the right equipment, get the right training and never stop practicing your self-defense skills.

HANDGUN MANUFACTURERS

The following is a list of U.S. and foreign handgun manufacturers. Some of these companies are small and might produce only one gun model. Others have a vast selection of handguns. The foreign companies have an American distributor (sometimes a subsidiary and sometimes a partnership with a domestic company) that handles U.S. sales and repairs. Not included are companies that no longer offer handguns or are out of business.

ACCU-TEK FIREARMS

1601 Fremont Ct.
Ontario, CA 91761
(909) 947-4867
www.accu-tekfirearms.com
This company produces variations of just one gun, a small, reasonably priced single-action, semi-automatic pistol in .380 ACP.

AMERICAN DERRINGER

127 N. Lacy Dr.
Waco, TX 76705
(254) 799-9111
www.amderringer.com
As the name implies, this company produces single-action and double-action two-shot derringer handguns (they also have two small semi-automatic pistols). A derringer has two barrels (and is limited to two shots) with a break-open design to load and unload.

AMT-HIGH STANDARD

5151 Mithcelldale St., B14
Houston, TX 77092
(800) 272-7816
www.highstandard.com
This company manufactures .22-caliber target pistols as well as 1911 pistols including a compact model. Most interesting for CCW is their AMT double-action-only backup pistol.

ARCUS CO.

219, Vassil Levski St.
5140 Lyaskovets, Bulgaria
+359 (619) 2 54 84
www.arcus-bg.com
Imported by Century International Arms (www.
centuryarms.com), this Bulgarian company offers full-sized and compact 9mm semi-automatic pistols with a classic single-action/double-action hammer-fired operation.

ARMINIUS

Hermann Weihrauch Revolver GmbH
Postfach 25
Mellrichstadt, Germany
+49 9776 707678
www.hermann-weihrauch-revolver.de
Imported by European American Armory Corp. (www.eaacorp.com), this company offers several models of German-made double-action revolvers.

ROCK ISLAND ARMORY

150 N. Smart Way
Pahrump, NV 89060
(775) 537-1444
us.armscor.com
This company primarily sells 1911-style handguns imported from the Philippines, including a compact model as well as a compact double-action 9mm and a small revolver.

AUTO-ORDNANCE

130 Goddard Memorial Dr.
Worcester, MA 01603
(508) 795-3919
www.auto-ordnance.com
This company sells originally styled 1911 full-sized pistols.

BERETTA U.S.A. CORP

17601 Beretta Dr.
Accokeek, MD 20607
(800) 929-2901
www.berettausa.com
Beretta is the oldest firearms manufacturer in the world and is still family owned and operated. It produces a wide array of full-sized, compact and pocket-sized semi-automatic handguns.

BERSA

González Castillo 312
Buenos Aires, Argentina
+54 11 4656 2377
www.bersa.com
Imported by Eagle Imports (www.eagleimportsinc.com), this South American company produces compact semi-automatic pistols.

BOBERG ARMS

1755 Commerce Ct.
White Bear Lake, MN 55110
(651) 287-0617
www.bobergarms.com
This company makes an extremely compact pistol with a very innovative design.

BOND ARMS

PO Box 1296
Grandbury, TX 76048
(817) 573-4445
www.bondarms.com
This company makes very high-quality and very safe derringer handguns.

BROWNING

One Browning Place
Morgan, UT 84050
(800) 333-3288

www.browning.com

Browning makes 1911-style .22-caliber pistols, as well as other .22-caliber target pistols and the famous Browning Hi-Power pistol.

CARACAL USA

7661 Commerce Lane
Trussville, AL 35173
(205) 655-7050
www.caracal-usa.com

Made in the United Arab Emirates, Caracal sells both traditional steel hammer-fired semi-automatic pistols and polymer-framed striker-fired pistols.

CHARTER ARMS

18 Brewster Lane
Shelton, CT 06484
(203) 922-1652
www.charterfirearms.com

Charter Arms offers a full line of double-action revolvers.

CHIAPPA FIREARMS, LTD. USA

6785 W. 3rd St.
Dayton, OH 45417
(937) 835-5000
www.chiappafirearms.com

Chiappa is best known for its innovative Italian-made Rhino revolver, which is available in several styles. The company also sells a full line of .22-caliber pistols and revolvers.

COBRA

1960 S. Milestone Dr., Suite F
Salt Lake City, UT 84104
(801) 908-8300
www.cobrapistols.net

Cobra makes a full line of very compact and economical handguns including derringers, semi-automatics and a revolver.

COLT'S MANUFACTURING COMPANY, LLC

PO Box 1868
Hartford, CT 06144-1868
(800) 962-2658

www.coltsmfg.com

One of the most famous names in firearms manufacturing, Colt produces a wide variety of 1911-style pistols from full-size to pocket-size and cowboy-style revolvers.

COONAN INC.

4501 103rd Ct. NE #120
Blaine, MN 55014
(763) 786-1720
www.coonaninc.com

This company makes one gun, a high-quality and very large 1911-style pistol in .357 Mag. Maybe not the best concealed-carry option.

CZ-USA

PO Box 171073
Kansas City, KS 66117-0073
(800) 955-4486
www.cz-usa.com

The United States subsidiary of this Czech company still produces its famous CZ-75 pistol in a wide variety of styles, as well as more modern and compact semi-automatic pistols.

DAN WESSON

5169 Highway 12 S.
Norwich, NY 13815
(607) 336-1174
www.danwessonfirearms.com

Dan Wesson is now owned by CZ-USA and the company produces high-quality revolvers and 1911-style pistols.

DETONICS

609 S. Breese, Suite 101
Millstadt, IL 62260
(618) 476-3200
www.detonics.ws

This company makes 1911-style pistols in both compact and sub-compact models.

DIAMONDBACK FIREARMS

4135 Pine Tree Pl.
Cocoa, FL 32926
(888) 380-2767
www.diamondbackfirearms.com

The company makes well-designed and solidly built pocket pistols chambered in .380 ACP and 9mm. It recently began producing a full-sized 9mm and an AR pistol.

EAA -EUROPEAN AMERICAN ARMORY CORP.

PO Box 560746
Rockledge, FL 32956-0746
(321) 639-4842
www.eaacorp.com

EAA imports a variety of Italian and German firearms, including CZ-75 clones and 1911s in a wide variety of styles, as well as revolvers.

ED BROWN

PO Box 492
Perry, MO 63462
(573) 565-3261
www.edbrown.com

This company produces a full line of exquisitely built custom 1911-style pistols. This level of care comes at a premium price, however.

EXCEL ARMS

4510 Carter Ct.
Chino, CA 91710
(909) 627-2404
www.excelarms.com

This company makes innovative .22-caliber pistols and rifles.

FNH USA

7918 Jones Branch Dr.
McLean, VA 22101
(703) 288-3500
www.fnhusa.com

This U.S. subsidiary of Belgium's Fabrique Nationale Herstal offers full-sized but very innovative and well-made semi-automatic pistols.

GLOCK INC. USA

6000 Highlands Parkway
Smyrna, GA 30082
(770) 432-1202
www.glock.com

Glock makes the most popular pistol among U.S. law enforcement personnel and has a reputation for reliability. The Glock pistol is available in a wide variety of calibers and sizes, including new compact models.

HIGH-POINT FIREARMS

8611-A N. Dixie Dr.
Dayton, OH 45414
(877) 425-4867
www.hi-pointfirearms.com
Budget-priced High-Point handguns are simple single-action blow-back-operated pistols.

HECKLER & KOCH USA

5675 Transport Blvd.
Columbus, GA 31907
(706)568-1906
www.hecklerkoch-usa.com
These are high-quality German-made semi-automatic pistols in several styles.

IWI US INC. (UZI)

PO Box 126707
Harrisburg, PA 17112
(717) 695-2081
www.iwi.us
IWI's Israeli website lists their handguns, which are occasionally available in the United States (www.israel-weapon.com). The UZI Pro pistol should be available soon.

METRO ARMS

Paranaque City, Philippines
www.metroarms.com
Imported by Eagle Imports (www.eagleimportsinc.com), this company produces 1911-style semi-automatic pistols.

JIMENEZ ARMS

5550 Reference St.
Las Vegas, NV 89122
(877) 241-9938
www.jimenezarmsinc.com
Inexpensive single-action only, small semi-automatic pistols.

KAHR ARMS

130 Goddard Memorial Dr.
Worchester, MA 01603

(508) 795-3919
www.kahr.com
Makers of well-made and very reliable semi-automatic pistols in a variety of calibers and sizes.

KEL-TEC

PO Box 236009
Cocoa, FL 32923
(321) 631-0068
www.keltecweapons.com
Makers of innovative, compact semi-automatic pistols.

KIMBER

555 Taxter Rd., Suite 235
Elmsford, NY 10523
(888) 243-4522
www.kimberamerica.com
Makers of a wide selection of outstanding 1911-style pistols and a sub-compact double-action only concealed-carry pistols.

KORTH USA

437R Chandler St.
Tewksbury, MA 01876
(978) 851-8656
www.korthusa.com
This small German company produces high-end pistols and revolvers.

LES BAER

1804 Iowa Dr.
LeClaire, IA 52753
(563) 289-2126
www.lesbaer.com
This company produces a full line of exquisitely built custom 1911-style pistols. This level of care comes at a premium price, however.

LIONHEART INDUSTRIES

7140 180th Ave. NE
Redmond, WA 98052
(888) 552-4743
www.lionheartindustries.com
This company manufactures a mid-size semi-automatic pistol with a light double-action-only hammer design.

MAGNUM RESEARCH

12602 33rd Ave. SW
Pillager, MN 56473
(508) 635-4273
www.magnumresearch.com
Now owned by Kahr Arms, this company makes the famed Desert Eagle pistol, as well as a smaller version and a sub-compact pistol.

METRO ARMS

Paranaque City, Philippines
www.metroarms.net
Imported by Eagle Imports (www.eagleimportsinc.com), this company produces 1911-style semi-automatic pistols.

NAA—NORTH AMERICAN ARMS

2150 S. 950 E.
Provo, UT 84606
(800) 821-5783
www.northamericanarms.com
This company is known for incredibly small and innovative revolvers and semi-automatic pistols.

OLYMPIC ARMS

624 Old Pacific Hwy. S.E.
Olympia, WA 98513
(800) 228-3471
www.olyarms.com
Olympic Arms produces a limited line of 1911-style pistols and AR pistols.

PARA USA, LLC

10620 Southern Loop Blvd.
Pineville, NC 28134
(704) 930-7600
www.para-usa.com
Formerly a Canadian company, Para USA is now part of Freedom Group and is best known for its double-action and high-capacity 1911-style pistols.

PHOENIX ARMS

4231 E. Brickell St.
Ontario, CA 91761
(909) 937-6900
www.phoenix-arms.com
This company makes small

single-action semi-automatic economical pistols.

REMINGTON
PO Box 1911
Madison, NC 27025
(877) 801-1911
www.remington.com
Out of the handgun business for a long time, Remington came back with well-made 1911-style pistols and a new compact pistol.

COMANCHE—REXIO
2011 Lasserre SA
Buenos Aires Argentina
+54 11 4201 1218
www.rexioarms.com.ar
Imported by Eagle Imports (www.eagleimportsinc.com), this company produces large revolvers and single-shot handguns.

ROHRBAUGH FIREARMS
PO Box 785
Bayport, NY 11705
(800) 803-2233
www.rohrbaughfirearms.com
Makers of high-quality small, innovative and lightweight semi-automatic double-action-only pocket pistols.

ROSSI
16175 N.W. 49 Ave.
Miami, FL 33014
(305) 474-0401
www.rossiusa.com
This Brazilian company is now owned by Taurus and sells a full line of economical revolvers.

ROCK RIVER ARMS
1042 Cleveland Rd.
Colona, IL 61241
(866) 980-7625
www.rockriverarms.com
Rock River Arms sells AR pistols and a brand new polymer-framed 1911-style pistol.

RUGER
Sturm, Ruger & Co. Inc.
411 Sunapee St.
Newport, NH 03773

(603) 863-3300
www.ruger-firearms.com
Ruger produces a comprehensive line of tough-as-nails and high-quality pistols and revolvers, including many ideal for concealed carry.

SCCY INDUSTRIES
1800 Concept Ct.
Daytona Beach, FL 32114
(866) 729-7599
www.sccy.com
This company produces a good-quality economical double-action-only sub-compact pistol.

SEECAMP
280 Rock Lane
Milford, CT 06460
(203) 877-7926
www.seecamp.com
This company makes high-quality and very small double-action-only pocket pistols.

SIG SAUER
18 Industrial Dr.
Exeter, NH 03833
(603) 772-2302
www.sigsauer.com
Austrian engineering meets German manufacturing in this excellent line of full-sized and compact semi-automatic pistols.

SMITH & WESSON
2100 Roosevelt Ave.
Springfield, MA 01104
(800) 331-0852
www.smith-wesson.com
The world's largest handgun manufacturer and one of the most storied names in firearms, S&W offers a complete line of excellent revolvers and pistols.

SPHINX
Gsteigstrasse 12
Matten Switzerland
+41 33 821 10 05
www.sphinx-systems.ch
Available from some limited dealers in the United States, this company offers a line of full-sized

and compact Swiss-made semi-automatic pistols.

SPRINGFIELD ARMORY
420 W. Main St.
Geneseo, IL 61254
(800) 680-6866
www.springfield-armory.com
Springfield Armory is the maker of very well-regarded 1911-style pistols and the Croatian-made XD line of polymer striker-fired pistols.

STEYR MANNLICHER USA
PO Box 840
Trussville, AL 35173
(205) 655-8299
www.steyrarms.com
Producers of excellent Austrian-made semi-automatic polymer-framed pistols.

STI INTERNATIONAL
114 Halmar Cove
Georgetown, TX 78628
(512) 819-0656
www.stiguns.com
Makers of high-quality 1911-style pistols, including high-capacity models.

STOEGER
901 Eighth St.
Pocomoke, MD 21851
(800) 264-4962
www.stoegerindustries.com
Stoeger produces the Beretta-designed Cougar compact pistol.

TANFOGLIO
Fratelli Tanfoglio S.N.C
via Valtrompia 39/41
Brescia Italy
+39 030 8910623
www.tanfoglio.it
Imported by European American Armory (www.eaacorp.com), this company makes a good-quality line of CZ-75 and 1911-style semi-automatic pistols.

TAURUS USA
16175 N.W. 49th Ave.
Miami, FL 33014

(305) 624-1115
www.taurususa.com
    This well-regarded company produces a full line of innovative and well-priced revolvers and semi-automatic pistols, including many ideal for concealed carry.

UBERTI
via Craftsman 1
Brescia, Italy
+39 030 834 1800
www.uberti.com
    Makers of reproduction cowboy revolvers.

US FIREARMS
United States Firearms Mfg.
Co. Inc.
453 Ledyard St. #453

Hartford, CT 06114
(860) 724-1152
www.usfasingleactions.com and www.usfirearms.com
    Makers of single-action cowboy revolvers and a new innovative .22-caliber pistol.

WALTHER AMERICA
2100 Roosevelt Ave.
Springfield, MA 01102
(800) 372-6454
www.waltheramerica.com
    Makers of the James Bond PPK, this company produces high-quality German-made semi-automatic handguns.

WILSON COMBAT
2234 CR 719
Berryville, AR 72616
(800) 955-4856
www.wilsoncombat.com
    This company produces a full line of exquisitely built custom 1911-style pistols. This level of care comes at a premium price, however.

ZASTAVA ARMS
4 Kosovska
Kragujevac Serbia
+381 34 301 137
www.zastava-arms.co.rs
    Imported by Century Arms (www.centuryarms.com), this company produces solid and well-priced, full-sized semi-automatic pistols.

APPENDIX II:

HOLSTER MANUFACTURERS

Here is a list of U.S. and foreign holster manufacturers. Some of these companies are small and might produce only a few holsters; others produce custom holsters to fit your specific needs and tastes. Many of the larger companies specialize in law enforcement gear and holsters, but have a good selection for the civilian concealed-carry market as well.

5-11
4300 Spyres Way
Modesto, CA 95356
(866) 451-1726
www.511tactical.com
    Tactical holsters and holster shirts.

5 SHOT LEATHER
18018 N. Lidgerwood Ct.
Colbert, WA 99005
(509) 844-3969
www.5shotleather.com
    Leather waist and ankle holsters.

ADAMS HOLSTERS
W8941 Newberg Rd.
Channing, MI 49815

(906) 662-4212
www.adamsholsters.com
    Fine leather belt holsters.

A. E. NELSON
38492 Gilkey Rd.
Scio, OR 97374
(503) 394-3412
www.nelsonleather.com
    Leather belt holsters.

AHOLSTER COMPANY
PO Box 1022
Jonesborough, TN 37659
(423) 972-1348
www.lefthandholster.com
    Kydex belt and pocket holsters.

AKER LEATHER
2248 Main St., Suite 6
Chula Vista, CA 91911
(800) 645-AKER
www.akerleather.com
    Fine leather belt holsters for law enforcement and civilian use.

AKJ CONCEAL COMPANY
PO Box 134
Rupert, Idaho 83350
(208) 436-7828
www.concealco.com
    Leather belt holsters.

ALESSI HOLSTERS
247 Cayuga N.
Cheektowaga, NY 14225
(716) 932-7497

www.alessigunholsters.com
Leather belt, pocket, shoulder and ankle holsters.

ALFONSO'S GUNLEATHER
1512 W. Magnolia Blvd.
Burbank, CA 91506
(818) 769-0362
www.alfonsosgunleather.com
Western-style leather holsters.

ALIEN GEAR HOLSTERS
827 W. Prairie Ave.
Hayden, Idaho 83835
(208) 215-2046
www.aliengearholsters.com
Kydex holsters.

ANDREWS LEATHER
22610 N.W. 102 Ave.
Alachua, FL 32615
(386) 462-0576
www.andrewsleather.com
Holsters in leather and exotic animals skins.

BANDERA GUNLEATHER
PO Box 1689
Bandera, TX 78003
(830) 612-3909
www.banderagunleather.com
Leather belts with built-in gun slots.

BELL CHARTER OAK HOLSTERS
PO Box 198
Gilbertsville, NY 13776
(607) 783-2483
www.bellcharteroakholsters.com
Leather waistband and pocket holsters.

BIANCHI
13386 International Pkwy.
Jacksonville, FL 32218
(800) 347-1200
www.bianchi-intl.com
Hip, shoulder and ankle holsters for concealed carry, law enforcement or Western wear.

BLACKHAWK
6160 Commander Pkwy.

Norfolk, VA 23502
(800) 379-1732
www.blackhawk.com
Kydex, nylon and leather holsters plus tactical supplies and accessories.

BLACK HILLS LEATHER
410 W. Aurora St. Dept. WWW
Laredo, TX, 78041
(877) 240-8274
www.blackhillsleather.com
Western leather belt and shoulder holsters.

BLADE TECH
5530 184th St. E.
Puyallup, WA 98375
(877) 331-5793
www.blade-tech.com
Waistband and pocket holsters.

BLUE STONE SAFETY PRODUCTS
3331 Hwy. 13
Wisconsin Dells, WI 53965
(888) 776-6220
www.bluestonesafety.com
Belly bands and Kydex holsters.

BOSTON LEATHER
1801 Eastwood Dr.
Sterling, IL 61081
(815) 622-1635
www.bostonleather.com
Leather holsters for firearms and less-lethal devices.

BRIGADE GUNLEATHER
33301 Osawatomie Rd.
Osawatomie, KS 66064
(888) 600-2377
www.brigadegunleather.com
Leather waist and shoulder holsters.

BROMMELAND GUNLEATHER
PO Box 813
Sneedville, TN 37869
(423) 733-1779
www.brommelandgunleather.com

Leather inside-the-waistband holsters.

BROWNING
5 AmeriBag Dr.
Kingston, NY 12401
(800) 237-3224
www.browningbags.com
Concealment bags.

BULLDOG CUSTOM GUN LEATHER
PO Box 282
Round Lake, IL 60073
www.bulldogleathercompany.com
Leather waist and pocket holsters, plus custom holster kits.

C5 LEATHER
(913) 209-2402
www.c5leather.com
Leather waistband holsters.

C. RUSTY SHERRICK CUSTOM LEATHER WORKS
507 Mark Dr.
Elizabethtown, PA 17022
(717) 361-7699
www.c-rusty.com
Leather holsters in waist, pocket, ankle, shoulder and ladies' styles.

CENTER OF MASS HOLSTERS
894 N. Hwy. 91
Firth, ID 83236
(866) 293-1002
www.comholsters.com
Kydex clip-on holsters.

CLEVELAND HOLSTERS
2192 S. 60th St.
West Allis, WI 53219
(414) 545-3323
www.clevelandholsters.com
Leather and Kydex IWB holsters.

COBRA GUNSKIN
1220 Tangelo Terrace, Bay 17

Delray Beach, FL 33444
(561) 455-2248
www.cobragunskin.us
  Leather belt holsters.

COMBAT GUN LEATHER
510 Swift St.
Buffalo, WY 82834
www.combatgunleather.com
  Leather belt, pocket, ankle and
shoulder holsters for pistols and
revolvers.

COMP-TAC
1307 FM 1960 Rd. E.
Houston, TX 77073
(866) 441-9157
www.comp-tac.com
  Molded Kydex waistband
holsters.

CONCEALED CARRIE
11261 Alpharetta Hwy.
Roswell, GA 30076
(844) 5CARRIE
www.concealedcarrie.com
  Fine concealment purses.

CORONADO LEATHER
San Diego, CA
(800) 283-9509
www.coronadoleather.com
  Fine leather holster bags.

CR SPEED
PO Box 11786
Queenswood, Pretoria, GP 0121,
South Africa
+27 12 333 4768
www.crspeed.co.za
  Competition holsters.

CROSSBREED HOLSTERS
224 N. Main
Republic, MO 65738
(888) 732-5011
www.crossbreedholsters.com
  IWB, ankle, belly and purse
holsters plus home defense
accessories.

CROSSFIRE
2212 Cortland Pl.
Nampa, ID 83687
(208) 461-8888
www.crossfiregear.com
  Soft nylon holsters for pocket,
waist, shoulder and leg.

CROSSFIRE HOLSTERS
West Palm Beach, FL
www.crossfireholsters.com
  Kydex holsters.

D.M. BULLARD LEATHER
11385 FM 730 N.
Azle, TX 76020
(866) 383-6761
www.dmbullardleather.com
  Waist holsters in leather and
exotic skins.

DEEP CONCEAL
PO Box 833
Layton, UT 84041
(877) HIDE-GUN
www.deepconceal.com
  Bra and shoulder holsters.

DEL FATTI LEATHER
907 S. Main St.
Greenwood, WI 54437
(715) 267-6420
www.delfatti.com
  Fine leather belt, pocket and
shoulder holsters.

DESANTIS GUNHIDE
Long Island, NY
(800) 424-1236
www.desantisholster.com
  Waist, pocket, ankle, thigh and
shoulder holsters.

DIAMOND D LEATHER
540 W. Hjellen Dr.
Wasilla, AK 99654
(907) 631-4212
www.diamonddcustomleather.
com
  Leather belt and shoulder
holsters.

DON DIEGO LEATHER
PO Box 4425
Kingshill, VI 00851-4425
(340) 513-3866
www.dondiegoleather.com
  Leather belt and shoulder
holsters.

DON HUME
500 26th St. N.W.
Miami, OK 74354
(918) 542-6604
www.donhume.com
  Leather waist, pocket and
shoulder holsters for law
enforcement and civilians.

DURANGO GUN LEATHER
Irving, TX 75062
(888) 751-6337
www.dgunleather.com
  Western-style leather holsters.

EAGLE INDUSTRIES
6160 Commander Pkwy.
Norfolk, VA 23502-2052
(888) 343-7547
www.eagleindustries.com
  Tactical gear and holsters.

ELITE SURVIVAL SYSTEMS
310 W. 12th St., PO Box 245
Washington, MO 63090
(866) 340-2778
www.shootingsystems.com
  Ankle, waist, shoulder and
pocket holsters in nylon plus
concealment bags.

EL PASO SADDLERY
2025 E. Yandell
El Paso, TX, 79903
(915) 544-2535
www.epsaddlery.com
  Fine leather belt and shoulder
holsters.

EVERYDAY TACTICAL GEAR
(855) 822-4327
www.everydaytacticalgear.com
  Concealment purses.

EZ HOLSTERS
810 Wilcox Rd.
Chattanooga, TN 37419
(423) 509-7496
www.ezholster.com
Holsters disguised as cell phone cases.

FIN DESIGNS
PO Box 1034
Burtonsville, MD 20866
(301) 928-1461
www.findesigns.net
Kydex holsters.

FIST
20 Jay St., Suite 211
Brooklyn, NY 11201
(800) 443-3478
Fist-holsters.com
Custom-made holsters.

FLASHBANG HOLSTERS
2124 S. Prospect Ave.
Oklahoma City, OK 73120
(800) 299-5667
www.flashbangholsters.
publishpath.com
Bra and waist holsters.

FOBUS HOLSTERS
(267) 803-1517
www.fobusholster.com
Paddle and ankle holsters.

FRONT LINE HOLSTERS
3951 E. 66th Ave.
Anchorage, AK 99507
(907) 317-8440
www.frontlineholsters.com
Leather and Kydex holsters.

GALCO GUNLEATHER
2019 W. Quail Ave.
Phoenix, AZ 85027
(800) 874-2526
www.galcogunleather.com
Fine leather concealment bags and cases, and ankle, belt and shoulder holsters.

GARRITY'S GUNLEATHER
PO Box 82664
Phoenix, AZ 85071
www.garritysgunleather.com
Belt, pocket and shoulder holsters in leather and exotic skins.

G-CODE HOLSTERS
Edge Works Manufacturing
Jacksonville, NC
(910) 455-9834
www.tacticalholsters.com
Kydex pistol and revolver holsters.

GHOST HOLSTER
1008 S. Center St.
Mesa, AZ 85210
(480) 969-1311
www.ghostholster.com
Adjustable clip holsters.

GHORMLEY HOLSTERS
118 1/2 N. Grand
Chariton, IA 50049
(515) 979-7725
www.willghormley-maker.com
DIY Kydex IWB holster kits.

GOULD & GOODRICH
709 E. McNeill St.
Lillington, NC 27546
(910) 893-2071
www.gouldusa.com
Waist, ankle and pocket holsters for law enforcement and civilian carry.

GRANDFATHER OAK CUSTOM CARRY
PO Box 421
Roxboro, NC 27573
(919) 612-8924
www.grandfatheroak.com
Shoulder, waist and pocket holsters.

GRASSBURR LEATHER WORKS
9534 Autumn Wind
Boerne, TX 78006
(210) 687-1717
www.grassburr.com
Shoulder holsters and concealment systems for home and the car.

GUN TOTE'N MAMAS
1303 Shermer Rd.
Northbrook, IL 60062
(847) 446-0700
www.guntotenmamas.com
Concealment bags and cases.

HAUGEN HANDGUN LEATHER
4159 25th St. N.W.
Douglas, ND 58735
(701) 529-4834
www.haugenhandgunleather.com
Fine leather belt holsters.

H.B.E. LEATHERWORKS
(801) 916-9248
www.hbeleatherworks.com
Custom leather holsters.

HEDLEY HOLSTERS
www.hedleyholsters.com
Handmade pocket holsters.

HIGH NOON HOLSTERS
PO Box 1923
Tarpon Springs, FL, 34688
(727) 939-2701
www.highnoonholsters.com
Leather waist, shoulder and pocket holsters.

HILLSMAN HOLSTER COMPANY
PO Box 307
Brookshire, TX, 77423
(713) 560-2454
www.hillsmanholster.com
Boltaron belt holsters.

HOFFNERS
21145 FM 529 #1103
Katy, TX 77449
(281) 855-8800
www.hoffners.com
Waist holsters for pistols and revolvers.

HOLSTERAMA
10100 Old Bon Air Pl.
Richmond, VA 23235
(855) 486-6298
www.jbpholsters.com
  Waist, ankle, pocket and
shoulder holsters.

THE HOLSTER STORE
1116 New York Ave.
Saint Cloud, FL 34769
(866) 998-7254
www.theholsterstore.net
  Belt and shoulder holsters.

HORSESHOE LEATHER
The Cottage, Sharow
Ripon HG4 5BP, England
+44 1765 605858
www.holsters.org
  Leather belt and shoulder
holsters.

I LOVE MY GLOCK
www.ilovemyglock.com
  Clip and sleeve holsters.

INTERNATIONAL HANDGUN LEATHER
3334 W. McDowell Rd., Ste. 26
Phoenix, AZ 85009
(602) 269-0202
www.
internationalhandgunleather.com
  Leather waist, pocket and
shoulder holsters.

J.R. ROSCOE
Fort Worth, TX
(817) 773-5459
www.shoulderholster.us
  Leather shoulder holsters.

JS HOLSTERS
1700 Sullivan Trail #385
Easton, PA 18040
(423) 257-3471
www.jsholsters.com
  Leather and Kydex holsters.

J.W. O'ROURKE LEATHER PRODUCTS
PO Box 1296
Hartselle, AL 35640
(256) 751-3387
www.gun-holsters.com
  Pancake holsters.

KELLEY GUN LEATHER
Phoenix, AZ 85032
www.kellygunleather.com
  Leather waist holsters.

KHOLSTER
1202 Highland Ter.
St. Louis, MO 63117
www.kholster.com
  Waist, shoulder and ankle
holsters and concealment bags.

KINETIC CONCEALMENT
116 E. Lafayette
Jackson, Tennessee
(731) 388-9693
www.kineticconcealment.com
  Kydex and hybrid IWB and
OWB holsters.

KIRKPATRICK LEATHER
1910 San Bernardo
Laredo, TX 78040
(956) 723-6893
www.kirkpatrickleather.com
  Leather belt, shoulder and law
enforcement holsters.

K. L. NULL HOLSTERS
161 School St. N.W.
Resaca, GA 30735
(706) 625-5643
www.klnullholsters.com
  Leather belt, shoulder and ankle
holsters.

KRAMER LEATHER
PO Box 112154
Tacoma, WA 98411
(800) 510-2666
www.kramerleather.com
  Leather ankle, belt and pocket
holsters plus concealment
undershirts.

KT MECH
16433 N. Midland Blvd. #105
Nampa, ID 83687
www.kt-mech.com
  Custom Kydex belt and IWB
holsters and belts.

KYTAC
PO Box 1911
Edmond, OK 73083
(405) 844-6040
www.kytac.net
  Competition holsters.

LIGHTNING ARMS SPORTS
PO Box 944
Beaverton, OR 97075-0944
(503) 643-8198
www.lightningarms.com
  Leather belt and pocket
holsters.

MASTER OF CONCEALMENT
4585 Murphy Canyon Rd.
San Diego, CA 92123
(800) 601-8273
www.masterofconcealment.com
  Belly bands, concealment
clothing and holsters for ankle,
thigh, waist and shoulder.

MERNICKLE HOLSTERS
1875 View Ct.
Fernley, NV 89408
(800) 497-3166
www.mernickleholsters.com
  Western leather belt holsters.

MILT SPARKS
115 E. 44th St.
Boise, ID 83714
(208) 377-5577
www.miltsparks.com
  Leather belt and pocket
holsters.

MITCH ROSEN
540 N. Commercial St.
Manchester, NH 03101-1122
(603) 647-2971
www.mitchrosen.com

Fine leather belt, pocket, ankle and shoulder holsters.

MOUNTAIN HOME LEATHER
(928) 751-0020
www.mountainhomeleather.com
Leather belt and shoulder holsters.

NEVADA GUN LEATHER
4012 S. Rainbow Blvd., Suite K-335
Las Vegas, NV 89103
(702) 362-9224
www.nevadagunleather.com
Leather concealment bags, cases and holsters for belt, shoulder, thigh and ankle.

PACIFIC CANVAS & LEATHER
Dept. WS, PO Box 291909
Phelan, CA 92329-1909
(760) 868-3856
www.pacificcanvasandleather.com
Historical replica holsters.

PAGERPAL
PO Box 700695
Dallas, TX, 75370
www.pagerpal.com
Waist and pocket holsters.

PETERS CUSTOM HOLSTERS
www.peterscustomholsters.com
Kydex belt holsters.

PISTOL PACKAGING
5350 Pioneer Creek Dr., Suite 2
Maple Plain, MN 55359
(763) 479-0440
www.pistolpackaging.com
Shoulder and belt holsters.

PISTOL WEAR
11063D S. Memorial #337
Tulsa, OK 74133
(800) 231-7385
www.pistolwear.com
Belly bands and shoulder holsters.

POCKET CONCEALMENT SYSTEMS
PO Box 10271
Baltimore, MD 21234
(410) 426-9004
www.pcsholsters.com
Leather pocket and belt holsters.

PRICE WESTERN LEATHER COMPANY
Ponsford Rd.
Minehead, Somerset TA24 5DX
UK
+44 (0) 1643 705071
www.pwluk.com
Waist, ankle and shoulder holsters and concealment pouches.

PURE KUSTOM HOLSTERS
(480) 924-6866
www.purekustom.com
Snakeskin and leather holsters.

PYLE MOUNTAIN HOLSTERS
www.holsterss.com
Concealment vests, belly bands and holsters for ankle, waist, pocket and shoulders.

PYTHON HOLSTERS
2733 E. Battlefield #156
Springfield, MO 65804
(417) 864-6644
Pocket, ankle, belt and shoulder holsters in nylon.

RAVEN CONCEALMENT SYSTEMS
(440) 508-9000
www.rcsgear.com
Kydex belt holsters.

RAY'S HOLSTERS
9135 109th Ave.
North Largo, FL 33777
(727) 393-2078
www.raysholsters.com
Concealment vests, purses, backpacks, and belt and ankle holsters.

RECLUSE HOLSTERS
PO Box 463
Gig Harbor, WA 98335
(866) 960-1264
www.recluseholster.com
Pocket holsters.

REMORA CONCEALMENT & SECURITY PRODUCTS, LLC
PO Box 990340
Naples, FL 34116
(239) 434-7200
www.remoraholsters.com
Pocket and IWB holsters.

R GRIZZLE LEATHER
(706) 265-0118
www.rgrizzleleather.com
Leather belt and pocket holsters.

RICK WALTNER HOLSTERS
404 Stillwater Dr.
Columbus, MT 59019
www.rickwaltnerholsters.com
Leather belt holsters.

RIDGE
2817 S. Grove St.
Eustis, FL 32726
(352) 357-2669
www.ridgeoutdoors.com
Men's and women's holster shirts.

RITCHIE LEATHER COMPANY
2465 Niagara Falls Blvd.
Amherst, NY 14228
(716) 691-6300
www.ritchieholsters.com
Leather holsters for belt, shoulder, ankle and pocket.

RIVERS WEST
3000 Lind Ave. S.W.
Renton, WA 98057
(800) 683-0887
www.riverswest.com
Holster jackets and vests.

RKBA HOLSTERS
Madras, OR 97741
www.rkbaholsters.com
Leather and Kydex belt and pocket holsters.

RM HOLSTERS
6567 N. Foster Dr.
Baton Rouge, LA 70811-6115
www.rmholsters.com
(866) 288-9778
Kydex belt holsters.

ROSS LEATHER
6112 33rd St. E., Unit 103
Bradenton, FL 34203
(800) 929-8270
www.rossleather.com
Fine leather belt, pocket and shoulder holsters.

SAFARILAND
13386 International Pkwy.
Jacksonville, FL 32218
(800) 347-1200
www.safariland.com
Tactical and law enforcement holsters.

SICKINGER
4901 Ottnang, Achleiten 6, Austria
(0043) 7676/7503
www.sickinger.at
Leather belt and shoulder holsters.

SIDEARMOR
Cedar Rapids, IA
(319) 775-5092
www.sidearmor.com
Kydex holsters.

SIDE GUARD HOLSTERS
Twin Cities, MN
(651) 263-1434
www.sideguardholsters.com
Belt, pocket and women's holsters.

SIMPLY RUGGED HOLSTERS
PO Box 10700

Prescott, AZ 86304
(928) 227-0432
www.simplyrugged.com
Leather belt and pocket holsters.

SMARTCARRY
940 7th St. N.W.
Largo, FL 33770-1112
(727) 581-7001
www.smartcarry.com
Belly bands.

SNEAKY PETE HOLSTERS
3 Andiron Lane
Brookhaven, NY 11719
www.sneakypeteholsters.com
Belt holsters disguised as cell phone cases.

SOUTHERN HOLSTERS
www.southernholsters.com
Pocket, shoulder, belt and ankle holsters.

STELLAR RIGS
PO Box 22132
West Palm Beach, FL 33416
(561) 616-5015
www.stellarrigs.com
Kydex pocket, waist and shoulder holsters.

STICKY HOLSTERS
4306 Arnold Ave.
Naples, FL 34104
(239) 434-1844
www.stickyholsters.com
Rubberized pocket, thigh and ankle holsters.

STRONG HOLSTERS
39 Grove St.
Gloucester, MA 01930
(978) 879-1050
www.strongbadgecase.com
Waist and shoulder holsters.

SUNRISE LEATHER
PO Box 18173
Sarasota, FL 34276
(941) 927-2544
www.sunriseleather.com
Leather waist and pocket holsters.

SURVIVAL SHEATH SYSTEMS
710 N.W. Friesen Ct.
Dallas, OR 97338
(503) 623-9538
www.survivalsheath.com
Shoulder holsters.

TAC PRO
14 Essex Ave., Unit 30,
Thornhill, ON L3T 3Z1 Canada
(905) 738-4711
www.tacpro.com
Kydex holsters.

TACTICAL TAILOR
12715 Pacific Hwy. S.W.
Lakewood, WA 98499
(253) 984-7854
www.tacticaltailor.com
Holster bags and IWB holsters.

TAGUA GUN LEATHER
2047 N.W. 24 Ave.
Miami, FL 33142
(866) 638-2482
www.taguagunleather.com
Waist, ankle and shoulder holsters.

TALON TACTICAL
149 Cagle Branch Rd.
Jasper, GA 30143
(770) 737-5054
www.talontactical.com
Kydex holsters.

TAURIS HOLSTERS
10 Compton Rd.
New Hartford, NY 13413
(315) 735-0530
www.taurisholsters.com
Leather waist, pocket, ankle and shoulder holsters.

TENNESSEE HOLSTER COMPANY
Granville, TN 38564
(931) 653-4117
www.tennesseeholstercompany.com
Waist, pocket and shoulder holsters.

TSC HOLSTERS

PO Box 1751
Apache Junction, AZ 85217
(602) 738-1682
www.threatsolutions.com
Waist holsters.

TT GUNLEATHER

(707) 260-4858
www.ttgunleather.com
Leather and exotic skin belt
holsters.

TUCKER GUN LEATHER

7027 Concho St., Ste. 100
Houston, TX 77074
(800) 308-6628
www.tuckergunleather.com
Concealment purses and waist,
pocket and ankle holsters in
leather and Kydex.

TUFF PRODUCTS

1060 Colorado Ave., #C
Chula Vista, CA 91911
(877) 883-3776
www.tuffproducts.com
Concealment cases and bags,
pocket and belt holsters.

UBG HOLSTERS

Stansbury Park, UT
www.ubgholsters.com
Waist, pocket and shoulder
holsters.

UNCLE MIKE'S

9200 Cody
Overland Park, KS 66214
(800) 423-3537
www.unclemikes.com
Waist, pocket and ankle
holsters in nylon and Kydex.

UNDERTECH UNDERCOVER

4585 Murphy Canyon Rd.
San Diego, CA 92123
(800) 601-8273
www.undertechundercover.com
Holster shirts and shorts, belly
bands, concealment bags.

VERSACARRY

1724 B Gooseneck Dr.
Bryan, TX 77808
(855) 278-9678
www.versacarry.com
Polymer IWB holsters.

VEGA HOLSTER

Via Di Mezzo, 31, 56030
Calcinaia, Pisa, Italy
+39 0587 489190
www.vegaholster.com
Belt, shoulder and ankle
holsters in Kydex and leather plus
concealment cases.

WILD BILL'S CONCEALMENT

2664 Timber Dr. #341
Garner, NC 27529
(919) 779-9582
www.wildbillsconcealment.com
Waist and pocket holsters.